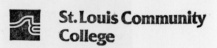

ORANGE ROOFS,
GOLDEN ARCHES

ORANGE ROOFS, GOLDEN ARCHES

The Architecture of American Chain Restaurants

Philip Langdon

Alfred A. Knopf · New York 1986

JUICE EAT A PIG SANDWICH

THIS IS A BORZOI BOOK PUBLISHED BY
ALFRED A. KNOPF, INC.

Library of Congress Cataloging-in-Publication Data

Langdon, Philip.
Orange roofs, golden arches.

1. Chain restaurants—United States—Buildings.
I. Title.
NA7855.L36   1986   725′.71′0973   85-45776
ISBN 0-394-54401-3
ISBN 0-394-74129-3 (pbk.)

Manufactured in the United States of America
FIRST EDITION

Overleaf: *Pig Stand drive-in at Pico and Western, Los Angeles, about 1927.*

For Maryann

Contents

Foreword

IN GREENVILLE, PENNSYLVANIA, WHERE I WAS BORN, a flat-roofed little Dairy Queen stand appeared in 1951 on the north side of Main Street, just a few blocks removed from the busy, squeezed-together business district. It was in one of those typical small-town transition zones where an occasional stone church sat among tall old houses that were gradually being converted to real-estate offices and funeral homes or being replaced by modern one-level stores, but where there remained enough trees and lawns so that the increasingly dissimilar buildings still looked as if they naturally fit together.

The Dairy Queen, a concrete block structure neatly painted white, with a long blue rooftop sign extending toward the street, was, for Greenville, the first of a new kind of chain restaurant or refreshment stand—an immediately recognizable, nationally standardized building surrounded by the pavement of its own parking lot. The stand became immediately popular, not only with four-year-olds like me but with the town's adults, who could drive to the Dairy Queen and not have to bother circling the crowded downtown blocks in search of an unoccupied parking spot.

I left that town along the Ohio border before finishing elementary school and grew up in the Erie area of Pennsylvania, a bigger place where roadside strips full of chain eating establishments were developing faster and more profusely, with fewer trees interrupting the onward rush of commerce and asphalt. McDonald's and Mister Donut, Arby's and Elby's, Bonanza and Red Barn, Ponderosa, Perkins, Howard Johnson's, Kentucky Fried Chicken—these became the franchised landmarks of everyday life for those of us who came of age in western Pennsylvania in the 1960s. They seemed entirely familiar, and yet in another sense they were mysterious. Where did they come from? Why did they look the way they did? How was it that a pair of illuminated arches came to perch on top of the McDonald's roof? What were the sources of the curious designs that dominated so much of the American roadside?

The usual explanations held that chain restaurants' boisterous shapes and colors were dictated by their need to catch the traveler's eye, or that the startling forms of oversize electrified signs simply popped out of the uninhibited imagination of sign-makers who knew nothing about "serious" art and architecture. But even if these assertions were accurate, by the end of the 1960s the colors, shapes, materials, and textures—the overall personality of restaurants and other roadside buildings—were becoming far different from what they had been during the first spurt of postwar growth. As these esthetic changes continued to accumulate, influencing the character of communities all across the United States, it became apparent that some fuller, more detailed exploration was needed. Not only had the evolution of chain restaurants become an intriguing subject in itself; it also displayed potential for illuminating the history of roadside commercial buildings in general. A vast number of business structures along America's highways had undergone a metamorphosis, and of all these buildings it was the ubiquitous chain restaurant that exhibited the changes most vividly. Consequently, I set out to tie together the history of chain-restaurant design and decor and to offer conclusions about its meaning.

This book holds to the thesis that chain restaurants have consistently embodied the spirit of their times. The span of American history in which these chains have developed is longer than even I had initially imagined; what's presented here is the story of chain restaurants from their beginnings in the 1870s to the mid-1980s. I have devoted special attention to chains and restaurants that made an especially large impact on society, most notably White Castle, the original nickel-hamburger restaurant; Howard Johnson's, the long-dominant family roadside establishment; and the arches-on-the-roof McDonald's, introduced in the early 1950s. I have also examined what it was about the design of such buildings as Howard Johnson's, Dairy Queen, Denny's, and Big Boy that made them so appealing to their millions of customers. And I have attempted to show what chain restaurants as a group have done to the character of American cities, suburbs, and towns.

The research for this undertaking took me to the headquarters of most of the major American restaurant chains, where I interviewed designers and executives, and to out-of-the-way places like Bedford, New Hampshire, where Richard J. McDonald, the retired surviving co-founder of the world's preeminent fast-food chain, gave me his account of how the McDonald's system and its 1950s buildings came about. Much additional information came from architectural journals and restaurant trade publications from the opening decade of the twentieth century to the 1980s.

This book is neither an economic history nor a general history of restaurant chains. But since no economic or general history has yet been written, I have incorporated into this architectural history what I hope will be useful basic information on most of the major chains that are discussed. Where I was able to make a reliable determination about a chain, I have told who founded it, where and when it started, and how it got its name.

Even in the 1980s the chain restaurant is something of a strange subject—considered outside the realm of significant architecture, yet swiftly reflecting shifts in popular taste and unquestionably making an impact on daily life. These buildings rarely show up in architectural journals, yet they have become some of the most numerous and conspicuous in the United States today. The men (and hardly any women) who set out to make money by establishing multiple eating places have ended up making entire environments in communities throughout the nation. Whatever the quality of the results, this is a design phenomenon worth examining.

ORANGE ROOFS,
GOLDEN ARCHES

CHAPTER ONE
Origins of the Chain-Restaurant Industry

Overleaf: *Still on wheels, Hayes-Bickford's Dining Car No. 1 operated near the Cottage Farm Bridge in Boston about 1925. The company also had a diner in Cambridge at that time.*

BEFORE THE AUTOMOBILE WAS INVENTED, before the streets were paved with asphalt, Americans had already started eating in chain restaurants. In New York, in Baltimore, in other major cities and in a series of towns along the western rail routes, chain restaurants began to become a fixture of life in the late nineteenth century. During the last three decades of the 1800s, urban populations were multiplying, industry was growing to vast new proportions, travel was becoming increasingly extensive, and all these changes helped restaurants thrive. With the expansion of travel, the boom in factory and office work, and the burgeoning size of cities, more and more Americans found themselves away from home at mealtime. They needed somewhere to eat—preferably a place known for reliability—and the result was a promising market for restauranteurs capable of organizing systems of eating establishments. This was an era of aggressive system-building—of the organization of massive steel and petroleum companies and of the rise of powerful railroads—and the restaurant business mirrored the changes taking place in the nation's industrial structure. Restaurants in the closing decades of the nineteenth century started to go well beyond the scale of a single shop. They developed into networks serving entire cities or spanning a broad section of the country.

The first large restaurant organization had its start in what was then the West—the sparsely inhabited state of Kansas—and was formed by an English immigrant of demanding standards, Frederick Henry Harvey. From the time he arrived in the United States in 1850 at the age of fifteen, Harvey began acquiring the experience that would enable him to establish a far-reaching restaurant chain, the Fred Harvey Company—an organization that continues to operate eating places, hotels, and other public facilities in the western United States today. Harvey entered the restaurant business as a $2-a-week dishwasher in a New York City café and soon headed south, finding employment in the finest restaurants in New Orleans and later working in St. Louis. Harvey had become co-owner of a St. Louis restaurant by 1859, but that ended abruptly when, during the Civil War, his partner absconded with the restaurant's funds. Harvey shifted to work as a mobile postal clerk, sorting mail on the trains running between St. Joseph and Quincy, Missouri, and then took a series of increasingly important positions as agent for railroads in Kansas and Missouri—the Hannibal & St. Joseph, the Northern Missouri, and the Chicago Burlington and Quincy.

The extensive travel required for his job exposed Harvey to many of the eating places along western rail lines, and he was hardly pleased. Lacking dining cars, most trains stopped periodically and let passengers order a quick meal in a depot or restaurant close by. Any stop could turn into an ordeal, for trackside restaurants often served badly prepared food, and some dealt in meals that literally could not be eaten: as soon as the meal was served, the customers would be ordered back on board because the train was pulling out. This was part of a manipulative arrangement in which the train crew received a percentage of the revenue from meals that went uneaten. Harvey, resolving to offer travelers better treatment, joined with a partner to operate three eating houses along the Kansas Pacific rail line, and after those became successful, he asked the Burlington to help him establish a series of dependable restaurants along its route. The Burlington, only recently recovered from financial trouble, turned him down, but suggested he try his idea on the Atchison, Topeka & Santa Fe, which was vigorously pushing westward. The railroad agreed, and in the spring of 1876 Harvey opened a restaurant in the Santa Fe depot at Topeka. A year later, Harvey went about 100 miles down the Santa Fe line and opened a refurbished hotel and restaurant in Florence, Kansas. Gradually, the system of Harvey Houses spread into Colorado, New Mexico, Arizona, and other states, filling its staff with attractive "Harvey Girls"—waitresses from eighteen to thirty years old who had been recruited through newspaper advertisements in the East and the Midwest and who lived in Harvey's supervised dormitories, subject to a ten o'clock curfew.

Some Harvey establishments were simply lunchrooms or newsstands. Others were hotel or railroad station dining rooms, where every man was required to wear a jacket and was supplied with a dark alpaca coat if he didn't have one with him. The food was invariably good; Harvey paid handsomely for provisions and made surprise inspections, on occasion firing restaurant managers who had failed to uphold his rigorous standards. To help the customers relax, he had managers circulate through the dining rooms, assuring everyone that there was no need to hurry—the train wouldn't leave until the travelers had finished their meals. There was adequate time for dining because Harvey had devised a system that enabled the kitchen to begin preparing each customer's meal even before the train pulled up to the station. A few miles prior to the stop, a conductor asked for each passenger's meal preference, and the engineer transmitted the orders to the restaurant through a succession of whistle signals. Thus when the travelers arrived at the Harvey House, their meals could be served almost immediately.

Harvey's meticulousness laid the groundwork for a consistently successful chain. By his death on February 9, 1901, forty-five Harvey restaurants were operating in twelve states, and the expansion would continue until the 1930s. In the first two decades after the opening of the restaurant in Topeka, Harvey Houses typically were frame structures, economical and efficient but architecturally undistinguished. In 1896, however, the company, in conjunction with the railroad, embarked on a much more ambitious program, opening a series of luxury station hotels in varied historical styles. In Hutchinson, Kansas, the hotel-restaurant was a many-gabled, three-story building of brick and half-timbering, fashioned after a Tudor manor house. The hotel-restaurant in Wellington, Kansas, took its inspiration from eighteenth-century Flemish design. The Harvey House in Needles, California, used a succession of classical columns on its long, two-story façade.

The most notable designs appeared in the Indian country of New Mexico—at Albuquerque, Lamy, Las Vegas, Vaughan, and Gallup. There, Harvey Houses incorporated elements with Indian and Spanish Colonial antecedents—stuccoed walls, tiled roofs, projecting rafters, and round-arched verandas prominent among them. Rather than climbing high, the buildings rambled horizontally, and what height they did have—usually two or three stories—took on a comfortable human scale because of porches and other low, inviting extensions. These were picturesque, approachable buildings, and the charm that was evident on the exterior continued inside, where often there were massive fireplaces in the dining rooms and ceilings with hefty exposed beams. Mary Elizabeth Jane Colter, an art teacher hired by the Fred Harvey Company in 1902 to decorate the interior of an Indian handicrafts museum and salesroom, within several years became the firm's chief designer, integrating Navajo rugs, Spanish chests, Indian sand paintings, wrought-iron wall lamps, and other Southwestern articles into the decor of structures that carried on the region's architectural traditions. Indigenous adornment, used with forethought, evoked a welcoming feeling without being ostentatious. In the dining room of the LaFonda Hotel in Santa Fe, weighty beams ran across the ceiling, supporting small hanging lamps, yet the walls were uncluttered, almost devoid of moldings; a decorative painted pattern was

Exterior of El Navajo hotel, station, and restaurant, Gallup, N.M., designed by Mary Colter. Opened 1923, demolished 1957.

Dining room of Harvey's Hotel Fray Marcos in Williams, Ariz., 1908.

all that embellished the dining room doorway. In the Fray Marcos Hotel in Williams, Arizona, guests sat at widely separated tables beneath coffered ceilings whose edges were softened by simple painted patterns. Overall, the Fred Harvey dining rooms of the Southwest had a sense of clarity and restraint—a character in tune with major esthetic currents in the opening years of the twentieth century, when the Arts and Crafts Movement, among others, similarly made a virtue of simplicity.

The architecture of the Harvey Houses conveyed strength and dignity. The atmosphere may have been slightly exotic—Spanish and Indian motifs were something out of the ordinary for travelers from back east—but the general effect was of soothing respect for tradition in service, in architecture, and in decor. English silverware and Irish linen on sturdy wooden tables under heavy-timbered ceilings—these represented the secure establishment of civilization in a harsh and mostly empty land. America was being made safe and sufficiently predictable for the long-distance traveler; a precedent was being set that would outlast the railroad age.

Yet the Harvey Houses, situated in remote towns about 100 miles apart, were far removed from the scene of the greatest early chain-restaurant growth in the United States. Most restaurant activity in the late nineteenth and early twentieth centuries took place in crowded eastern and midwestern cities, where people needed a quick, inexpensive meal within walking distance of where they worked or lived.

In the cities, only a limited number of establishments initially served food to people on a workingman's budget. One such establishment was the old-time saloon or tavern, which often provided free food to any man who paid for a beer. Another source of nourishment was the lunch wagon, a horse-drawn cart that first appeared in 1872 traveling the streets of Providence, Rhode Island. Some lunch wagons operated from dusk to dawn, others during daylight hours, dispensing food near factories, ball parks, race tracks, and other places where people worked or congregated. The typical operator handed sandwiches, slices of pie, beverages, and a few other items through an open window to waiting customers. By 1884, operators were beginning to introduce wagons wide enough so that customers could step up into them and be protected from rain, snow, and wind while they ate. Many of these cars had an eating area with stools at one end and a tiny kitchen at the other; the kitchen also had a window or two for handing food to customers who preferred to stay outside.

Eventually, most lunch wagons quit making daily journeys through the streets, settling instead on small plots of land and evolving into factory-made buildings known as dining cars, or "diners." By about 1910 the demand for a larger menu and greater seating capacity resulted in a new interior layout, with the kitchen placed against a long wall and an eating counter running down the car's center. Customers, sitting on round metal stools, faced the cooking operation.

During the same period, soda fountains became a much-appreciated part of American life. After the Civil War, a small number of drugstores operated soda fountains, serving beverages made of a mixture of soda water and sweet cream syrup. In 1874, the operator of a soda fountain at the Franklin Institute Exposition in Philadelphia ran out of the syrup, so he substituted ice cream and created a delicious new concoction—the ice cream soda. The new drink captivated the public, and soda fountains rapidly proliferated until by 1908 there were an estimated 75,000 of them, usually with counters of marble and pumps and fittings of nickel. Chicago alone supported more than 3,500 fountains. Inevitably, some operators began serving sandwiches, cakes, and other items, so that by 1912 many soda fountains had evolved into another institution, the "luncheonette," and by the 1920s other counter-service establishments advertised themselves as "coffee shops."

But taverns, lunch wagons, luncheonettes, soda fountains, and coffee shops couldn't satisfy all the burgeoning demand for fast, low-priced eating places. Much of the inexpensive nourishment was provided by yet another kind of restaurant, the humble institution known as the "lunchroom." These were small and often cramped shops, too utilitarian to enter the national folklore; they possessed neither the romance of the soda fountain nor the proletarian charm of the diner. Nonetheless, they achieved enormous success, largely because they were so economical. From the 1880s to the 1920s, many of the better-managed lunchrooms developed into chains, some—

like the Ueata Lunch Company in Detroit—serving only a single city, others operating in extensive areas of the nation.

In 1893, John R. Thompson, who had gone to Chicago with his bride to see the World's Columbian Exposition, purchased his first lunchroom on South State Street in that city; by 1920 there were 104 Thompson's lunchrooms in a score of cities. James A. Whitcomb started the Baltimore Dairy Lunch in the 1880s in Baltimore and by 1921 he, too, had 104 lunchrooms in a number of cities. William and Samuel Childs opened their first Childs Unique Dairy Lunch on Cortlandt Street in New York City in 1889 and had 86 restaurants in operation by 1920. In Springfield, Massachusetts, in 1904, Harry S. Kelsey opened his first Waldorf Lunch, its name reputedly inspired by a passer-by's facetious suggestion that he name the lunchroom after New York's famed Waldorf-Astoria; by 1920, 75 Waldorf Lunch outlets were feeding people in Springfield, Providence, Boston, New York, Buffalo, and other cities.

The face that a lunchroom presented to people walking by was relatively nondescript. Generally, lunchrooms occupied a sliver of ground-floor space in a building that contained other businesses at street level and on the floors above. The building's sidewalls were usually pressed against adjoining buildings. Consequently, lunchrooms had little potential for achieving distinctive architectural identities. Lunchrooms were not freestanding structures; they had only a façade with which to announce their presence, and not even the façade of an entire building.

Inside, a few basic layouts prevailed. Where the interior was long and narrow, a lunchroom might adopt the typical luncheonette or coffee-shop configuration—a long counter and a line of stools running from the front of the shop to the back, so that customers, as they ate, faced the counterman and a food preparation area that hugged the sidewall. Heavier cooking often was done out of sight, in a kitchen at the rear. In some narrow Childs lunchrooms, tables for four, with bentwood chairs, were placed on each side of the long center aisle, and waitresses delivered food from a preparation area at the rear. Where the space was more generous, row upon row of tables—each row consisting of as many as ten tables accommodating two persons each—occupied the center of the restaurant. This created an air of mass feeding, yet it was still less spartan than the restaurants run by chains like Thompson's, Waldorf, and Baltimore Dairy Lunch. In those, customers did without tables and eating counters and sat, instead, at one-armed chairs like those used in classrooms. Upon entering a "one-arm lunch" shop, the customer might receive a ticket from an attendant and then walk to the far end of the restaurant, where roasts and other foods—often prepared in a kitchen to the rear—were carved or portioned out at a small counter. The

Original Waldorf Lunch in Springfield, Mass., soon after it opened in 1904. Turnover was rapid in "one-arm" lunch places like this.

At the Waldorf Lunch on Niagara Street in downtown Buffalo, 1919, most customers either sat at "settles" along a side wall or straddled metal tubing that held a tray in front of them.

counterman handed the customer his order and punched a section of the ticket indicating how much to pay. The customer then carried his tray of food to one of the chairs, which were set with backs to the walls, facing an aisle busy with other customers coming and going. The noise and constant motion gave the customer little incentive to linger over lunch, and that was fine as far as owners were concerned. They could generate a heavy volume of business in a shop of minimal size. Overhead was reduced by the self-service procedure, which eliminated the need for waiters and waitresses, and by having much of the food preparation done by a commissary in a low-rent area outside the central business district. By 1907 there was even a machine called the "automatic cashier" that dispensed tickets near the door, thus eliminating the need for an attendant as well.

The quest for more efficient and occasionally more comfortable designs became a major preoccupation of low- and moderately-priced restaurants. Waldorf Lunch introduced a metal stool with two curving supports at the front that held a metal tray-table in front of the customer; the customer's legs had to straddle the supports, but since most lunchroom patrons were male, that was acceptable. The advantage of this stool with an attached tray was that each customer received an eating surface of his own—thus accommodating single diners efficiently—and yet friends could face each other as they ate, since the trays were clustered in groups of two or four. In 1915 the Waldorf's founder obtained patents for still another lunchroom innovation, an improved "settle"—basically a device combining the features of a one-armed chair and a one-person booth. Kelsey's settles were a series of high-backed seats placed with their backs against the wall, with wooden partitions between each seating compartment so that a customer would neither see nor be seen by people sitting on either side. Each settle was equipped with a table surface almost identical to that of a one-armed chair, but detachable for cleaning or refinishing. Settles permitted convenient maintenance, provided some privacy, and required less space than tables and chairs. John H. Mink, who entered the lunchroom business in New York in the 1890s, recognized that many customers felt awkward perching on tall stools at tall counters—a carryover from tavern furnishings—and so he introduced low counters and low stools. Others followed his example, not only in the lunchroom business, which catered primarily to men, but also in soda fountains, luncheonettes, and coffee shops, which served a greater proportion of women and children, who had more difficulty maneuvering high stools. Restauranteurs began to recess the base of the counter to provide more adequate foot room. They started to arrange the counter not as one straight run but as a series of connected horseshoes; customers could more easily carry on conversations with one another at a U-shaped counter, and more importantly, the employee standing inside the "U" could serve a half-dozen people almost from a stationary position.

Below: *By 1924, when the Sani Products Company ran this ad, shiny white materials had become a hallmark of budget restaurants.* Right: *J. Willard Marriott's Hot Shoppes started in 1927 behind this modest storefront on Fourteenth Street N.W. in Washington, D.C.*

Is it *still* 1910 in your restaurant?—

This intense concern with efficiency and labor productivity was characteristic of much of the business world at the turn of the century. In the late nineteenth and early twentieth centuries, a Philadelphia engineer, Frederick W. Taylor, methodically studied the work processes of American industry and recommended ways to achieve greater output per employee through a smoothly coordinated succession of actions or techniques. Taylor's approach, summed up in 1911 in his influential book *The Principles of Scientific Management,* turned the nation toward time and motion studies and incited a widespread passion for eradicating wasteful procedures.

One of the most notable expressions of the interest in systematization was the development of the cafeteria. Essentially, the cafeteria represented the restaurant industry's first attempt at emulating the assembly line, by having a line of customers put together their own meals in a continuous, moving operation from start to finish. If the cafeteria typically promised more efficiency than it delivered—a couple of indecisive customers or a shortage of mashed potatoes could bring the entire line to a halt—it compensated with other advantages: the owner could do without waitresses, tipping was eliminated, and the customers could see every item before buying. Self-service lunchrooms, of course, had much the same advantages and might have been called cafeterias if they had had a more varied selection, a longer service line, and larger seating capacity.

The first cafeterias appeared in the 1890s, usually operated by the Young Women's Christian Association (YWCA) and other groups with at least semi-philanthropic objectives. By 1906 cafeterias were being run as profit-making enterprises in Los Angeles, where Boos Brothers established a chain that soon expanded northward to San Francisco. From California, commercially operated cafeterias spread eastward. In 1918 in Kansas City, Missouri, a lunchroom operator named Clarence M. Hayman started the Forum Cafeteria chain, which eventually expanded south to Houston, north to Minneapolis, and east to Cleveland. In 1920 in Waterloo, Iowa, Benjamin Franklin Bishop started Bishop's Cafeterias, now known as Bishop Buffets, and Charlotte, North Carolina, saw the founding of the S & W Cafeterias, another chain still in business. In Mobile, Alabama, J. A. Morrison and a financial backer, G. C. Outlaw, started Morrison's Cafeterias, today the largest cafeteria organization in the U.S.

The key to a cafeteria was its large scale of operation. If the cafeteria was to achieve optimal efficiency, it required a bigger investment and a higher volume of customers than other kinds of restaurants. With its ample kitchen, large seating capacity, and a service counter often 75 feet long, it also required much more space than the typical lunchroom, luncheonette, or coffee shop. Sometimes it occupied an extensive ground floor and mezzanine, at other times a commodious basement, but rarely could it do business in narrow shops, where the rent was lower. The cafeteria's elephantine space requirements and its need to be centrally located allowed little flexibility for dealing with the real-estate market. The cafeteria was best at providing a heavy, hot, full meal, but the public taste headed in other directions as the 1920s progressed. More women workers, less physically strenuous jobs, an increasing so-phistication about fitness and nutrition—all these factors shifted the public appetite toward lighter midday meals. Consequently, although some cafeteria chains contin-ued to prosper and expand, a growing number of customers went to counter-service restaurants such as coffee shops. There they could get light lunches—salads, soups, sandwiches—and without the inconvenience of standing in line. Counter-service res-taurants could achieve an acceptable level of efficiency in quarters much smaller than those of cafeterias. Depending on how closely the counter stools were placed to one another and whether they had backrests, counter-service restaurants could to some extent regulate, through design, their customers' length of stay. To attract women and groups of diners, some coffee shops did add tables and booths—two kinds of seating associated with slower turnover—but the counter itself generated a rapid succession of customers.

What else could be done to maximize efficiency? In 1925 a restaurant magazine provided an answer: "There's more profit if you can get them to stand up." The Hard-ing Sandwich Shops in Chicago and a few other establishments had started taking orders at a counter, from which the customer carried the food to one of a series of high tables and high shelves throughout the restaurant. The shop contained no chairs, no stools. With only a high table or a shelf attached to the wall or to a pillar, there was often barely enough room for a nine-inch plate and a cup of coffee, and the customer risked losing his place if he went back to the counter for another serving. The advantage to the operator was that the customer took up very little space for a brief amount of time; the average person rushed through a meal in less than ten minutes.

Mechanical and electrical power offered still other possibilities for increasing efficiency. In Philadelphia, the Linton Lunch chain installed electrically operated button boards in eighteen of its sandwich shops by the early 1930s. A number was assigned to each luncheon combination, and employees silently transmitted orders to the kitchen by pushing the appropriate buttons. For special instructions, the employ-ees used speaking tubes. Conveyor belts sent the food out from the kitchen at the rear of the restaurant and carried back the dirty dishes.

In 1921 Lazarus Muntean of Highland Park, Michigan, invented an "eat-as-you-go" lunchroom mechanism. Tables and chairs were set on a platform that slowly moved around the room, past serving counters from which the customers took whatever portions they wanted. In the center of each table was to be a spigot dispensing ice-cold drinking water. Each table was also to be fitted with a lamp and with an electric motor which, at the push of a button, would turn on a fan.

Whether anyone ever put such a restaurant into commercial operation is doubtful. Muntean failed to grasp one crucial element: from the standpoint of power consumption and mechanical simplicity, it was better to place the food rather than the diners in motion. Thus, by 1930 in Long Beach, California, the Merry-Go-Round Cafe chain was seating customers at a circular counter. After being served a small meat order, customers could reach forward and help themselves to the salads, fruits, vegetables, and desserts that continuously revolved in front of them. By March 1931, thirteen Merry-Go-Round Cafes sprang up from Southern California to Seattle, charging a set price of fifty cents a meal. Instead of a circular counter, which required a building twice as wide as the typical urban storefront, the newer cafés used an oval counter, which could be accommodated behind a single standard storefront.

Self-service emerged as a central idea of the twentieth century; self-service ho-

A glass cover shielded the revolving foods at the Merry-Go-Round Cafe.
The chain remained in business until the late 1930s.

tels, self-service grocery stores like A & P and Piggly Wiggly, and countless home appliances that took the place of servants reflected the widening acceptance of the self-service concept. Within the restaurant industry, one form of self-service ultimately came to possess an aura of glamour, of big-city sophistication. This was the Automat, an invention that arrived in the United States when the century had barely begun.

Two Philadelphia lunchroom operators, Joseph Horn and Frank Hardart, ordered the first Automat mechanism from a German firm that installed food-vending machines in European train stations. Their original purchase sank on a ship that went down near the coast of England in 1901, but the loss was insured, and on June 9, 1902, a $30,000 Automat opened at 818 Chestnut Street in Philadelphia. Exulted *The Evening Bulletin:* "The horseless carriage, the wireless telephone and the playerless piano have been surpassed. . . . Artistically, it is a glittering, though effective, combination of plate glass, marble tiling, weathered oak wainscoting and hammered brass trimmings. Practically, it is a boon to thousands of hungry business men and women."

In an Automat, as in a cafeteria, food was cooked in advance, and the customer had the satisfaction of seeing what he was getting before he bought it. The difference was that in an Automat, unlike a cafeteria, employees did not wait on customers and the customers did not have to queue into long lines. They simply stepped up to the rows of glass cases and dropped coins into the slots. A nickel bought a ham sandwich, a slice of apple pie, or a dish of rice pudding. Heated or refrigerated compartments could deliver everything from soup to ice cream. The glass-fronted compartments and shiny, nickel-plated fittings created an impression of clean, sparkling conditions and also gave an illusion of effortlessness; all the labor went on behind the scenes.

By May 1912 Horn & Hardart had four Automats operating in Philadelphia. The partners then developed and patented their own apparatus and opened the first Automat in New York on July 2, 1912, at 1557 Broadway on Times Square. Behind the Broadway Automat's symmetrical, moderately Beaux-Arts–style façade with its tall, arched, flanking doorways and its weighty cornice lay an interior more than grand enough for the selling of inexpensive meals. A great wall of stained glass with "Automat" lettered in its center supplied decoration and partial illumination for the high, wide interior, which was much more generous than the typical cramped lunchroom. A vinelike pattern in plaster climbed a center column and radiated onto the ceiling, the decoration interspersed with clusters of light bulbs like pearls set in a piece of jewelry.

Along the side and rear walls stood the Automat mechanism—not just machinery but machinery with splendor, its ornate wooden framework sparkling with beveled mirrored surfaces, its uppermost edges alternating between swelling arches and horizontals, so that the entire room was enveloped in an ennobling, continuous rhythm. Placed on the mosaic-tiled floors were large, round, marble-topped tables, each accompanied by four sturdy wooden chairs with rounded backs. Here was efficiency enshrined, daily necessity given an atmosphere of glory. It was an exceedingly effective first effort at winning the loyalty of New York.

People from all levels of society ate in Automats at least occasionally. Movies often cast their cosmopolitan stars dropping coins in Horn & Hardart's slots, and tourists felt compelled to visit an Automat. The core of the Automats' constituency, however, was the lower-middle class—clerical workers and others who had to eat cheaply.

Expanding rapidly in New York, Horn & Hardart sometimes erected new buildings, as it had on Broadway, usually with at least one floor containing income-producing rental space. At other times, the company occupied space in existing buildings. Although a few Automats continued the use of stained glass on the façade, fronts with plate glass predominated, often with the company name discreetly painted in the center of the window. A big metal sign might extend above the sidewalk, but until the 1930s, most restaurants, Horn & Hardart's among them, gave their windows an air of composure. Vases of flowers, pyramids of fruit, collections of garden produce, cardboard displays—these were the sorts of things featured in a respectable restaurant window.

In the two decades after Horn & Hardart's arrival in New York, most Automats fell short of the original Broadway outlet's grandeur. Their ceilings achieved considerable height, since tall ceilings were common in the years before sophisticated mechanical ventilation, but generally they had plain walls, patterned tile floors, smooth-plastered ceilings, and a series of pillars and beams for support. Some Automats even sat humbly in basements.

Still, they were usually more spacious than lunchrooms, and the company was flexible enough to recognize that a mechanized delivery system was not always the best way to meet patrons' needs. In the early years, customers could deposit coins in certain slots and a short while later receive food that had been cooked to order—bacon and eggs, for example. It wasn't long before some foods became available without the use of coin slots, and by 1920 Horn & Hardart had set up cafeteria service as an auxiliary to all its Automats, especially to provide hot foods.

Success in Philadelphia and New York led Horn & Hardart to introduce the

Above: *Behind the scenes at the Waldorf System's Automat in the Little Building, Boston, about 1919.* Right: *Street view of Horn & Hardart's first New York Automat, Times Square, soon after its opening in 1912.*

Automat to Boston and Chicago around the middle of the 1910s. It also led to imitation by others, like the "Autometer" in Washington, D.C., in 1924. But the Boston Automat operation (run by the Waldorf system) and the Chicago venture both failed within a few years, perhaps partly because impersonal service had limited appeal but perhaps also because of inadequate management or inconsistent food quality. The company vigorously contested the right of any other restaurant to use Automat mechanisms or a name containing the prefix "auto." In the end, the Automat remained a phenomenon restricted to New York and Philadelphia.

One issue that all restaurants had to deal with was sanitation. Through the middle and late nineteenth century, scientists and public health experts had accumulated a growing knowledge of how disease was transmitted. By the 1880s, surgeons dressed in white while performing operations, and the public was coming to realize that germs had to be eradicated or at least controlled. By 1906, when Upton Sinclair's book *The Jungle* exposed deplorable conditions in the meatpacking industry and sparked the uproar resulting in the Pure Food and Drug Act, it was obvious that restaurants, too, would have to respond to the widespread alarm.

Conscientious restauranteurs began to consider new instruments of sanitation, such as electrically powered dishwashing machines, and they put more effort into scouring their tableware, their equipment, and the surfaces of kitchens and dining areas. They wanted to impress customers with their efforts, and new materials helped make their achievement more noticeable. In 1905 a "white-alloy" metal of copper and nickel, capable of retaining its silvery finish after years of use, was first produced at a copper plant in New Jersey. The new material, given the trade name "Monel Metal," promised sparkling, corrosion-resistant surfaces. Later, stainless steel arrived on the market, presenting similar bright, shiny surfaces at lower cost. Sinks, refrigerators, dishwashers, coffee urns, steam tables, and ice-cream cabinets could proclaim their cleanliness to the sanitation-minded customer.

But restaurants started experimenting with a white, sanitary look even before Monel Metal and stainless steel began to make an impact. The Dennett chain of restaurants in New York City introduced gleaming white interiors in the 1880s, using a new process by which white glass was pasted onto the walls. The Childs restaurant chain, from its founding in 1889 until the 1920s, made shiny white walls one of its trademarks, relying first on white glass, then on tile.

More than walls could take on a brilliant whiteness. The counters of soda fountains customarily were constructed of white marble, and not long after 1910 nearly every surface in a restaurant could be given a spotless white finish. A foundry in Chicago introduced "Sani-onyx" table tops of sturdy, snow-white glass, and "Sani-metal" table legs, bases, and stools, made of cast iron coated with white porcelain enamel. Porcelain-enameled stools and table bases would not absorb dirt and grease; they also resisted the deteriorating effects of wet brooms and mops. As the obsession with cleanliness grew, questions arose about whether even marble was good enough. Counters were developed with glasslike white materials that resembled marble but were impervious to stains and scratches. "Better than marble" was the slogan used by Chicago's Vitrolite Company in promoting its glasslike product. Even the mahogany one-armed lunch chair was rechristened the "sanitary lunch chair" and outfitted with shiny nickel feet and a white glass surface for the tray.

By the 1920s, floors with exposed wood were no longer acceptable. Many floors were tiled and others were covered with linoleum or a troweled-on substance resembling terrazzo. The new materials withstood wear better and were easier to clean. Some of them also presented a choice of colors and patterns, along with the advantages of fire resistance, noise reduction, and fewer cracks for insects and dirt.

Restaurants set out to improve the quality of their air as well. At the turn of the century, kitchen odors, smoke, and stale air permeated many eating places. By the

1920s, restaurants were investing in exhaust fans and, after some unsuccessful installations, learning how to place them so that the air would be constantly fresh, especially in the public portion of the restaurant. Even with ventilation, however, restaurants suffered a downturn in business every summer. In hot weather, people were less inclined to go into restaurants, and when they did go in, they didn't eat as much as in winter. The solution lay in air conditioning, which became available in the 1920s and commonplace in the 1930s.

This ceaseless stream of experimentation and modification indicates just how progressive the restaurant industry had become by the opening decades of the twentieth century. Customary ways of doing things were continually open to challenge. New methods and materials found an appreciative audience, especially in the chain organizations, which were adept at taking an innovative idea and transforming it into standard practice. Chain restaurants placed an emphasis on sanitation and helped bring about a crisp-and-clean esthetic, a style of design that drew upon the smooth-surfaced products of foundry and factory rather than old-fashioned handicrafts. Some conscious artistry did make an appearance; floor tiles and metal furnishings, for example, were often worked into decorative patterns rather than left entirely plain. But function and economy were the driving forces. Indeed, the lunchroom was one of the common structures that attracted the admiration of architectural modernists. Like grain elevators, which were often cited as outstanding specimens of unadorned, functional design, lunchrooms seemed generally not to have relied on past styles. They embodied the contemporary boldness of the machine age. Lewis Mumford, one of the twentieth century's most perceptive observers of architecture and urbanism, surveyed the latest Childs restaurants in New York in 1921 and found "a fresh tradition" on the rise. Cheap, popular lunchrooms, he declared, constituted one of the "main sources of the modern style at present."

One curious aspect of this lunchroom modernism was that for most chains, as of 1921, it remained restricted almost entirely to interiors. Small restaurants generally occupied part of a large building, reducing the realm of their exterior architectural effects to a façade, and the façades tended to borrow from a variety of historical styles. The Childs chain was an exception. From early on, Childs recognized the merchandising potential of storefronts. It had often sought to attract attention by stationing an employee next to the front window, making pancakes. By around 1910, Childs, whenever it was able to do so, put white tile on its façades to advertise the bright, clean atmosphere inside.

Most restaurants didn't put much emphasis on exterior building design. What they did use to make themselves noticed were signs. As early as 1907, flashing electric signs intended to "attract attention 24 hours a day" were distributed by at least one manufacturer. "They literally burn your ad into the minds of the people," an advertisement insisted. Companies like Buffalo's Flexlume Corporation nudged the signs toward ever-greater dimensions until sometimes they rose higher than the buildings to which they were attached. "A Flexlume Electric sign," the company said, "will make your restaurant stand out and be seen far and near." The raised white letters against a dark metal background looked crisp, said the manufacturer, and, more than that, "sanitary."

By the late 1920s and the 1930s, many urban restaurant chains had decided to do something about their restrained façades, which had contributed more to the continuity of design along the street than to the corporate profile. Horn & Hardart sent crews out to renovate the façades of older Automats, enlarging the windows. Ever-larger expanses of plate glass, manufactured by new processes that reduced the price and improved the quality, were the key to up-to-date merchandising. Passers-by should be able to peer in and see how attractive the restaurant was—so went the thinking. To pull the pedestrian out of the hurrying sidewalk traffic, glass façades angled inward in the direction of the door. The pedestrian who lingered, looking inside, found himself almost automatically at the restaurant's entrance. Subtly manipulative design did everything but open the door for him.

Compared to the staid storefronts of the turn of the century, the new ones had a vibrant liveliness. For the front of a Chock Full o'Nuts coffee shop at 62 Broadway in 1934, Jules Kabat, a young designer working for New York architect Horace Ginsbern, used his skill in lighting and styling to design an angled entrance of plate glass, glossy black Carrara glass, bronze bands, and molded shapes exuding the geometric sophistication of Art Deco. In later years, the height and width of the meticulously cleaned plate glass in Kabat's Chock Full o'Nuts façades grew until the restaurant was transparent from floor to ceiling—as open, visually, as some of the celebrated houses of the Modern Movement.

In this way, modernism marched out of the kitchen and dining area and into the street, into an increasingly public domain—the façade, in effect, representing the final frontier to be conquered. But by the time it made a major impact on restaurant exteriors, modernism had shown itself to encompass more than one particular style. Art Deco proved to be one of the most popular varieties in the late 1920s and '30s. At the Forum Cafeteria that opened in Cleveland in 1931, the smooth, gleaming surfaces took on jazzy Art Deco effects, with interior walls covered in Vitrolite, the glass-

Chock Full o'Nuts at 62 Broadway, New York, 1934, the company's first move toward sleeker modern styling.

Chock Full o'Nuts at 1350 Broadway in 1952 employed what the glass manufacturers called a "visual front," putting the entire interior on display.

like material that had been used for white countertops a decade earlier. Here the Vitrolite was installed not in a single color but in a careful gradation from black and green near the floor to gray and ivory near the ceiling. A band of wavy lines in bright colors formed a shoulder-height border. Pilasters and columns were surfaced with up to a dozen narrow vertical black Vitrolite strips, and the dazzling effects were reinforced by an extensive array of mirrors.

Perhaps the finest Art Deco restaurant exterior belonged to the Automat that opened in August 1938 at 104 West Fifty-seventh Street in New York. Designed by Ralph Bencker, it exuded an exuberant modern spirit in curving pink terra-cotta. A stack of blocky squares at each end of the façade conveyed stability and strength, countering the thrust of three curves in the façade's center. As the façade rose, it stepped back with a combination of curving and rectilinear shapes surprisingly intricate for a building only two stories high. The restaurant's several signs, saying "Automat" and "Horn & Hardart," were mounted at nearly every level, vertically and horizontally, but not one of them seriously marred the quality of the robust yet complex design. The West Fifty-seventh Street Automat and a few others constructed in the 1930s succeeded—in combination with the entire chain's up-to-the-minute graphics—in reinforcing Horn & Hardart's prestige.

The Art Deco style helped bring about some of America's most captivating restaurants, but the same kinds of materials could also be shaped into lighter, more austere compositions. In 1939 the Kansas City–based Forum organization opened its first Chicago cafeteria. A long sign bearing the chain's slogan, "Save $104 a Year," projected from a two-story façade that consisted of little more than great sheets of plate glass and planes of lustrous reddish-brown granite and shiny blue Vitrolite. Designed by G. B. Franklin with assistance from Frank Sohn, the Chicago Forum wholly avoided the weightiness of Art Deco. Great circular lamps seemed to hover like flying saucers against the acoustic ceiling of the immense cafeteria, which had seats for 474 and could accommodate 8,000 customers a day. A huge mirror spanned the dining room's entire wall and reflected the Vitrolite structural glass of the opposite wall. Like many cafeterias, this Forum had a balcony dining area, but it was a structure whose curving edge seemed to float effortlessly above the serving counter.

Restaurants like the Forum, Horn & Hardart, and Chock Full o'Nuts seemed to represent a clear triumph of modernism. But the restaurant industry always contained conflicting currents, in part because of the variety of its clientele. In 1922

A conspicuous glossiness characterized the Forum Cafeteria in Cleveland in 1931.

William Childs, who had skillfully used a white-and-bright look to help his chain grow to 101 restaurants, observed that "the white, the really sanitary features, have their limitations . . . soft materials, for some purposes, are more pleasing to the senses than hard materials." Within six years, he started a series of more expensive restaurants that shifted away from modern materials and contemporary atmosphere. Close to Symphony Hall in a fashionable section of Boston, behind an imposing façade redolent of Beaux-Arts classicism, Childs in 1928 began operating a restaurant intended to convey the charm of a rural French village. The main dining room imitated a village square. Tables were set on a floor of stone, surrounded on three sides by quaint, half-timbered façades with weathered shingle roofs. In diminutive upper windows, a faint light glinted, giving the illusion of a never-ending dusk—an illusion reinforced by concealed bulbs that cast light onto a ceiling painted to resemble sky. A few leaning street lamps and old wall lanterns shed a feeble light around the perimeter, and in one of the second-story openings hay was stacked, as if ready to be fed to the livestock. The Boston restaurant was called Old France, to be followed by Old Algiers and Old London in a series of restaurants striving for a romantic atmosphere.

On the West Coast, Clifford E. Clinton, who had grown up in a family that operated San Francisco cafeterias, similarly was attracted by the idea of eating places with an atmosphere divorced from everyday reality. In 1931 in downtown Los Angeles, he opened the first Clifton's Cafeteria, its name an amalgam of his first and last names, and by 1935 he was doing so well that he could afford to open a second cafeteria and give it a novel decorative scheme. This "Brookdale" Clifton's, which continues to do business today on Broadway near West Seventh Street, captured the feeling of a redwood forest. Structural posts were covered with genuine redwoods, and walls were painted with murals that accentuated the effect of looking through a forest. A flowing brook, a waterfall, a wishing well, and a little stone chapel filled out the interior. The crowning touch was a great lamp that had been recessed into the wall to create the illusion of the moon gleaming through the boughs of the trees.

In 1939 Clinton took a vacation in Hawaii, and when he came back, he knew what to do to his original cafeteria on Olive Street: turn it into a tropical paradise. He furnished it with a thatched hut and tropical plants, and far above the diners' tables he had neon tubing form enormous pastel flowers. On the mezzanine, a simulated rainfall burst forth every twenty minutes. The exotic effect extended outside, where cement stucco over steel and wire mesh made the façade look as if it were composed of huge boulders. Where other buildings had second-story windows, Clifton's

Clifton's "Pacific Seas" Cafeteria, 618 S. Olive Street, Los Angeles, in the 1940s, when customers could "dine free unless delighted."

sprouted tropical plants—a surprising sight, but not so startling as the waterfall that rippled down the center of the façade, glowing blue, green, pink, and yellow in the evenings. Clinton, whose chain eventually numbered six cafeterias in Southern California, called this his "Pacific Seas" Clifton's.

Neither the air of fantasy at Clifton's nor the Old World nostalgia of Childs represented the dominant theme in chain-restaurant design. In the 1930s the prevailing spirit in restaurant design, as in much other architecture and industrial design, drew from one or another form of modernism. The machine age had at last come to maturity, generating esthetic possibilities that enriched daily life. What most restaurants of the 1930s did have in common—whether their designs were rooted in modernism, nostalgia, or fantasy—was an appreciation of the importance of the facade. Even in dense urban locations, the exterior—the storefront—had emerged as an effective merchandising tool, helping to attract the attention of potential customers and, in many instances, to signal what would be found inside. All that was missing from chains like Childs, Forum, and Horn & Hardart was the standardization of an entire restaurant organization's appearance. That was the aim of a different group of chain restaurants.

CHAPTER TWO
Standardizing the Image

Overleaf: *Postcard view of Howard Johnson's at a traffic circle in Portsmouth, N.H., built in 1940, photographed in the 1950s.*

IN THE EARLY YEARS OF THE TWENTIETH CENTURY, the hamburger was not yet a favorite American food. Quite the contrary, ground meat had a dubious reputation, made worse by muckraking journalists' exposés of the meat-processing industry. Even if people had not been suspicious of what they contained, hamburgers would still have had their popularity limited by another consideration: they didn't have much flavor. Food stands that specialized in hamburgers, many of them at fairs and amusement parks, usually cooked the meat slowly, in thick lumps, a method that left the meat bland and dry.

Walter Anderson, an itinerant fry cook who had settled in Wichita, Kansas, was one of the first restaurant operators to aim at making hamburgers more appealing. The secret, he discovered, lay in flattening the meat into thin patties and then searing them on both sides to seal in the natural juices. In 1916 he opened a shop where, for a nickel apiece, he served hamburgers prepared by the new method, hamburgers whose freshness was assured by twice-a-day deliveries of meat and buns. The shop itself was a makeshift affair—a remodeled streetcar that Anderson equipped with a counter down the middle, three stools for customers, and, for a griddle, a flat piece of iron that initially didn't even have its edges turned up to prevent surplus grease from dripping onto the floor. But the hamburgers, fresh and flavorful, broke down the public's resistance—so much so that Anderson succeeded in opening a larger shop in the summer of 1920 and still another in December of that year.

To continue expanding, Anderson needed a partner and more capital, so he teamed up with a local real-estate and insurance man, Edgar Waldo "Billy" Ingram, and, with a $700 loan, opened a fourth shop in March 1921. Like the stand erected three months earlier, this one was constructed of blocks with a rough, rocklike face—rusticated concrete, a material that at the time was popular and inexpensive. The newest shop added two architectural features not found in the others—at the top of the walls was a chunky imitation of the crenellations found on castles, and toward the back of the building rose a crenellated turret. Painted on the façade for the first time was a name suggested by Ingram: "White Castle."

This was a clever piece of merchandising. By being called a "white castle," the little 10-by-15-foot stand laid claim to both cleanliness and importance, and the unusual profile commanded more attention than a typical lunchroom exterior. For well over twenty years, lunchrooms had been furnished with white interiors, both for easier cleaning and for impressing customers with how sanitary their surroundings were. White Castle, like some units of the Childs chain on the East Coast, cleverly took this technique a step further by proclaiming the white, sanitary atmosphere on the outside.

Later in 1921 four more White Castles were opened in Wichita, and the following year two more there, two in El Dorado, Kansas, and three in Omaha. The White Castle System of Eating Houses then grew fast, entering Kansas City in 1924; St. Louis in 1925; Minneapolis and St. Paul in 1926; Cincinnati, Louisville, and Indianapolis in 1927; Columbus, Detroit, and Chicago in 1929; and Newark, New Jersey, and New York City in 1930. By 1931 the chain owned and operated 115 units.

Unlike other chains that had been developing since the 1870s, White Castle had its own unique style: a standard freestanding building erected in a territory spanning half the nation. This was the first extensive restaurant organization to have a completely uniform architectural image, and the company presented its visible standardization as proof that White Castles had broken free of the unpredictability found in other lunchrooms. The repetitive look emphasized White Castle's commitment to consistency in food, service, and every other aspect of its business. The avoidance of design variations, White Castle believed, could not only magnify the chain's impact but also help win the public trust.

"When you sit in a White Castle," declared a brochure distributed to customers in 1932, "remember that you are one of several thousands; you are sitting on the same kind of stool; you are being served on the same kind of counter; the coffee you drink is made in accordance with a certain formula; the hamburger you eat is prepared in exactly the same way over a gas flame of the same intensity; the cups you drink from are identical with thousands of cups that thousands of other people are using at the same moment; the same standard of cleanliness protects your food. . . . Even the men who serve you are guided by standards of precision which have been thought out from beginning to end. They dress alike; they are motivated by the same principles of courtesy."

Left: *Original White Castle in Wichita, built in 1921, shown in 1929.* Below: *Two stuccoed second-generation Castles, both built in 1925, were in St. Louis (left) and Wichita.*

A White Castle employee was expected to wear a clean, white shirt with the sleeves folded neatly and all the buttons buttoned; a necktie that was not dirty or frayed; clean trousers with no patches on the seat; and an apron. His hair was to be kept trimmed and covered by a cap. Initially, the company provided its employees with linen caps; but these shrank when washed, with the result that they either started out too large or ended up too small. The company met this chronic if minor problem by developing a plant to manufacture disposable paper caps, which would adjust to fit every employee every time. It was a solution typical of the innovative spirit that White Castle also brought to issues of restaurant design and construction.

The buildings remained small. The original 10-by-15-foot design allowed for a

Before Going On Duty

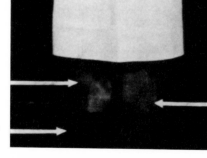

3. Be ready to make suggestions.

5. Be prepared to speak pleasantly.

7. Correct bad breath.

8. Get rid of chewing gum.

11. Wear clean shirt.

13. No body odor.

14. Fold shirt sleeves neatly.

17. No patches in trousers seat.

20. Wash hands.

21. Clean fingernails.

22. Wear clean trousers.

24. Wear comfortable shoes.

1. Cap should cover hair.

2. Keep hair trimmed.

4. Have clean shave.

6. Brush teeth.

9. Wear clean collar.

10. Be sure tie is not frayed or dirty.

12. Button all shirt buttons.

15. Fasten apron neatly.

16. Have shirt neatly tucked in trousers.

18. No wrist watch.

19. No flashy jewelry.

20. Wash hands.

21. Clean fingernails.

23. Turn up trousers if too long.

The appearance of White Castle employees was regulated from head to toe. This was the checklist as of 1931.

counter and five stools, and in 1935 the gross floor area of a new White Castle was still only 400 square feet. But not an inch was wasted, even on the griddle; the patties and buns were square, to utilize the entire cooking surface.

By the mid-thirties, the restaurant had accumulated the features that would earn it the nickname of "porcelain palace." The interior featured walls of white porcelain-enameled steel; a white porcelain-enamel backbar with nickel trim; and a counter with a linoleum top and a porcelain-enamel front. It also contained a tile floor, opal glass shelves for displaying merchandise, and an electrically operated heating, ventilating, and cooling system.

The only significant disruptions in the uniformity of White Castle's appearance were those caused by the introduction of new building designs. In 1922 the company made what it thought was an improvement, putting a surface of white stucco over a structural exterior of smooth concrete block. As a result, the new buildings didn't look as coarse as those made of rusticated concrete block, but neither did they lend themselves to ornamentation. They were plain. In 1926 the company shifted to another design, one that achieved more elaborate detailing by using white-enameled brick. Buttresses projected outward at the base of the building, and a corbeled cornice stepped out from the top of the corner tower. Above and below the windows, a course of black brick was laid vertically, to contrast against the white. "White Castle" was lettered in Gothic style in a leaded-glass pane of the restaurant's main window.

By far the most significant change in the building design came in 1928, when White Castle's construction superintendent, L. W. Ray, developed a movable building made of porcelain-enameled steel panels. The prototype, manufactured in Chicago, was shipped to Wichita and set on a vacant lot to see whether it would develop problems in the sweltering Kansas summer or the frigid winter. Not only did it survive exposure to the weather; when barrels of tar were lighted around the building's base, the company learned that a porcelain-steel structure would also withstand the intense heat of a fire and would prevent water from high-pressure hoses from penetrating the interior. What's more, the soot from the fire reportedly washed off the enamel easily. Consequently, in 1929 the new design became the company's standard. White Castle commissioned a number of companies to manufacture its buildings until 1934, when the restaurant organization established its own subsidiary, the Porcelain Steel Buildings Company in Columbus, Ohio, to produce all future Castles.

The building's interchangeable steel panels were secured with a locking device that dispensed with the use of rivets or bolts, thus making it easier to take the structure apart and move it. Wooden strips inside the walls prevented condensation and

Above: *A marble-streaked porcelain-enamel White Castle on Southern Boulevard, Bronx, N.Y., 1931.* Right: *White porcelain-enamel Castle on Hempstead Turnpike, Queens, N.Y., 1936. A larger, less toylike white-enameled building was introduced in the 1950s.*

eliminated the hollow sound of the usual metal structure. The porcelain-steel design made it possible for White Castle to extend a spotless, sanitary atmosphere from interior to exterior with maximum consistency, and it provided the entire building industry with a significant technical advance. The White Castle prototype appears to have been the first use of porcelain steel for a whole building exterior, an innovation soon borrowed by manufacturers of filling stations and those searching for modern ways of constructing houses and other buildings. Oddly enough, for the first three years, instead of achieving a truly gleaming whiteness on the exterior, White Castle used its new system to produce a porcelain enamel with the appearance of streaked marble. It wasn't until 1932 that the company switched to an all-white porcelain-enamel exterior.

White Castle never operated in more than about thirteen metropolitan areas, but nearly every aspect of the company and its buildings served as inspiration for other restauranteurs. Throughout almost the entire United States, local or regional chains took as their model one or more attributes of White Castle—the name, menu, operating procedures, construction techniques, materials, and design. In 1926, five years after White Castle was founded, White Tower began in Milwaukee. In 1927 the Little

Tavern chain began in Louisville. In 1929 White Tavern Shoppes started in Shelby-ville, Kentucky. The same year, in Houston, Jacob Cox Stedman started the Toddle House chain, which would eventually spread throughout much of the eastern half of the country. In Chattanooga, Krystal began in 1932, ultimately expanding through much of the Southeast. In 1935 White Hut restaurants began appearing in Toledo. In 1936 the Rockybilt chain was established in Denver, and the first unit of the Mem-phis-based chain of Hull-Dobbs Houses opened in Richmond, Virginia. Royal Castle appeared in Miami Beach in 1938. Indeed, in the 1980s, White Castle, now a chain of about two hundred restaurants in nine metropolitan areas, has become such an object of nostalgia that it has had to fend off new restaurants called West Castle and Lite Castle.

Some chain organizers made no secret of their debt to White Castle. Rody B. Davenport, a businessman who in 1932 was looking for an enterprise more Depres-sion-resistant than his high-fashion Davenport Hosiery Mills, acknowledged that he inspected a White Castle before joining with J. Glenn Sherrill to open the first Krystal that October in downtown Chattanooga. The new ten-stool restaurant featured square, one-ounce, five-cent burgers virtually identical to White Castle's. It also emu-lated White Castle's image of spotlessness; thus the name—derived from the saying "clean as a whistle and clear as crystal"—and the abundance of shiny surfaces. Inside and out, Krystal's walls were white porcelain enamel, and above one corner of the building sat the company symbol, a silvery Krystal ball. The building was smoother

The first Krystal takes shape in a Chicago factory, 1932.

A streamlined Krystal on 12th Street in downtown Columbus, Ga., 1936.

and much less ornamented than White Castle, but like White Castles, the early Krystals were prefabricated. Components of the original Krystal were manufactured and assembled in a Chicago factory, then taken apart and shipped to Chattanooga for reassembly on the business site. The rationale was to have a building that could be moved if necessary. Nearly every hamburger chain wanted its restaurants to be portable. In fact, one story has it that Jacob Cox Stedman's chain started under another name and was rechristened Toddle House as a result of a remark overheard when one of the first of the chain's restaurants was being moved through a tight intersection; a little boy watched the building swaying and exclaimed, "It's toddling." Whether that story is to be believed or not, portability was a decided advantage. It eliminated the need to purchase permanent building sites. The restaurants could adjust to changes in automobile traffic and public-transportation routes, and they could occupy lots that real-estate speculators were willing to lease only on a short-term basis—in some instances a mere thirty days at a time. Any chain that could pick up its building and move would obviously have a stronger hand in negotiating with landowners.

Since the new chain operations pioneered by White Castle typically aimed to do business twenty-four hours a day, some of the companies put their restaurants close to factories, whose two or three daily shifts would generate a steady stream of customers. Toddle House and Hull-Dobbs House, though much less enamored of factory neighborhoods, did try to locate on the "work side" of the street—the side that people traveled when heading toward downtown jobs in the morning. On the work side of the street, a restaurant could get more people into the habit of stopping for breakfast; sales were said to be slower on the opposite side of the street.

Like the urban chains that had grown up between the 1880s and 1920, the new standardized-image restaurants generally pushed up right against the sidewalks and attracted customers who arrived on foot or from trolleys, subways, and other mass transportation systems. But instead of sharing sidewalls with neighboring buildings, the new restaurants often pulled away from other structures—not far at first, but far enough to permit a fundamentally different approach to exterior design. Here, in its incipient stage, was one of the critical changes in twentieth-century chain restaurant design: the beginning of the abandonment of tight, densely urban patterns of development. Standing as separate objects, the new restaurants had the potential to achieve strikingly individualized personalities. It is no accident that this transformation began in the 1920s. By 1920 the number of motor vehicles in the United States had nearly quadrupled in just five years, to a total of 9.2 million cars, trucks, and buses. The automobile, a curiosity several years earlier, had by then become commonplace. A restaurant that could magnify its presence through distinctive architecture would capture the attention of the new legion of motorists. And the proliferation of cars and trucks demanded more gaps in the urban landscape—more driveways, more parking spots—thereby helping the new chain restaurants to stand apart from their neighbors. In the 1920s, some White Castles stood at the edge of lots where customers could park their cars. Sometimes a curb was built a short distance from the restaurant's walls to prevent drivers from bumping into the Castle. No space was allotted for shrubs or other greenery. White Castle and some of its imitators—White Tower, especially—had their restaurants surrounded by a bed of concrete.

If the automobile influenced the architectural character of chain restaurants, helping to bring about conditions in which buildings could adopt standardized images, the menu made an impact as well. The selection of foods varied somewhat from one standardized-image restaurant to another, and included such items as chili, waffles, hot dogs, sandwiches, ham and eggs, and a few beverages. But the heart of the relatively limited menu was the "hamburger sandwich"—ground beef on a bun. Popularized by White Castle, hamburgers presented a set of efficiencies that helped a restaurant earn a profit in a building of diminutive size. Hamburgers required little space for preparation and cooking, and they could be produced systematically, so fast there would be almost no waiting. As a result, turnover would be swift, and the size of the eating area could be reduced to a minimum. Toddle House, while prohibiting the cooking of orders in advance, aimed to have the average customer in and out in twelve minutes. Moreover, the hamburger was a perfect carry-out food. It was hot, it was easy to package, it required no utensils. Nearly every chain encouraged customers to "buy 'em by the sack" or "take home a bagful," and this substantial carry-out trade enabled the restaurants to operate with a much smaller seating capacity than would otherwise have been feasible. All these factors meant that a restaurant serving five-cent hamburgers could be a fraction of the size of a typical urban lunchroom. The small size, in turn, further increased the ease with which nickel-hamburger restaurants could be put on sites where they would stand apart from other buildings. It also magnified the opportunities for prefabrication of the buildings, and in a design that attracted attention and was uniform throughout the chain. In the chain-restaurant business, small was beautiful.

By the end of the 1920s, the principle of chain-wide architectural uniformity had become so well established that even when a nickel-hamburger outlet did rent space in an existing building, it succeeded in communicating its corporate identity. Chains used their company's materials and shapes on the storefront, sometimes installing the restaurant façade so that it projected a few inches from the rest of the building, all the more aggressively announcing its presence.

With few exceptions, the image presented on the exterior of the early hamburger chains was either quasi-historical or cozily domestic. White Castle latched onto medieval imagery and, with the exception of the plain stucco buildings constructed from 1922 to 1925, never let go. As the company increased its technical prowess, advancing from a traditional exterior material such as brick to newer materials like porcelain-enameled steel, it sought no corresponding advances in the style of its exterior. On the contrary, the buildings became ever more literal in their use of medieval forms. The marble-streaked porcelain building, of which fifty-five were constructed, attempted to duplicate on a smaller scale the stone battlements and turret of the Chicago Water Tower, which itself was built in 1869 in an imitation of forms used in Europe centuries earlier. When White Castle shifted its color back to white in the early 1930s, the styling remained loyal to its medieval borrowings—a reflection, perhaps, of Americans' mixed attitudes about tradition in buildings. People took satisfaction in modern materials if the materials served an obvious purpose, such as the accentuation of cleanliness, but they also found reassurance in designs that had the patina of history. White Castle's combination of medieval and modern was similar, after all, to the domestic architectural practice of installing bright metallic surfaces in a residential kitchen while giving the exterior of the house a decidedly traditional character. If a building could have a recognizably historical shape, a shape that was also entertaining, why not use it? As Billy Ingram recognized, a castle represented "strength, permanence, and stability," the newness of porcelain enamel notwithstanding.

White Castle's strongest competitor adopted almost the exact same historically based image. Twenty-three-year-old Thomas E. Saxe, his father, John E. Saxe, and an associate, Daniel J. O'Connell, inspected two White Castles in Minneapolis in 1926 before going back to Milwaukee, where the Saxes lived, and attempting to duplicate White Castle's success. That November, on Wisconsin Avenue near the Marquette University campus, they built and opened the first of a series of white, bright, one-story restaurants with an entrance in a corner tower, and they named it White Tower. The fledgling company, which under the Saxes' leadership would become one of the country's largest chains in the 1930s, did not engage in mere offhand imitation; it obtained measurements, photographs, specifications, and plans of a White Castle stand and supplied them to White Tower's architect.

A 12-by-24-foot Toddle House goes toddling through Memphis in 1938. Some Toddle Houses were veneered with a cement coating scored to resemble brick, making them lighter and easier to move.

Toddle House and its spin-off, Hull-Dobbs House, both of which were operated from Memphis from the 1930s on, projected soothingly domestic images. A typical Toddle House or Hull-Dobbs House was a small building of brick or clapboard with a pitched roof and traditional detailing, such as a broken pediment over the entrance. In front was a lawn, sometimes protected by a white picket fence. All of this made for a settled, sedate impression—appropriate for restaurants that sometimes operated in the more affluent parts of town, where they could aim for a clientele more genteel than factory workers. The most distinctive feature of Toddle House and Hull-Dobbs House was a pair of identical chimneys, one at each end of the building. The chimneys were strikingly large for such tiny buildings and were also, as customers discovered, thoroughly deceptive. On the interior, the typical chimney contained only a small heater, if that. Metal stools, tiled floors, and an array of stainless steel equipment behind the counter left no doubt that this was a modern restaurant, but on the outside there wasn't a hint of the metallic and industrial—only a suggestion that there might be oversize fireplaces inside. The buildings looked like cottages, and Toddle

First Hull-Dobbs House, Richmond, Va., 1936.

The interior of a Toddle House about 1939.

House's practice of installing few or no exterior signs enhanced the houselike character.

Little Tavern, which Harry F. Duncan extended from Louisville to Washington and Baltimore by 1930, erected cottage-like buildings with whitewashed brick walls and steeply pitched roofs. In December 1930 Duncan began developing plans for more modern materials—porcelain-enamel white walls on both interior and exterior and porcelain-enameled kelly green shingles on the roof. These modern materials soon predominated, yet the form remained that of a Tudor cottage on a city street. The shape of the building, like its name, was meant to bestow a cozy, friendly atmosphere upon even the hastiest lunch.

The disparity between hard, shiny, metallic modern surfaces and distinctly traditional exterior images persisted in many chains. But the early 1930s marked a turning point. In Tennessee, Krystal broke free of nearly all historical associations. The company, starting with its first outlet in Chattanooga, chose to build flat-roofed structures with none of the leaded glass, brickwork, or clapboard of other chains. Streamlining was emerging in the early thirties as a style that captured the essence of speed—a visual antidote to the dismaying lack of forward momentum in the economy—and Krystal embraced streamlining wholeheartedly. On Krystal façades, dark horizontal bands alternated with broad expanses of white porcelain enamel. The chromed lettering, the chromed Krystal ball, the chromed parapet edge, and, it might be argued, even the occasional chromed downspout brought ornament into the age of fluid motion. Some Krystal buildings had curved corners. Even when the company operated in storefront locations rather than in freestanding structures, it created a sense of streamlining by having a front window end in a quarter-circle curve, or, if the storefront was especially small, by installing a single circular window.

White Tower, too, arrived at a thoroughly modern image, but in a manner that has never been fully explained. In the late twenties, the company expanded at breakneck speed, using a building design borrowed from White Castle, and it wasn't long before the two nearly identical chains were competing in the same cities. In 1929 White Castle sued White Tower, accusing it of unfair competition. Later, White Tower sued White Castle in Detroit, contending that since White Tower had opened a string of shops in the Motor City before White Castle arrived there, the Towers should be protected from their nearly identical competitors. Legal proceedings disclosed how thoroughly White Tower had copied White Castle. White Tower not only had used one of the White Castle stands as a model but had hired a White Castle counterman, at substantially more than his Castle salary, to install the equipment. The counterman brought with him White Castle interior measurements, accounting forms, a specially designed White Castle spatula, and bits of metal used in a White Castle griddle.

Legal wrangling dragged on for years. In 1930 a Minnesota court ordered White Tower to change its name, its slogan, and its style of building in that state to avoid misleading the public. In 1934 a Michigan court also decided in White Castle's favor. White Tower appealed the Michigan decision, and two and a half years later, in May 1937, the Sixth District U.S. Court of Appeals ruled again in White Castle's favor. White Tower was now under orders to alter the name, slogan, and style of architecture of its Detroit outlets significantly enough to eliminate any confusion with its rival.

More than half a century after the legal confrontation began, it is impossible to track down the litigation's precise impact on White Tower, but it seems revealing that from 1933 on, White Tower increasingly diverged from White Castle in appearance. Between 1933 and 1935, White Tower energetically experimented with reflective sheet materials—Vitrolite and porcelain enamel—and employed them in less traditional ways than White Castle. Roofline crenellations disappeared. Leaded glass no longer appeared in the windows. Buttresses along the walls assumed an expression more Art Deco than medieval.

During this period, White Tower's owners began hiring a variety of architects and testing their ideas. In 1935 a prominent designer, B. Sumner Gruzen of New York, produced a curving restaurant in the streamlined Art Moderne style. Others tried designs that combined the flowing lines of Moderne and the ziggurat effects of Art Deco. The tower moved from the corner of the building—where it had been in White Castle as well as White Tower designs—to the center, and it took on a new function: it told time. For ten years, the chain had used the tower solely for image and visibility, but in 1936 and 1937 the tower began to display a clockface, yet another element that set it apart from White Castle.

Considerable experimentation was still going on in 1937, but by then the new White Tower units had achieved a clear differentiation from White Castle. The Tower had left the Middle Ages and landed confidently in the modern world. Surely some of this progress was the result of the legal challenge. From the filing of the first lawsuit in the summer of 1929 and certainly from the initial decision against White Tower in July 1930, the chain's owners must have realized they were in an untenable position and would have to search for an alternative identity. The impetus of court challenges spurred White Tower into achieving an architectural presence that was unusually powerful for a little building capable of seating only seven to twelve customers at its counter and a few more at its windows. Its mix of streamlined and Art Deco motifs was enhanced by handsome proportions and by ornamentation in keeping with machine-made materials. The thirties represented the summit of White Tower design.

The chain continued to evolve in the 1940s, following the architectural profession's general trend toward a rectilinear modernism of flat surfaces and more boxlike configurations. This was a brand of modernism possessing far less romance, however, and it had an especially unfortunate effect on small buildings like White Tower's. The reductionist approach, with its hard right angles and unembellished surfaces, robbed White Tower of its ability to convey a sense of richness. The flat surfaces of the increasingly austere Tower hinted, in fact, at the flatness of spirit that would come to characterize many urban business areas once corporations erected innumerable boxy office buildings in the International Style.

What might be said in acceptance, if not defense, of the boxier, stripped-down Tower is that there was a certain inevitability about it: finally the customer was getting a building entirely consistent with the hamburgers—ungenerous, reduced to essentials, a kind of portion-control applied to food and architecture alike. From the beginning of the restaurant industry's quest for efficiency, there had always been a danger that intense systematizing would reduce everything to basic functionalism and leave little room for pleasure. The self-service lunchrooms that proliferated just after 1900, with their one-armed chairs lined up against the walls and their coin-operated ticket

Before the White Tower at left, built in Boston in 1931, was refashioned in Art Deco style in 1938, it bore an even stronger resemblance to the brick White Castle at right, photographed in 1930 on Broadway in New York.

dispensers by the door, had made mealtime a routine, mass-feeding process, and now White Tower developed a similar monotony in its architectural image. Unwittingly, the stark designs that began appearing in 1940 emphasized just how exceptional White Tower's buildings from 1933 to 1939 had been.

Another legacy of the 1920s and 1930s was a profusion of funny or strange-looking buildings, designed to look like teapots, ice-cream cartons, and other household objects. Throughout America, giant versions of everyday objects appeared on sites where they would draw plenty of attention, usually along highways outside the cities. More of these were built in California than in any other part of the country. The mild California climate was kind to contortions executed in malleable stucco, and Californians had a relaxed attitude toward the unconventional. In Southern California, amazing sights showed up even in central business districts, as exemplified by Clifton's "Pacific Seas" cafeteria, that streetcorner tropical paradise in downtown Los Angeles.

Probably the most famous oddity in the Los Angeles restaurant field was the Brown Derby, erected on Wilshire Boulevard near Alexandria in 1926 by Herbert Somborn, a motion-picture producer who felt that if the food was delicious, a restaurant would succeed no matter what it looked like. Somborn eventually opened several other Brown Derbies, but the original remained the only one shaped like a hat.

A meat delivery man named Arthur Whizin was more committed than Somborn to the use of unusual buildings. In 1931 on Crenshaw Boulevard in Los Angeles, Whizin opened the first Chili Bowl, which, as the name implied, was a building shaped like a bowl, but with windows and doors puncturing its rounded shell. Inside, college-age youths in white pants and T-shirts served customers at a curved counter with twenty-six stools. Whizin succeeded in expanding his restaurant business—featuring chili, spaghetti, soups, steaks, and other dishes—until 1941, when twenty-three Chili Bowls dotted the roadsides of Southern California. Then World War II took away most of his manpower, and Whizin closed nearly all the restaurants.

Upper left: "Size" on the Chili Bowl was a California term for a hamburger patty smothered in chili beans and onions. Upper right: Built in 1926, the Brown Derby was moved in the 1930s. Bottom: Postcard view of the Coon Chicken Inns in 1938; the chain disappeared in the 1950s. Postcard by permission of Curt Teich Collection, Lake County Museum, Lake County, Ill.

Nationally Famous - COON CHICKEN INN - 2950 Highland Drive - SALT LAKE CITY. UTAH

Eccentric buildings are often remembered fondly now. What is forgotten is that scattered among the visual jokes were a few buildings that took their supposed humor from unattractive stereotypes. In 1924 the small chain of Coon Chicken Inns was founded, and by 1934 there were inns in Salt Lake City, in Portland, Oregon, and on the outskirts of Seattle. These restaurants, specializing in Southern fried chicken, were unexceptional log-walled buildings, notable only for a visual gimmick: on the front of each was a face—at least 10 feet high—of a black bellhop or waiter, one eye closed in a perpetual wink while his mouth gaped open in a monstrous grin. At the Coon Chicken Inn in Salt Lake City, customers walked through the mouth to enter the restaurant, where they were served by black waiters. The theme was reinforced by presenting the same black stereotype on menus and dinner plates.

But novelty, even novelty free of offensiveness, wasn't what people most wanted when they were on the road. There was a need for someone to do for automobile travel in the 1930s what Fred Harvey had done for western rail travel in the 1870s: make it predictable and pleasant. By the early 1920s, automobile tourism had gained enormous popularity, but while it broadened the horizons of average Americans, it complicated such mundane matters as eating. Families getting away from home packed their meals, ate canned foods, tried roadside stands, or took from farmers' fields. None of these represented an entirely satisfactory solution to the problem of eating while traveling, nor were roadside eating establishments a trouble-free alternative. Small, individually operated cafés offered food of uncertain quality. Rural tea rooms had an emphasis on daintiness that didn't appeal to many travelers, and tea-room prices could be high.

Manufacturers of prefabricated diners saw travelers as a huge potential market. As one of the leading manufacturers observed in the spring of 1929, "20,000,000 families will again be skimming along the broad sunlit highways. They will be hungry—thirsty! There will be traffic tieups. . . . millions will be forced to get their food where they can find it. And that will be, in many cases, in attractive O'Mahony Dining Cars located at strategic points on the highways and catering to tourists, truckers, and all-year-round drivers."

What the O'Mahony advertisement failed to mention was that diners also had drawbacks. Each one had to be judged individually; the food might not measure up, and the preponderantly male atmosphere of many diners added another source of uncertainty for traveling families.

In 1931, B/G Sandwich Shops, a Chicago-based chain of about forty restaurants in downtown areas, decided to test the roadside market by opening a "B/G Eating Inn" in a dining car manufactured by Ward & Dickinson of Silver Creek, New York.

The plan was that if the first venture—on a plot shared with a filling station—succeeded, B/G would consider establishing a series of roadside outlets in suburban and rural areas. But diners failed to catch on as chain restaurants. Resembling too many dining cars operated by independent operators, they couldn't announce their corporate identity as effectively as an instantly recognizable White Castle or White Tower. Besides, there was something incongruous about the diner as a symbol of roadside eating: auto touring had initially been portrayed as a romantic escape into a countryside untainted by industrialism. People had been propagandized with the notion that exploring by automobile would liberate them from the restricted travel offered by railroads. The diner, looking as if it were ready to go clacking down the tracks, borrowed its appearance from the very vehicle that people had been told thwarted their ability to discover the genuine America. Even aside from the railroad image, there remained the question of why people who were trying to get away from cities and factories for a vacation would be pleased to eat in buildings with industrial overtones. The truth was, many people would stop at diners, and some enjoyed the atmosphere, but there was a market for an alternative place to eat, someplace more homey, more traditional.

It was this yearning that Howard Deering Johnson had the shrewdness to satisfy. Johnson had been a businessman for about fifteen years before he developed the formula that would alter the nation's habits of roadside dining. He took over his father's cigar-wholesaling business and then purchased a marginal drugstore-newsstand-soda fountain in Wollaston, Massachusetts, the Boston suburb where he'd grown up. The soda fountain experience led him to concentrate in 1925 on producing a superior-tasting high-butterfat ice cream, which sold well. Soon Johnson began opening ice cream stands along beaches and roads in the Boston area, using orange paint and his own name to make the nondescript little buildings identifiable. In 1929 he also opened a full-service restaurant on the ground floor of the Granite Trust Company's new bank building in neighboring Quincy, struggling for a long while to make it profitable.

In 1935 Johnson's great moment of opportunity arrived when he decided for the first time to use a business method already common in other kinds of enterprises—franchising. Reginald Sprague, a yacht captain who had gone to school with Johnson, offered in January of that year to sell Johnson a property in the Cape Cod village of Orleans. Sprague thought the property, located on a popular tourist route, would be a good spot for another Johnson ice cream stand. Johnson, however, thought an ice cream stand combined with a good restaurant would make more money, and since he couldn't finance it himself, he persuaded Sprague to construct and run the restaurant

An early Howard Johnson's stand. In the amateur tradition of commercial design, nearly every surface was a candidate for advertising.

while purchasing ice cream and other products from Johnson. The restaurant would be owned by Sprague but would bear Johnson's name.

On May 11, 1935, this first franchised Howard Johnson's Restaurant, built to Johnson's specifications and operated in accordance with his policies, welcomed the public. It achieved immediate success, and Johnson rapidly expanded, using the same method in most instances. The restaurants were built primarily with the franchisees' money but designed by Johnson's architects, led by Joseph G. Morgan. Modifications were permitted to suit the franchisee, but essentially the buildings followed company guidelines. By the fall of 1940, more than 130 restaurants were in operation—two of them in Florida, the rest spread from Maine to Alexandria, Virginia.

These were conspicuous restaurants. Johnson had a knack for selecting sites that would be visible from a great distance. They stood at major intersections, at traffic circles, along gradual curves—wherever they were sure to be noticed. There had been public outcries in the twenties and early thirties against billboards and other roadside signs, and Johnson was reluctant to resort to such crude advertising devices. He set out to make the building its own advertisement—complemented, however, by a big sign directly out front.

The Johnson's buildings prior to World War II had more variety than is commonly remembered today. Shapes, sizes, and detailing varied from one restaurant to another. Some had gabled roofs, others hip roofs. Cupolas varied in degree of elaboration. One converted inn had a windmill on its façade. The general practice was to develop a workable design for a particular location and then, at other sites, reproduce it with modifications—a wing to one side, wings to both sides, a rear projection. Johnson's designers experimented with Art Moderne, giving at least a couple of restaurants flat roofs, smoothly rounded corners, and some windows of glass block. The large sign near the highway often adopted a streamlined esthetic. Horizontal bands of neon wrapped around the sign, and more bands set each message apart from the one above or below, announcing "grille," "cocktail lounge," "fried clams," and "28 flavors." Even the name was streamlined, each *n* of "Johnson" set in lower rather than upper case, maximizing the number of curves.

But Howard Johnson's basic style consisted of Georgian architectural elements applied to a building whose shape, while not Georgian, was in character with New England's past. Even the streamlined, round-cornered restaurants had tall spires with traditional ornamentation rising from their flat roofs. These contributed visibility along with a pleasant suggestion of New England church and town hall architecture.

The orange paint used on the ice cream stands was applied to the roofs of the roadside restaurants, including Sprague's franchised shop on Cape Cod. On asphalt shingles, however, the paint produced a dull finish, and Johnson searched for improvements until he obtained porcelain-enameled metal shingles that glinted in the sun. To balance the bright orange, he chose white for the exterior walls and blue-green for such surfaces as window shutters, awnings, and cupola roof.

Opening day in Mineola, N.Y., in 1938.

The typical Howard Johnson's combination of civic, religious, and residential architectural elements succeeded in part because Morgan—who remained Johnson's chief architect until World War II terminated the company's construction program—had the skill to make the buildings rise grandly but gradually upward. Even as the buildings called out to customers, they reassured with a measured succession of dignified elements, from the projecting entrance to the set of usually three second-story dormers, and on up to the cupola, the steeple, and the weathervane with its "Simple Simon and the Pieman" figures. The proportions seemed right. Horizontal elements—the base or balustrade of the cupola, the ridgelines of the dormers, the cornice or balustrade of the entrance—offered a calming counterpoint to the roof's long slope and the spire's upward thrust. Moreover, the sense of dignity and order was reinforced at ground level by the careful planting of shrubbery, geraniums, and other vegetation around the building's foundation and at the base of the roadside sign, which had its own little island of greenery. The parking area, usually in front of and on one or both sides of the restaurant, was neater than most travelers were accustomed to. By 1936 Johnson was specifying asphalt paving, whereas competitors often used just dirt with a coating of oil. The rear of Johnson's building was somewhat less attractive because of the barrels in which refuse was put out for removal. But most of his restaurants did not have parking in the rear, and those that did stationed the barrels away from the building, with a wooden fence around them.

Howard Johnson's strove for symmetry, and although perfect symmetry could rarely be attained, the company consistently achieved the next best thing, a serene balance between left and right. In some Johnson's restaurants in the 1930s, there were exactly the same number of windows to the left of the front door as to the right, and they were almost evenly matched in size, even though strictly functional considerations would have dictated otherwise. If more space was needed for the dining areas at one end than for the counter service at the other, Howard Johnson's preferred to provide it in a lower-roofed wing that was set back several feet from the front wall of the main structure. This classical organization, with the cupola placed precisely in the center of the roof crest, carried an innate dignity, so that a Howard Johnson's building held its own against the constant motion of the highway. Even with cars whizzing past and nearby buildings looking scruffy, a Howard Johnson's looked solidly and properly planted.

The impression of stateliness was accentuated by an array of careful detailing. Morgan's blueprints called for such decorations as fluted pilasters on the front walls, garlands above the windows, and wooden urns on the balustrade. In the larger outlets, the ornament made for a rich composition.

Upon entering a Howard Johnson's, the first thing a customer encountered was Simple Simon and the Pieman—the company logo—inset in brass in the vestibule floor. On one side, the vestibule opened into what the company called the "dairy"— the counter-service area specializing in ice cream, desserts, beverages, and quick meals. Portable stools were positioned so that customers could eat lunch at the counter, and after lunch the stools were moved away so that the hordes of people coming in for ice cream could crowd up to the counter. It wasn't until after World War II that most Howard Johnson's dairy areas had fixed stools with upholstered backs, allowing customers to sit there comfortably while facing a mirrored backbar on which the most popular Howard Johnson's specialties were etched. Behind one end of the counter, a grill man cooked hot dogs—"frankforts," in Howard Johnson's dignified parlance—and passed most of them through a cutout in the wall separating the dairy area from the kitchen. From the kitchen, waitresses would then deliver the frankforts to dining room customers.

To the other side of the vestibule, but shielded from the glances of customers waiting to be seated, was the main dining room, often furnished with a combination of booths along the perimeter and tables and chairs in the center. To the rear of this dining room might be another, the "Lamplighter Room," which had a slightly different decorative scheme and sometimes a bar against the back wall. The front dining room served most of the families with children. The rear dining room handled overflow crowds, couples, groups of adults, and banquet parties. Floors throughout were of terrazzo or asphalt tile, and walls in the dining rooms were covered with grooved wooden "Pickwick paneling" or knotty pine. The subdivision of the restaurant into separate dining areas, sometimes with additional alcoves and wings, helped keep Howard Johnson's from seeming too massive and institutional for its predominantly middle-class customers.

The second story existed mostly to make the exterior visually complete, but since it existed, the company tried to find uses for it. In some restaurants, much of the second floor was made into a meeting room where banquets and other gatherings could take place. The most common uses, however, were to provide lavatories, dressing rooms, and an office or apartment for the manager.

Howard Johnson's was by no means unique in its architectural tastes. Dutchland Farms, a New England restaurant chain founded several years earlier and known for its yellow roofs, once accused Johnson of copying most of the Dutchland design. And the Friendly Ice Cream Company, established in Springfield, Massachusetts, by Curtis L. Blake and S. Prestley Blake, found Georgian architectural elements equally

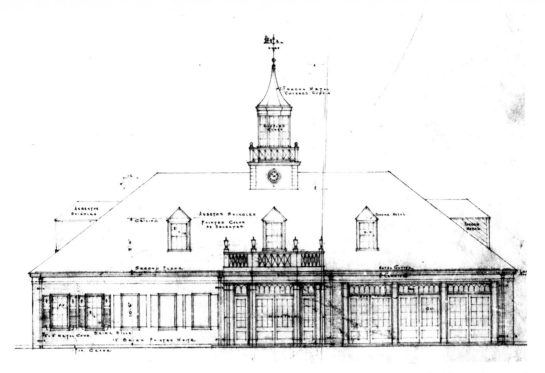

A Joseph G. Morgan design for Howard Johnson's, 1937. Soon afterward, the company switched from asbestos roof shingles to metal shingles coated in a brilliant orange porcelain enamel.

attractive for the exterior of its shops, which sold ice cream and sandwiches at horse-shoe-shaped counters. The Blake brothers, after forming their company in 1935, initially leased space from others, an arrangement that gave them little control over the style of their storefronts. But by the end of the Second World War, the Blakes had determined what sort of design they would have.

As Curtis Blake recalled years later, one of the advantages of a building using Georgian features was that although it seemed fitting in New England, it also contrasted with most buildings constructed in the 1940s. "We'd be next to ugly gas stations and we'd be next to other stores and strips of storefront locations, all kinds of stuff. . . . The crummier the stuff that was around, the better we looked." In addition, the Blakes anticipated that in the long run, a traditional exterior would be more economical than a modern one. "We realized that contemporary architecture was a very transient thing," Curtis Blake observed. "In the late thirties, you had to have glass block in your building, and then they got into those curved corners. And by golly, after the war—in ten years—it was totally obsolete. Nobody used it. We felt we couldn't afford to build new buildings every ten or fifteen years. This was a conscious decision to use an architecture that would have a long life."

Anyone familiar with architectural history could tell at a glance that the postwar Friendly shops were far removed from authentic Georgian design. Their windows were modern, extending almost from floor to ceiling and divided into panes much larger than those of the eighteenth century. The large panes helped attract people's attention to the interior, and large panes were the only practical form of insulating glass—almost a necessity in New England winters. On top of the roof perched a toylike cupola, too small to carry any real authority. Still, Friendly presented a symmetrical façade to the highway, and it had exterior walls predominantly of brick. Little keystones embellished the tops of some of the windows and there were other traditional touches, such as dentils under the eaves or columns supporting a pedimented entrance. For the average customer, this was enough to establish Friendly's respectability.

Inside, Friendly made no attempt to re-create a Georgian atmosphere. Under a ceiling of acoustic panels with their aluminum framework visible, customers sat at Formica counters. Walls generally were surfaced in butternut to a height of about six feet, and above that, the walls consisted of painted gypsumboard, decorated with pictures. As time went on, Friendly became increasingly concerned about authenticity, not so much inside as outside. Windows assumed proportions more like those of the Georgian era. Brick quoins appeared at the corners, the cupola was brought into scale with the rest of the building, and exterior shutters were installed in a manner that was historically accurate. The louvers, unlike those in most twentieth-century decorative shutters, slanted downward *toward* the building. Theoretically, if open shutters with louvers in that position were then pulled over the windows, they would shed water, as was true of shutters used for more than decoration in earlier centuries. To Friendly executives, the question of how closely to adhere to tradition was a serious matter. "It's like the quality of the food," the head of the company's engineering division observed in 1983. "You can always go to a lesser quality of food. Most of the people won't know it, but if you degenerate the quality of all of your food products, it becomes apparent. And we felt the same way about the architecture, that if you constantly nibble at these little things, pretty soon you end up with a barn."

After World War II, Howard Johnson reached a different conclusion about Georgian styling. Rationing during the war years slashed ice cream production and eliminated most automotive leisure travel, so most of the chain's restaurants had to be boarded up. Even a colossal outlet on Queens Boulevard in New York, constructed at a cost of more than $500,000, closed its doors. Johnson kept the company alive by supplying food for workers in factories and by processing food for the armed forces.

After the war, Johnson decreed "no more roadside cathedrals." He began to omit most of the ornamentation that was becoming expensive, and was going out of fashion anyway.

Johnson's new chief architect, Joseph A. Cicco, turned out designs with much simpler finishes and far less formality. The old rules were disregarded. The entrance might be shifted to one end of the main structure, or a wing might be positioned with its gable facing the street. Symmetry became less obligatory. Windows came to consist of fewer but larger panes, some stretching six feet high on the front of the dairy section. The dormers now looked puny, out of proportion to the large expanses of glass below.

The chain continued to make architectural adaptations for various reasons: to fit the site, to suit the franchisee, to accommodate markets of differing size, and to satisfy state turnpike commissions. (Howard Johnson's had become a concessionaire along the Pennsylvania Turnpike in 1940, and after the war the company won contracts to run restaurants on toll roads in many other states.) These conditions further expanded the variety of Howard Johnson's restaurants until in 1984 a company architect was able to observe that "we've got eighty-nine different building styles."

But there was a predominant Howard Johnson's look in the postwar years, and it resulted largely from the chain's aggressive expansion throughout Florida. In a state possessing a warm climate and not embracing New England architectural traditions, the usual Howard Johnson's designs encountered problems. Floridians were becoming accustomed to spotting successful stores and restaurants by looking through glass fronts and seeing lights and people. Johnson had been compelled to put up signs on his Florida outlets saying "Open." When, about 1948, the company asked Miami architect Rufus Nims to design another restaurant along the lines of what had been done before, Nims declined. He argued that by looking at a restaurant from the outside, people should be able to get an idea of the type of service and prices. Nims presented an architectural concept for an alternative design, and when he did, Johnson agreed to build it. The Miami architect banished Georgian styling and during the next ten years created a series of sleek, low-slung buildings for Howard Johnson's locations in Florida. Long ribbons of plate glass were recessed under the eaves, putting the interior on display and breaking down the tight sense of enclosure. Dormers disappeared and the cupola was abstracted into a simple modern ornament that sat on a pad in the center of the roof, exhausting stale air. By the mid-1950s, this was adopted as the company's nationwide prototype. Of course, there were variations from one building to another; the cupola was tinkered with, and in most instances it didn't double as an exhaust vent. But the basic image never wavered: it was a building of unquestioned modernity, praised by the architectural press, lauded by a restaurant journal, liked by the public.

The sleek Howard Johnson's carried its newfound smoothness into the interior. Tiny lamps of traditional design continued to be mounted by each booth, but lamps suspended from the ceiling were simple spheres in plastic, and the ceiling itself was a thin plane of suspended acoustic tiles, much simpler than the beamed ceilings of prewar years. The dining room had a feeling of lightness, with its thin draperies at the windows, its thin Formica tabletops, and its thin manufactured partition of re-peated circles. The feeling of handcraftsmanship—of objects laboriously con-structed—was gone. Howard Johnson's now represented the surmounting of many traditional restraints. Even the clock at the end of a row of booths was no longer a clock in the conventional sense of a three-dimensional container with a bulky mech-anism inside. Now it was simplified into an elemental starburst pattern of twelve radiating lines and two moving hands, pressed almost flat against the wall.

The change at Howard Johnson's was no mean accomplishment. The company had renewed itself, presenting a fresh image at a time when its clientele was ready for something more daring and up-to-date than New England Georgian. The new sleekness was well suited to America's selective but widespread embrace in the 1950s of technological advances and nontraditional aspects of living. The decade that de-voted itself to putting a TV set and a picture window in seemingly every living room would find Howard Johnson's boldness and simplicity perfectly appropriate. There remained enough softness in the restaurant's interior color schemes to avoid undue harshness, and on the exterior the restaurant did not break as radically with the past as might be presumed. The roofline avoided the flat-topped austerity of the Interna-tional Style and instead took on a kind of Prairie Style modernism that traced its roots all the way back to houses that Frank Lloyd Wright had designed in the centu-ry's opening decade. The Howard Johnson's roof was not all that different from the roofs of tens of thousands of suburban ranch houses built in the fifties. Its lines were soothingly horizontal, hovering low above the earth.

Equally important, Howard Johnson's maintained threads of continuity with its own past even while shifting toward 1950s tastes. The roof remained bright orange, the spire blue-green. Indeed, this was to be one of the tests of a restaurant organiza-tion's talent: Could it preserve something of its restaurants' original character (which benefited from high recognition and an established base of customers) while simul-taneously tapping new currents in popular taste?

To be sure, not every chain conducted itself like Howard Johnson's, or had to.

Howard Johnson's windows were large even when the view, as in this dining room in Fairfax, Va., in 1959, focused on nothing more than a gas station.

Exterior in Louisville, Ky., 1960. The size and proportioning of the by-now-abstracted cupola varied from one restaurant to another.

Chains like Friendly Ice Cream, which achieved increasing success with quasi-Georgian restaurants during a peak period of modernism, demonstrated that there was enough diversity in American taste to support more than one esthetic within the restaurant industry—especially if the esthetic was as firmly implanted in the American mind as Georgian architecture. Some chains stayed with a seemingly outdated esthetic for an extraordinarily long time. Krystal continued constructing shiny white streamlined buildings until the 1970s, as if to flaunt the fact that a chain would rarely fail solely because of the passé style of its architecture. Food quality, prices, and other vital aspects of restaurant operation nearly always outweighed the importance of architecture and decor.

Nonetheless, there was an undeniable connection among restaurant design, the spirit of the time, and the general pattern of which chains would achieve the greatest success. Friendly, after all, remained restricted to a few northern states, and the chains that did little to move beyond the white porcelain-enamel stage—White Castle, White Tower, Krystal—lost their leading role in the industry by the 1970s. The dynamic growth belonged to chains that could adapt their standardized images to the tastes of the current era.

FRIED CHICKEN
SANDWICHES
FOUNTAIN

Stans

LUNCH
DINNER

CHAPTER THREE
The Rise and Demise of the Drive-in

Overleaf: *Stan's drive-in, Fresno, Calif., early 1950s.*

AT THE START OF THE 1920s, THERE WERE EIGHT MILLION cars on the road, and their numbers were growing by three thousand a day—more than a million a year. They threatened pedestrians, they got in the way of streetcars, they broke down at critical moments, but they also promised liberating changes in Americans' living patterns—changes that would bring new opportunities for businessmen with vision.

One such businessman was J. G. Kirby, a Dallas candy and tobacco wholesaler who once remarked, "People with cars are so lazy they don't want to get out of them to go eat." Kirby devised the idea of a restaurant that would serve people sitting in their automobiles and then persuaded a prominent local physician, Dr. Reuben Wright Jackson, to supply the capital to get the venture established. With Kirby as its manager, the first Pig Stand drive-in opened on the Dallas–Fort Worth Highway in September 1921.

For some time, restaurants and drugstore soda fountains had occasionally delivered meals and snacks to people waiting in vehicles at the curb, but the Pig Stand, specializing in barbecued pork sandwiches, is believed to have been the first restaurant designed and constructed solely to serve people in automobiles. It proved so popular that three years later a second Pig Stand opened in Dallas, and by the 1930s there were more than sixty Pig Stands, most of them company-owned but several franchised, doing business not only in Dallas, Houston, San Antonio, and other Texas cities but also in Oklahoma, Louisiana, Mississippi, Florida, New York, and California.

Soon the Pig Stands Company faced competitors. Roy W. Allen, an Illinois native who began his career by purchasing, remodeling, and then reselling old hotels and restaurants, had already opened a small walk-in root-beer stand in 1919 on a downtown corner in Lodi, California. He expanded to nearby Sacramento the following

Above: *"Tray boys" and "tray girls" line up at an A & W stand in Salt Lake City, 1925. A & W also used outlets shaped like root beer barrels, as at left.*

year and in 1922 formed a partnership with one of his employees, Frank Wright. Together they opened three walk-up root-beer stands in Houston with the name "A & W"—A for Allen, W for Wright. By 1923, there were three concessions in Sacramento, one of them a drive-in featuring "tray boys" who brought the customers their five-cent mugs of root beer. Wright disposed of his interest in the company a year later but the corporate name continued unchanged, and Allen initiated an aggressive program of selling franchises, mostly in the West and Midwest. By 1933 A & W had 171 outlets.

Some were small, hipped-roof structures with side panels that could be propped open, allowing the tray boys and tray girls to get drinks without ever stepping inside. The economical construction of these small wooden stands allowed operators to recoup their costs quickly and earn a profit even though the stands were closed during the winter.

In Los Angeles about 1927, the Pig Stands Company, which had erected many rectangular drive-ins, opened its first round building, but even this was a relatively inexpensive and unself-conscious design, its exterior surfaces covered with advertising from the top of the parapet to the top of the windows and from the bottom of the windows to the ground. The operators found it more important to post the menu, promote their Maxwell House coffee, display silhouettes of pigs, and repeat the company's favorite exhortation, "Eat a Pig Sandwich," than to emphasize a distinctive

Simon's, built in 1936 on Wilshire Boulevard in Los Angeles, served customers either in their cars or inside the restaurant.

building form. The circular Pig Stand was a sort of half-step in the progression toward more memorable buildings.

Consistent with the flourishing of roadside oddities in the twenties and thirties, a number of early A & W stands were shaped like lighthouses, Indian heads, or root-beer barrels. These effectively attracted attention, but conspicuousness could also be achieved, and at less expense, by splashing a bright color on an otherwise common-place building. J. Willard Marriott had displayed the orange A & W logo in 1927 on the front of his first franchised establishment in Washington, D.C., a tiny walk-in unit called a "Hot Shoppe" because of the Mexican food it sold along with root beer. By 1930, Marriott had branched out along the Washington area's major streets with a series of Hot Shoppes operating in routine rectangular buildings, but with roofs painted an eye-catching orange. Marriott and Howard Johnson were later to argue about whose orange roofs had appeared first.

The finest drive-ins were reserved for California. Everything about the state favored drive-ins: the mild climate that permitted year-round operation, the dispersed cities and suburbs, the widespread reliance on automobiles, the willingness to experiment. California not only welcomed the Pig Stand organizers from Texas but also inspired development by such drive-in chains as Stan's, which Stanley Burke started in Sacramento in 1934, and Carpenter's, founded by the Texan Harry Carpenter. In addition, chains like Pig 'n Whistle, which had begun about 1910 as a Los Angeles tea room, started building drive-ins, sometimes in combination with coffee shops, which in California often offered seating both at counters and at tables and booths. All these chain restaurants erected circular drive-ins—buildings that in the 1930s and early 1940s captured the streamlined, sophisticated aura of Art Moderne.

Although signs near the street or highway would help attract customers, a tall, vertical element on the roof was considered far more effective. Visible from a great distance, it gave motorists plenty of time to slow down and turn in. The rooftop pylon became such an accepted element of California drive-in design that in 1946, *Architectural Record* published a Van Nuys, California, design whose pylon succinctly and unceremoniously urged, "EAT." A circular Pig Stand in Beaumont, Texas, raised two pylons, each embellished with nearly three dozen horizontal bands of neon.

In the most impressive of the streamlined drive-ins, thick circular canopies floated, seemingly weightless, over walls consisting almost entirely of glass. The old, visually inescapable reality of construction—the fact that buildings were heavy and required substantial walls to prevent collapse—appeared to have been magically transcended.

On Wilshire Boulevard in Los Angeles stood a drive-in that represented California's main alternative to the circle: the octagon. This drive-in, part of the Simon's chain started by Bill Simon and eventually acquired by Stanley Burke, rose in a series of steps like an Art Deco skyscraper until it culminated in a pylon vertically proclaiming "SANDWICHES." The stepped-roof design made the pylon seem a natural upward extension of the building; by contrast, circular drive-ins like Pig 'n Whistle sometimes gave the impression that the rooftop shaft was an afterthought, unrelated to the shapes below. But the octagonal, stepped designs, with their graduated, mountain-like effect, forfeited the lightness that was so compelling in the circular drive-ins, a lightness that was a major part of the streamlined esthetic's emotional appeal.

Conventional rectangular buildings were much less at home in the highway environment. Custom dictated that a rectangular building concentrate its most elaborate architectural effects on the front, and yet the front was glimpsed only briefly by people in passing vehicles. It was the long and usually plainer sides that the motorists saw for most of their approach. Here was a built-in frustration; people had been trained since childhood to want to see the front of the building, to read the façade to determine what sort of operation it housed, but motorists didn't want to slow down to do so. Howard Johnson's overcame the problem by erecting its restaurants at curves, traffic circles, and major intersections and by giving the buildings spires, cupolas, orange roofs, dormers, wings, and projecting entrances; the ensemble retained much of its impressiveness when seen from an oblique angle rather than head-on. But Howard Johnson's was, of course, a full-service restaurant, with enough architectural bulk to achieve a strong roadside presence. The typical drive-in was necessarily much smaller, and if its shapes were rectangular, it was out of place on the open road. Circular and octagonal drive-ins, on the other hand, each formed a complete composition no matter what the motorist's perspective. Moreover, a rounded building seemed a perfect counterpart to the curve a car would follow as it drove around the drive-in.

In some respects, a circle or octagon was also more functional once the vehicle came to a stop. A rectangular drive-in had a front and a back, and few people wanted to park in the back—unless they were couples looking for an undisturbed place for necking, an activity that added nothing to the drive-in's profitability. A circular or octagonal drive-in, unlike a rectangular one, had no area that was considered inferior or out of the way, since there was no front or back. Customers would park all the way around the building, and this meant that the distances to be walked by those delivering food and drinks would be kept to a near-absolute minimum. When the drive-in was busy, a second and sometimes a third circle of cars would bunch up around the

Late in the 1930s, the once-utilitarian Marriott began to put some flair into its Hot Shoppes.

innermost group. "The car in back would be happy to move to let the first one out," Burke recalled, "because then he could pull in closer to the building."

One attraction of the inner ring was the shelter of the broad overhang above. More important was the social atmosphere, which intensified in the inner circle. The drive-in was a gathering place, and one that embodied deeply ingrained American attitudes about proper spatial relationships. Americans enjoy opportunities to be outgoing, to congregate in a friendly setting, and this the drive-in enabled them to do. But Americans also prefer to keep a certain distance between themselves and others—and this, too, the drive-in made possible. Just as the preferred American housing pattern of separate single-family dwellings serves to offset the tension of coexisting with neighbors of different religious, ethnic, and class backgrounds, the drive-in's assemblage of individual vehicles ensured a similar physical buffer zone, allowing a person to keep his or her privacy essentially intact. Inside the movable capsule of space that was an automobile, protected by a shell of metal and glass, an individual or family could act gregarious without risking too great an involvement with other people. Customers were free from being bumped, jostled, or pressed too closely, vexations that occurred all too frequently in indoor restaurants.

Much of the drive-in's appeal rested on considerations other than social psychology—most notably, convenience and a love of the automobile, that status symbol on wheels, so quick to deliver its owners to places they'd never been before. But certainly part of its success grew out of its unusual ability to satisfy conflicting desires: the impulse to gather together and the psychological need to stay somewhat apart. It is no accident that there remains a reservoir of popular affection for memories of drive-in eating; the drive-in allowed Americans to think they were rubbing shoulders when in truth they were clustering fenders.

The key participants in the drive-ins' sociability-at-a-distance were the "tray boys" and "tray girls," known as "carhops" by the 1930s because of their practice of hopping up on the cars' running boards. Since the drive-in's atmosphere could not be firmly regulated through the design and decor of an interior dining room, it became all the more important to have carhops maintain an agreed-upon standard of dress and behavior; in the customer's mind, the carhops rather than the architecture epitomized the drive-in's character. This was more than a matter of having carhops dress alike; operators like Harry Carpenter introduced showmanship. Carhops put on bright uniforms that included military-style caps and pants with a stripe down the side—costumes that had much in common with the dress of movie ushers during the same period. A drive-in was a theater out-of-doors. "Houston's Drive-in Trade Gets

A carhop in 1955 at Stan's in Bakersfield, Calif. (above), and another (right) at a Clock drive-in in Los Angeles in the early 1950s.

Girl Show With Its Hamburgers," reported a 1940 issue of *Life,* which displayed on its cover a carhop at the drive-in of Mr. and Mrs. J. D. Sivils. At Sivils Drive-in, carhops had to be women aged eighteen to twenty-five with high-school diplomas, good figures, and "come-hither" personalities. They dressed in satin majorette costumes with white boots and abbreviated skirts. To prevent the girl show from being taken too far, carhops were instructed on how long they could talk to a customer and on the necessity of avoiding physical contact; change was to be placed on the tray, not in the customer's hand. Most drive-ins adopted an extensive list of "do's" and "don't's" which regulated the carhops' behavior and gave them a degree of responsibility for keeping the lot clean and seeing that cars were parked in an orderly fashion.

Order, in most drive-ins outside of California, came to mean having the cars lined up in rows according to lines painted on the pavement. The predominant arrangement, especially in the Northeast and Midwest but also in many drive-ins in the South, was rectangular—long rectangular parking areas for the cars being served, following the rectangular shapes of the buildings, which were softened occasionally

Above: *The every-surface-a-signboard approach to design at an A & W stand after World War II.* Right: *White Tower, in its ultimately unsuccessful attempt to capture a suburban clientele, added drive-in canopies to some of its restaurants.*

by slightly curved corners. The prevalence of rectangular designs outside of California may have stemmed from narrower lots or more traditional attitudes toward architecture, or perhaps from climates that limited the drive-ins' profitability, thus discouraging departures from standard, economical building configurations. What the drive-ins throughout the country did share was the use of a pylon to gain the attention of oncoming motorists; usually the pylon rose from the front of a rectangular building and was embellished with neon.

By the late 1940s, American architecture was undergoing a major change, discarding the leading styles of the 1920s and 1930s and settling on newer kinds of design. With the death of Art Deco and the decline of streamlining, some designers experimented with styles that seemed crisper and more forceful, such as the structurally expressive modernism employed in 1949 for a Tiny Naylor's drive-in at Sunset Boulevard and La Brea Avenue in Los Angeles. There the Los Angeles architect Douglas Honnold had a long cantilevered canopy aggressively jut out from the building toward the street and culminate in a dynamic wedge-shape. In 1947 the prominent architect Pietro Belluschi used a more austere form of modernism for Waddle's drive-in and coffee shop near Portland, Oregon, creating a composition that consisted largely of vertical and horizontal planes. Rising from the flat-roofed restaurant like a broad untapered chimney stack was a flat, rectangular signboard—essentially the familiar drive-in advertising pylon, but much wider than before. On a smaller and less artistic scale, the same technique was adopted by A & W Root Beer, which raised a rectangular signboard through the roof of some of its buildings.

If drive-ins took on varied architectural expressions, they also differed in the kinds of service they offered their customers. Many combined carhop service with conventional indoor dining. In 1934 in Normal, Illinois, A. H. "Gus" Belt began a chain of Steak n Shake drive-ins that in time advertised "four-way service"—car, counter, dining room, and carry-out, or, as Steak n Shake preferred to call the latter, "Takhomasak." The kitchen area was open so that customers on the interior could see how clean it was, and it was positioned alongside large windows so that even the curb-service customers could watch their orders being prepared. "In Sight, It Must Be Right" was the company slogan.

In 1936, Robert C. Wian, Jr., three years out of high school, opened Bob's Pantry, a ten-stool restaurant on Colorado Boulevard in Glendale, California. After inventing a "Big Boy" double-decker hamburger in 1937 for a group of orchestra members who demanded something different, Wian started a chain of Bob's Big Boy drive-ins that offered some coffee-shop–style indoor seating in addition to curb service. Around 1936, White Tower also began adding curb service to some of its new suburban units. The combination of two or more kinds of service enabled a restaurant to broaden its appeal. If bad weather hampered drive-in activity, the inside restaurant would still do well. The general rule was to separate the circulation areas of different kinds of service as much as possible; carhops often had a separate entrance and sometimes a separate kitchen so they wouldn't get in the way of counter-service or dining-room customers.

The drive-in enjoyed a phenomenal boom during the postwar years. Suddenly in the late 1940s this form of restaurant—once concentrated mostly in warm states like California and Texas—began to flourish even in the Northeast and Great Lakes regions. The emergence of the drive-in as a truly national institution came at a time when millions of young families were buying houses in the suburbs and getting around increasingly by private automobile. In the five years after the war's end, the number of cars on the nation's highways jumped by 15 million, reaching a record 40 million, and in the next seven years the number rose by 15 million more, helping to fuel explosive growth by chains like A & W, which tripled in size, from 450 outlets in 1950 to 1,400 outlets by 1957.

By the beginning of the 1950s, however, the carhop-service chains no longer had the roadside eat-in-your-car trade all to themselves. They competed with a rapidly expanding number of chain refreshment stands that had no carhops but that were generally called "drive-ins" all the same. The refreshment stands had the advantage of being simple and economical to operate, with none of the problems of hiring and managing a corps of adolescent carhops. The items they served were immensely popular and easy to prepare—mostly beverages and ice-cream specialties, some of which were relatively recent concoctions. In Green River, Illinois, J. F. McCullough developed a semi-frozen ice cream in 1938. In August of that year, the new soft ice cream was test-marketed with an all-you-can-eat-for-ten-cents promotion at a store in Kankakee, Illinois. The store's owner, Sherb Noble, found himself with an instant hit; 1,600 servings were sold in two hours. In June 1940 Noble opened the first outlet named for McCullough's product: Dairy Queen. World War II, with its rationing of dairy products, gasoline, and other commodities, halted the company's expansion, but after the war Dairy Queen quickly surpassed established chains like A & W and became the leader of this branch of the restaurant industry. From 17 outlets in 1946, the franchise-based organization grew to 1,400 stands in 1950 and 2,500 stands in 1953.

The typical Dairy Queen was a rectangular concrete-block building painted white, with a flat overhanging roof that curved at the corners—the curves probably a vestige of the now-fading streamlined esthetic, which was also evident in the rounded letterforms of the company slogan, "Nationally Known, Locally Owned," and in objects as mundane as the round-topped trash receptacles. Mounted above the front end of the building was a cool-blue Dairy Queen sign showing a tilted cone of soft ice cream with a curl on top.

The utilitarian attributes of the Dairy Queen building are hallmarks of "vernacular" design—the straightforward construction characteristic of ordinary people, functional and unself-conscious, dictated by the need for economy rather than by sophisticated cultural aspirations. This simplicity has a certain charm. Dairy Queen's low, flat roof—probably attributable to the limited finances of the franchisees—gave the building a calm, soothing profile and in general a feeling of modesty, which could offer a welcome respite from an aggressively commercial landscape. Yet the attractiveness of the Dairy Queen stand was not entirely artless. There were just enough features—the rounded overhangs, the brick base under the windows, the consistent absence of clutter on the concrete-block walls—to indicate that the building was consciously intended to project an image. These simple decorative touches made the stand just gracious enough to avoid looking pinched and severe.

The pattern set by Dairy Queen was followed by a number of other chains. In 1949 Tastee-Freez was founded in Chicago by Leo S. Maranz, a mechanical engineer who had designed an automatic freezer and then learned that the freezer was too

Dairy Queen on Main Street in Greenville, Pa., built 1951. A cone tilted forward became a favorite symbol of postwar custard stands.

expensive for businesses to buy unless it came with a franchise to sell soft ice cream. By June 1953 Tastee-Freez had grown into a national chain with 600 outlets, their roofs flat, with a bow in the front overhang.

In 1948 the Richardson Corporation of Rochester, New York, introduced a small root-beer stand consisting of a rectangular kitchen of stuccoed concrete block at the rear and a smaller serving area at the front, with flaps that opened on three sides so that customers could sit on red metal stools at an open-air counter. Frostop Products, a root-beer franchiser established in Rochester two years later, also used a simple rectangular building, which was modified in the mid-1950s when a Louisiana franchisee installed an 8-by-10-foot revolving mug on the roof and extended the roof overhangs to as much as 16 feet to protect customers from sun and rain.

A more architecturally aggressive chain was Carvel Dari-Freeze, which traced its beginning to the summer of 1934, when Thomas Carvel, who had been selling radios, hitched a home-built trailer full of ice cream and cones to a 1929 Graham and headed north from New York until, according to a company story, a flat tire stopped him in nearby Hartsdale and he sold his product on the spot. Tom Carvel then began to open ice cream stores, using his savings to perfect an electric freezer, and by 1952 he had developed a chain of 200 Carvel outlets. In the early 1950s the company introduced a building whose glass and metal façade leaned forward under a roof that tilted upward toward the street. On top was an oversize replica of a cone of soft ice cream. By the mid-1950s, Tastee-Freez too had tilted its roof upward toward the road, and in 1960 Dairy Queen abandoned its flat roof for a barnlike new design with a bright red gambrel roof. The era of low-profile refreshment stands was over.

But during the brief reign of architectural modesty, refreshment stands made a pleasant, low-key addition to the landscape, one that suited the baby-boom years especially well. To children, who spent much of their time in the monumental realm of schools, libraries, churches, and other intimidating institutions, a diminutive Dairy Queen was a relief. The older chains specializing in hard ice cream, like Isaly's in western Pennsylvania, occupied conventional stores where service took place inside, where there were rules, written or unwritten, about how noisy a person could be, where to sit or stand, and other aspects of behavior. Such regulation of daily life becomes second nature to adults, but to young children and adolescents, interiors can be uncomfortably constricting, and refreshment stands offered the attraction of a much freer outdoor environment. Everyone but the employees stayed outside the building, in an informal atmosphere. At the Dairy Queen, people relaxed on summer evenings under a fluorescent-lighted overhang, watching as the ice cream flowed from stainless steel machines into a succession of ice cream cones, while in the background intermittent crackling sounds emanated from a device that invariably fascinated youngsters—the electric bug-killer. The parking lot provided an uninhibited area for socializing. Not only was this a friendly, entertaining place for young children

In the 1950s and 1960s, Carvel constructed ice cream stands with roofs that rose toward the highway, as on this building along the Berlin Turnpike in Connecticut, photographed in 1983.

Owners of a Dairy Treat stand on Route 12 north of Binghamton, N.Y. Dairy Treat also operated in other parts of upstate New York.

and a relatively unrestrictive environment for teenagers; it was also comfortable for parents, who didn't have to worry about how they were dressed or whether their children would be quiet.

While refreshment stands were prospering in the form of simple little buildings on open parking lots, carhop-service drive-ins, on the other hand, were becoming increasingly elaborate, investing in more comforts for customers and more labor-saving devices to reduce the running between kitchen and cars. In 1931 the Pig

Stands organization in Texas had installed its first canopy for customers' cars—a brown canvas structure—and by the early 1950s, canopies, usually made of metal, were becoming commonplace in the South. They offered protection from the rain, but more important, they provided shade, helping drive-ins attract more business, especially in the heat of late afternoon.

The canopies were part of a widespread quest among drive-in operators for better ways of doing business—pulling in more customers, serving them faster, selling bigger orders, maximizing revenue-per-carhop. A few operators suspended air-conditioning apparatus from their canopies, with flexible hookups that could be attached to each car's windows. In the North, a few attached infrared heaters to extend the selling season through the cold months. The 30-foot-wide canopy at an A & W drive-in in Hammond, Indiana, sheltered not only two rows of cars but also a "Driv-O-Matic" conveyor belt, which delivered the food and drinks to carhops who remained at outside work stations close to the cars, using microphones to tell the kitchen what was needed. Drive-in conveyor belts failed to catch on, although they attracted widespread attention. What did win acceptance were electronic ordering systems; they were the rage of the 1950s. From 1951 to 1959, a succession of electronic call-in systems appeared: Aut-O-Hop, Auto-Dine, Dine-a-Mike, Dine-a-Com, Electro-Hop, Ordaphone, Fone-A-Chef, Servus-Fone, Teletray, TelAutograph, and the Lindley Wireless Expeditor. Drive-in operators were infatuated with the new gadgetry. The electronic speaker system installed about 1954 at Troy Smith Jr.'s Top Hat Drive-in in Shawnee, Oklahoma, inspired that drive-in's slogan, "Service with the Speed of Sound." Four years later the slogan led Smith to use the name "Sonic Drive-in" for the chain he began developing—a chain that entered the 1980s as America's largest surviving drive-in organization, with more than 1,100 units in twenty states from North Carolina to Nevada.

Most of the electronic ordering systems required the customers to call in their own orders, thus saving the carhop the first trip to each car. This eliminated some of the effort involved, especially in serving a rectangular lot, where the outermost cars were a substantial distance from the kitchen. Cincinnati-based Frisch's Drive-ins, an early franchisee of Bob's Big Boy, adopted the electronic method because it allowed the number of carhops to be cut by at least one-fifth and because it provided a permanent menu display next to the car window, along with a speaker that made it easy for customers to keep requesting more items. As a result, sales at some Frisch's drive-ins rose 20 to 30 percent.

By itself, electronic equipment did little to alter a drive-in's appearance, but the canopies that often accompanied the electronic systems resulted in hundreds of drive-ins being disfigured, all in the cause of convenience and efficiency. Usually the canopies ran from the front of the lot to the building that housed the kitchen. Consequently, the utilitarian canopy structure gained an esthetically unwelcome prominence while the building sat half-hidden in the canopy's shadow. Indeed, by installing low, flat canopies, drive-in operators achieved the doubly dubious result of making an outdoor setting feel dark and closed-in, and of putting the flimsiest part of the drive-in's structure in the most visible position. This could not be tolerated. The solution lay in raising at least a portion of the canopy and giving it more flair. Dog 'n Suds, a root-beer chain founded in 1953 by two high-school teachers in Champaign, Illinois, bent its canopy into something of a butterfly shape. The two wings spread upward and outward from a long center spine, creating a sense of openness while also exposing the bulbs on the canopy's undersides so that motorists, like moths, would be lured by light. The canopy was supported by a series of yellow I-beams that jutted up, pierced the canopy at an angle, and extended four more feet into the sky. If bright lights didn't capture customers' attention, such structural jabs in the air would.

A canopy industry arose to offer an assortment of increasingly stylized products. One manufacturer in the early 1960s formed the edges of canopies into diamond shapes. Another hung the canopies from hexagonal I-beam frames with flags flying from their tops. A third manufacturer advertised a selection of five new designs: curved, canted, pitched, folding-plate, and lazy boomerang. A fourth introduced the "Mountain Range," which had a series of abrupt peaks and valleys also known as folding-plate; the "High 'n Hailing," which put the canopy under what looked like a series of oversized croquet hoops; and the "Rock 'n Roll," which rose and fell like an ocean wave. The roof decking of the Rock 'n Roll could be painted in contrasting colors above and below to make it stand out even more. A Pig Stand in Austin, Texas, a White Tower in Richmond, and a Jerry's Drive-in in Louisville all installed the Rock 'n Roll or close imitations of it.

The appearance of an ocean wave was a fitting image, for the drive-in segment of the restaurant industry had reached its crest and was soon to crash. In November 1963 Lyndon Johnson became President. Not long afterward Lady Bird Johnson, with her husband's support, began leading a fight to beautify America, especially the America visible from highways. The most flagrant offenders were billboards and junkyards, but the environmental consciousness that Mrs. Johnson embraced quickly developed into a critical way of looking at the totality of American surroundings. Drive-ins became a major target, and by the latter half of the 1960s the uproar against them resounded throughout the land.

Some of the complaints were directed at the drive-ins' visual disorder—bright

In the 1950s, Dog n Suds had used small pipes to support its butterfly canopies, but by about 1962 the chain discovered the advertising power of exaggerated structural elements, as at this Missouri drive-in.

colors, treeless expanses of asphalt, litter left behind by customers. But much of the disenchantment went beyond the visual and had to do with behavior ranging from adolescent high spirits to serious social disorder. By 1966 there were 78 million cars roaming the nation's streets, many of them driven in the evenings by teenagers who did not always concern themselves with maximizing tread life or miles per gallon. They honked, they yelled, they turned the radio up. Some vandalized the drive-in. Some brought alcohol or drugs or got into fights. An estimated one-quarter of the nation's drive-ins suffered serious problems in trying to control teenagers. Defenders of drive-ins turned the statistics around, pointing out that three-quarters of the drive-ins did *not* have serious difficulties in maintaining order, but this was little consolation. The public had heard plenty in the 1950s about a threatening phenomenon called "juvenile delinquency," and by the latter half of the 1960s, youth had become far more numerous and restless. Drive-ins were vulnerable to teenagers who decided to ignore the law.

The difficulties were exacerbated by the typical lot layout, which created a continuous traffic-circulation pattern around the drive-in and placed much of the parking in areas that couldn't be monitored by employees inside the building. Drive-ins were usually situated so that cars turning from the road entered a driveway that looped all the way around the building and onto the street again. The cars held up traffic while their adolescent occupants looked for familiar faces amid the vehicles under the center canopies and along the perimeter of the lot. Teenagers made the loop of one drive-in after another in the cruising circuits of the sixties, and adult America grew angry at the exhibition. This anger took the form of neighborhood complaint, and the neighborhood complaint led to municipal ordinances, which sought to hold drive-in operators responsible for what happened on their premises and sometimes for what happened a few hundred feet off their premises as well. Ordinances demanded that drive-ins keep their own and adjoining properties clear of litter, and erect fences around their lots. They required landscaping and fewer signs. Cities and towns tried to force drive-ins to close earlier or to stop carhop service entirely.

To keep order, many drive-ins hired police officers to supervise the lot after dark, and a few drive-ins installed automatic gates that prevented each vehicle from departing until a quarter or a token had been deposited. Tokens were supplied free to those who purchased food or drinks; those who came just to cruise got stuck paying for the privilege. Where gates were installed, they cut cruising dramatically, but they were expensive and they constituted an inconvenience even for legitimate customers—this in a business that had been founded on convenience.

Faced with public protests, even the industry's spokesmen could no longer deny that most drive-ins presented a harsh appearance. An editor of *Drive-in Restaurant*

Tastee-Freez in Delaware and Maryland started the 1960s with this folded-plate-roof prototype.

Under the rock-'n-roll-style canopy of a Pig Stand drive-in, Austin, Tex., 1958.

magazine admitted that of the thousand or more drive-ins he had inspected in the previous several years, no more than six or seven had well-landscaped, litter-free grounds. From their earliest days, drive-ins had stood out, but the old ways were now unacceptable; the time had come to settle down and seek respectability. *Drive-in Restaurant* began urging operators to plant trees, shrubs, and flowers. "An orderly, appealing exterior implies that the inside of your place is kept the same way," the magazine argued. "If planned with imagination, landscaping can help the owner achieve better conduct by his customers." Bushes, perhaps with thorns, "can be planted in a favorite place where teenagers loiter on foot." Landscaped pathways to the carry-out window could narrow what had been a wide, congested, littered area. Kim's, a chain of nine drive-ins in the vicinity of Waco, Texas, began putting in landscaping and giving its buildings softer textures in 1965. The message affected the canopy manufacturers, who once more began promoting shelters that were calmly horizontal, now with the natural look of cedar shakes on their edges.

None of these techniques improved the drive-ins' prospects, however, for curb-service drive-ins also had serious economic problems. In the 1950s, land on Wilshire Boulevard and many less-renowned streets in California became too expensive for glorious older drive-ins like Stan's, Simon's, and Pig 'n Whistle to continue operating, or for new drive-ins to be built. Coffee shops with considerably more indoor seating and no outdoor service brought higher revenues. Even in the mild climate of Southern California, a drive-in's volume in winter fell as much as 60 percent below what it was in summer, and cold or rainy weather produced unpredictable daily fluctuations in patronage. Coffee shops, by contrast, attracted a steady flow of customers regardless of day or season. They generally did business around the clock and they benefited from the fact that people spent more generously once they came inside. The lesson was not lost on drive-in operators like Bob Wian; in 1964 he built his last drive-in. The future of Bob's Big Boy—a bright one—lay with coffee shops and family restaurants.

By the late fifties, carhop drive-ins also competed against another kind of restaurant: the self-service "fast-food" outlet where customers got out of their cars and stood in line for food, which they carried back to their cars. Fast-food outlets enjoyed some of the same economies as refreshment stands, and they had hamburger-based menus that competed head-on against the carhop establishments. The turnover of vehicles on a self-service lot was twice as fast as at a drive-in—the average customer left about ten minutes after he arrived—and the number of employees was much lower.

Legislated against for rowdiness and litter, squeezed economically by coffee shops and fast-food places, the drive-in rapidly declined in most metropolitan areas. Not even the drive-ins run by the Sivils, who had captured the country's imagination in 1940 with their carhops in majorette uniforms, were immune to the growing difficulties. In 1967 the land occupied by one of their drive-ins on Fort Worth Avenue in Dallas was converted into a sales lot for mobile homes. Sonic Drive-ins survived, partly because of their strength in small towns, where real-estate costs were lower, where competition was less intense, and perhaps where the control of teenagers was less of a problem; but in the early 1980s, Sonic's profits fell drastically and by 1984 the number of outlets had slipped below 1,000. The company arrived at what must have been a wrenching decision: it would start offering customers the option of eating indoors.

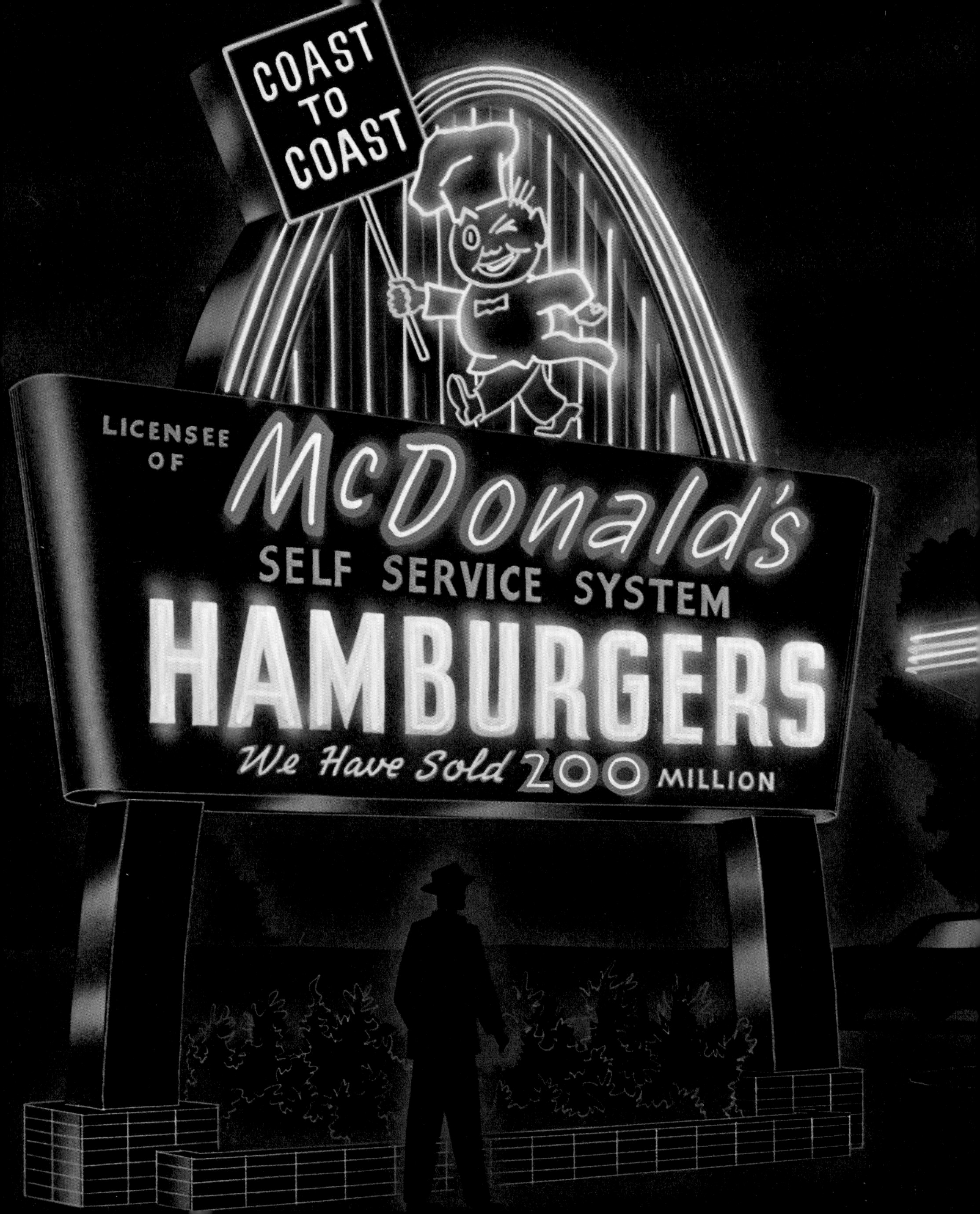

COAST TO COAST
LICENSEE OF
McDonald's
SELF SERVICE SYSTEM
HAMBURGERS
We Have Sold 200 MILLION

CHAPTER FOUR

Handlebars, Boomerangs, and Arches That Flash in the Night

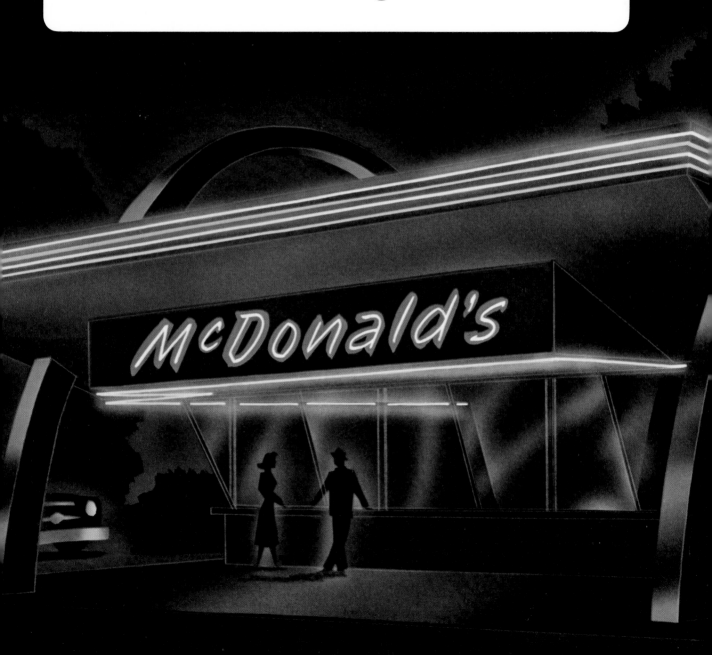

Overleaf: *Night sketch of the new McDonald's prototype was used by Richard and Maurice McDonald in 1953 to enlist franchisees. The company was then strictly a western operation which had sold about 9 million hamburgers, but the messages on the sign foretold the future.*

RICHARD MCDONALD SAT IN THE OFFICE behind his drive-in in San Bernardino, California, sketching what he hoped would be the restaurant of the future. On a sheet of typing paper, he drew a building with columns like those of the spacious two-story colonial house where he lived with his wife and his business partner-brother, Maurice. The sketch left him dissatisfied. Colonial lacked the power he wanted, and besides, the columns would get in the customers' way.

The McDonald brothers—Richard, 43, and Maurice ("Mac"), 50—needed a new design because, in that autumn of 1952, they were about to begin selling franchises for the "McDonald self-service system," a method of restaurant operation they had pioneered with enormous success for nearly four years.

From their hometown of Manchester, New Hampshire, the brothers had migrated to Southern California in the late 1920s and after finding work driving trucks, moving scenery, and doing other unglamourous jobs for a Hollywood studio and later operating a small movie theater, they decided to enter the restaurant business. For three years, the McDonalds ran a little octagonal drive-in in Arcadia near the Santa Anita race track. Then they cut the building in two, transported it some forty miles farther inland to San Bernardino, and enlarged it to accommodate what they expected would be a larger volume of customers. Their location in San Bernardino was a good one on E Street, the city's main thoroughfare, only four blocks from San Bernardino High School; so with Mac supervising the daytime shift and Richard taking over in the evenings, the carhop-service drive-in manned by some twenty employees produced a comfortable income.

After World War II, however, a fundamentally different labor market was shaking up the restaurant industry. In 1940, restaurants had paid out 27 percent of their gross income as wages. This constituted the highest percentage for wages for any sizable segment of retailing, and by 1947 the figure had climbed to the worrisome 35-to-40-percent range. Returning veterans could settle into more attractive jobs or use their service benefits to go to college; drive-ins were having a harder time attracting and holding reliable employees. In December 1948, tired of "drunken fry cooks and dishwashers," restless for a new way of doing things, Richard and Mac McDonald introduced a limited and rigidly standardized menu and dismissed the carhops. Self-service was the dominant trend in retailing; in clothing stores, for instance, customers could pick through merchandise displayed in the open instead of always having to ask clerks for assistance. Why shouldn't it work at a drive-in?

Actually, in the transition to self-service, McDonald's Drive-in nearly died. Customers parked their cars on the lot and honked their horns, signaling in irritation for carhops who no longer came. Those customers who got out of their cars and walked up to the order windows, as they were supposed to do, discovered they would have to accept a hamburger with a standard collection of condiments or get no hamburger at all. Trade dwindled so drastically, Richard McDonald recalled, that "our old customers would come in and say, 'You're really swamped, aren't you?' They heckled us."

Within a few months, though, the McDonald's Drive-in's exceptionally fast service, combined with low prices and the elimination of tipping, attracted a growing number of customers—at first, painters, carpenters, mechanics, and clerks who wanted lunch quickly, then teenagers and families looking for something inexpensive to eat in the afternoon and evening. Lines began to form at the windows where fifteen-cent hamburgers, ten-cent French fries, and twenty-cent milk shakes were dispensed. Word of the remarkable new system spread through the restaurant industry.

In May 1952 the makers of Primex, a shortening used by the McDonalds, took out a two-page advertisement in *American Restaurant* magazine to tell about this compact, self-service drive-in capable of selling 30,000 orders of French fries a month. Two months later, McDonald's, the restaurant whose self-service system had slashed labor costs to less than 17 percent of gross sales, was featured on the magazine's cover. By that time, the sign out front announced that McDonald's had sold six million hamburgers, and the brothers had been pestered by so many people interested in the details of their operation that they had begun preparing a franchise program. The cover story in the restaurant industry's premier publication bolstered their confidence. "When this hit all over the country, that is when people really began to flock out, so we knew that we had something that was going to make us some money," Richard recalled. "Sometimes there'd be probably seven or eight different people from different parts of the country out there with a piece of paper, sketching." The

Above: *McDonald brothers' octagonal stand in San Bernardino in 1949, after conversion from carhop service.* Right: *The brothers ran this ad in* American Restaurant *in September 1952, when they were still debating what shape to give the franchised restaurants.*

brothers occasionally became perturbed at people who would buy a hamburger and sit in their cars, surreptitiously taking notes, but even the clandestine copiers reinforced the McDonalds' conviction that the restauranteurs would be willing to pay a fee to duplicate the San Bernardino drive-in's equipment, procedures, layout, and menu. Richard McDonald knew the franchising package needed one more thing: "I wanted a building that when people saw it, they knew this was McDonald's. There would be no doubt about where they were going to eat."

The existing eight-sided building wouldn't do—octagonal drive-ins had been commonplace in California for nearly twenty years—but the shape of the new building was slow to crystallize. That much was clear when the brothers bought a full-page advertisement in *American Restaurant*'s September 1952 issue to promote "the new 'McDonald Self-Service Drive-in'—the most revolutionary development in the restaurant industry during the past 50 years!" The ad showed an airbrush rendering by San Bernardino artist Sal Cruz that depicted a rounded building with the message "We Have Sold Over 8 Million" above its three serving windows. The building—a design conceived by Richard McDonald—rose in diminishing concentric circles and was topped by a pylon displaying a cartoon-like chef and a free-form sign saying "McDonald Self-Service System." "We almost went into the franchising program with this circular building," Richard recalled. But round buildings, like octagonal buildings, were already in frequent use as drive-ins in California, so even as the magazine ad was being readied for publication, Richard continued to search for something more daring.

He consulted a couple of architects and was disappointed when they suggested what he considered to be "low, squatty little buildings." He drove to Los Angeles to talk to Douglas Honnold, an architect known for imaginative drive-ins, but it proved to be an icy encounter. After listening to McDonald lay out his ideas, Honnold replied, according to McDonald, 'If you're going to tell me how to design a building, you'd better do it yourself."

"I said, 'Thank you very much,'" McDonald recalls. "'I'll maybe do that.'"

So McDonald went on sketching. "I thought there has to be some way to spark these buildings up." One rainy night when business was slow, he drew a building with the roof tilted upward toward the front. "I was trying to give the building some height. Tilting the roof with a big overhang helped, but it was still on the low, squatty side." To the tilted roof he added a single arch across the front. "Well, this didn't look too bad, but it didn't look too good either. So then I sketched in the two arches running from the front of the building to the back, and well, that seemed to pick the building up. So at that point I showed it to my brother, and he said, 'Hey, that looks pretty sharp.'

"So we took it to one architect, and he said he thought it was terrible. The basic building, he said, wasn't bad, but the terrible arches, those have got to come out. So we didn't do any business with him."

Next McDonald went to Stanley C. Meston, an architect in nearby Fontana who had worked in the 1930s with Los Angeles restaurant architect Wayne McAllister, and showed him his increasingly detailed idea for a rectangular building that would get structural support as well as visibility from two large arches. "He wasn't too enthused about the arches, either, so I told him, you go draw the building, leave the arches off." Then McDonald visited his neon sign supplier, George Dexter in San Bernardino. Dexter liked the arches and encouraged McDonald to insist on them, as decoration if not as structural support. By then it was clear that if Meston wanted the McDonald brothers' commission, he would have to work with their ideas, and he did. He accentuated the roof shape by designing a thick, tapered soffit, for a strong wedge-like profile. He specified large windows canted upward and outward, like those of an airport control tower, and he accommodated the McDonalds' request for exterior walls surfaced with shiny horizontal bands of red and white tile. These would be sleek, conspicuous, and easy to maintain, and the cherry-red on the walls would not be far removed from the color preferences of the architectural profession in the fifties.

In 1954 *Architectural Record* not only published photos of a San Diego drive-in with vivid red panels facing the road but justified the color selection by saying, "Gay colors catch the eye and help offset the disadvantage of a rather narrow frontage."

Richard McDonald's sketch had called for rounded arches. By the end of the design process, the arches instead projected upward in a sharp parabolic curve, a shape that strikingly evoked the spirit of modernism. Any recent architectural graduate, indeed anyone familiar with modernism in design, would by that time have seen parabolic arches. Meston's chief draftsman, Charles Fish, the man who worked on the McDonald's project, had used a parabolic curve a year earlier in one of his student projects at the University of Cincinnati. Simple parabolic curves had been marching into the architectural mainstream for more than three decades, ever since the French engineer Eugène Freyssinet designed parabolic vaulted dirigible hangars at the Orly airport outside of Paris in 1916. The most celebrated of modernists, Le Corbusier, proposed using a huge parabolic arch to support an auditorium for a Palace of the Soviets in Moscow in 1931. Eero Saarinen's 590-foot-high arch on the Mississippi riverfront in St. Louis, though not constructed until the 1960s, received extensive publicity in 1948 when it won the Jefferson Westward Expansion Memorial national competition. The acclaimed architect Matthew Nowicki had decided in 1949 to use two gigantic parabolic arches to support the roof of the North Carolina State Fair stadium. The sheetmetal arches at McDonald's—fabricated whole and tied to the walls, with the roof built around them—might be smaller than their illustrious predecessors, but they would share the same buoyant spirit: a feeling of skyward momentum, symbolic of an aerospace age in which man could hurtle himself into the heavens.

The enthusiasm for bold forms and modern ways that McDonald's exploited was by no means confined to the narrow ranks of the architectural profession. It had become part of the national outlook, an expression of the potential of the twentieth century. Propaganda aimed at making a dynamic modern vision acceptable to the great mass of Americans had been disseminated since the 1930s, in no instance more effectively than at the 1939 New York World's Fair. In a single summer, five million people trooped through the fair's most popular exhibit, General Motors' Futurama. In lines up to a mile long, they waited for a sixteen-minute excursion into a tomorrowland where abstract buildings would be glimpsed from radio-controlled cars gliding along expressways separated into 50-, 75-, and 100-mile-an-hour lanes—"magic motorways" they were called by their designer, Norman Bel Geddes. If Richard McDonald had visited Futurama (which he didn't), he might have noticed that the farm of the future contained a tall building in the shape of a parabolic arch. Nor did

Above: *Open-air ordering at McDonald's in Downey, Calif., soon after its opening in 1953.* Right: *Downey McDonald's in 1985, still outlined in neon. Speedee rises from a special 60-foot sign built in 1959.*

Right center: *Sign and logo featuring Speedee were commonly used from 1953 to 1962.* Above: *An outlet built about 1964 in Syracuse, N.Y., with plastic-covered arches, an enclosed ordering area, and no references to Speedee; photo 1983. Next step was to put shingles on the roof-wedge and brick on the walls, as at a McDonald's photographed in Cheektowaga, N.Y., in 1982.*

Above: *A variation on the mid-1960s shingled roof.* Left: *Ronald McDonald in Matteson, Ill., 1969.* Below: *A mansard-roofed McDonald's with drive-thru and McDonaldland Park in Corning, N.Y.; photo 1985.* Bottom: *Custom urban design for San Francisco; photo 1983. Roof-wedge was removed from the logo in 1969.*

the propaganda cease when the fair closed. World War II, in a curious way, put the seemingly wondrous potentialities of the man-made world even more strongly in the spotlight. With people being forced to make sacrifices and postpone normal civilian activities for the duration of the war, the natural tendency was to focus attention on the better times coming once the fighting was over. The heightened air of anticipation had enough basis in fact—in the arrival of commercial television, for instance, and the construction of "superhighways" and extraordinary buildings—to continue into the 1950s and to convince business owners that an appearance of modernity could be to their benefit, especially if it was a kind of modernity that caught everyone's eye.

The propagators of structurally adventurous modern design—such architects and engineers as Freyssinet, Le Corbusier, and Italy's Pier Luigi Nervi—had wanted to span great distances without obstructions or to explore new technologies or to enclose a maximum volume of space with a minimum of material; but the restaurant industry felt free to ignore these considerations. What mattered was the futuristic *look*. Richard McDonald, in injecting the appearance of dynamic structural modernism into a roadside hamburger stand, wasn't bothered when the arches, as finally built, had no function other than the strictly visual. He said later that it was probably fortunate the arches were not structural, since if a vehicle had run into one of them, it might have done serious damage to the building.

The McDonald brothers considered painting the arches red, but, according to Richard McDonald, chose yellow because it offered contrast against the red and white of the walls. Attached to each arch was neon tubing in white and reddish-pink, a color combination that Richard McDonald believed "gave the entire building a pleasant glow at night." In the fifties, architects began to equate neon with commercial vulgarity, but the public as a whole had not yet turned against it. After the austerity of the Depression and the scarcities of the war years, an explosion of light and color was more cheery than irritating. The arches, incidentally, were occasionally called "golden arches" by the McDonald brothers, but the term didn't become widely known for several years, perhaps because they were golden only during the daytime. When restaurant magazines searched for a way to describe the building, they usually referred instead to "rainbow-shaped arches illuminated in neon," which, at McDonald's locations in the West, insistently flashed on and off in the night. The pink and white of the neon in the arches were repeated in a sign near the street—a single arch with a little chef, "Speedee," who had what was called "a round hamburger face."

Meston contended in 1984 that the arches idea had been his own. "It became evident," he said, "that something was required to give the basic elements another dimension, and at the same time make a statement that would have distinction. After many sketches, it was decided the arches would be the answer." This claim is unconvincing. Meston's office may have contributed such refinements as the parabolic curve, but the initial impetus to use arches of any kind clearly came from McDonald. Richard McDonald was a man who enjoyed sitting in his office, toying with design ideas. Art Bender, who went to work at the San Bernardino drive-in in 1948 and later opened several McDonald's restaurants of his own in Fresno, California, recalls that even before the decision to franchise McDonald's was made, McDonald considered constructing a restaurant called "The Dimer," where everything on the menu would sell for multiples of dimes and where there would be a machine to polish all the dimes the customers received as change. "He drew a round building," Bender said, "with serrated edges like a dime has, and with a single arch."

What's more pertinent is that Charles Fish, now an architect in San Diego, recalls that the McDonald brothers "had pretty well researched this thing before they reached the stage of wanting a prototype. They had the basic plan worked out in rather meticulous detail." A drawing of the building, on wrapping paper or butcher paper, was presented to Meston and Fish. "We thought it was a little gaudy," Fish acknowledged. "I did a few sketches of alternative designs that we thought were more architectural, but they held firm. The colors, the arches were asked for by the McDonalds. The red-and-white striped tile was something they wanted. . . . Dick McDonald was not interested in professional design services. He felt all he needed was someone to translate it to paper."

The first of what came to be called "candy-striped" buildings was a franchised unit that opened in Phoenix, Arizona, in May 1953. A second franchised McDonald's, conforming to the same design, opened in August 1953 in the Los Angeles suburb of Downey. In Los Angeles, Sacramento, Pomona, Alhambra, Azusa, and elsewhere in California, the McDonalds granted additional franchises. A system of standardized, eye-catching buildings was well into development when in 1954 the McDonalds were visited by Ray A. Kroc, a Chicago distributor of milkshake mixers who had heard of the brothers' phenomenal business.

Although Kroc was slower than thousands of other people in discovering the McDonalds, timing served to his advantage. The McDonalds wanted to avoid the travel that a franchising program required, and illness had recently forced their first franchise agent, William Tansey, to resign after working less than three months. So Kroc became the McDonald brothers' second franchise agent, with rights to license outlets throughout the United States. He accepted the building essentially as the McDonald brothers had designed it, adding only such elements as a basement and tiled built-in benches along the side windows when he erected the first McDonald's of his own in Des Plaines, Illinois, in 1955—the same year the McDonald brothers demolished the octagonal restaurant in San Bernardino and replaced it with a standardized building.

About 1959 Kroc began fitting the arches with fluorescent bulbs and yellow plastic covers, not only making them more sturdy than neon but also producing a consistent color—bright yellow, day or night. Advertising began to urge: "Look for the Golden Arches." The shape of the arches also underwent modification. The parabolic shapes rising through the roof took on a more gradually rounded profile. The change appears to have been made because the company started having the arches manufactured in segments, but it was a decision imbued with symbolism: by the end of the fifties, the buoyant spirit represented by structural modernism was beginning to erode. The parabolic shape remained only in the single-arched sign near the street and in the corporate logo.

For several years, a constant series of long-distance conversations and Dictaphone tapes connected San Bernardino to Chicago as Kroc and his organization cleared their ideas with the McDonald brothers, who had retained the right to review Kroc's initiatives. In 1961, Kroc bought out the brothers for $2.7 million, but even after doing so, he clung to the basic elements of the design the McDonald brothers had conceived in 1952.

The extraordinary success of McDonald's made it a model to follow and gave it an enormous impact on the character of both the restaurant business and the man-made environment. Entrepreneurs throughout the United States launched competing chains with similar formulas: walk-up windows, low prices, limited menus, simple cooking procedures that could be easily taught to inexperienced, low-wage workers, and an absence of carhops and indoor seating. Many of them copied either the specifics or the spirit of the McDonald's building.

The basic shape of the building—leaning forward, looking as if it were poised for a leap toward the highway—was what some chains mimicked. Hardee's, a fifteen-cent hamburger chain established in 1960 by Wilbur Hardee in Greenville, North Carolina, was by 1961 using a red-and-white-tiled building with a tilted roof and a tapered soffit much like McDonald's, except that poles extended from the ground into the soffit to provide the support that McDonald's received from a cantilever. Hardee's, however, had no arches.

In 1954 the Bresler Ice Cream Company of Chicago started a chain of self-service hamburger outlets named Henry's in honor of one of the Bresler brothers who had died the previous year. By 1958 Henry's Hamburgers—the term "drive-in" was gradually abandoned by self-service operators—adopted the tilted roof, the thick, tapered soffit, and the horizontal bands of tile used by McDonald's. Henry's didn't have arches, either, but it did erect a metal sign framework that was made to appear as if it had burst through the center of the roof.

In 1956 in Gary, Indiana, the Tastee-Freez Company of Chicago built the first outlet of a hamburger chain that Tastee-Freez chairman Leo S. Maranz named Carrols in honor of his daughter. Customers ordering fifteen-cent hamburgers at Carrols stood out-of-doors under an extended, sloping roof, the same as they did at McDonald's, Henry's, and Hardee's. Behind a kitchen exposed by large windows on the front and sides was a boxy rear area for storage and lavatories, the walls decorated with the ever more common red-and-white stripes—in this instance with the stripes running vertically instead of horizontally. The most striking architectural feature, however, was a pair of big blue boomerangs—"wings" or "fins," the company called them—one attached to each side of the building, as if ready to fly into the sky. Here, for the first time, was a major fast-food chain exploiting dynamic modern architectural imagery just as aggressively as McDonald's.

In 1958, after two years of experimentation, the executives of a restaurant equipment manufacturing company in Indianapolis started Burger Chef, a chain that at its peak in the late 1960s would have 1,000 outlets. Its standard building, designed by Indianapolis architect Harry E. Cooler, and its roadside sign, devised in conjunction

Original Carrols design in early 1960s in Syracuse, N.Y., and (left) restaurant with enclosed ordering area near Poughkeepsie, N.Y., photographed in 1981. Carrols peaked at 163 restaurants in 1973, but two years later the company began converting most of its outlets to Burger King franchises.

with the Grate Sign Company of Joliet, Illinois, had what signmaker Tony Grate called "the kite look." "McDonald's had the arches that added height to their building," Grate recalled. "We did the same thing, but Burger Chef didn't have the financial capability of McDonald's, so we had to do it cheaply." A vaguely kitelike or diamond-shaped framework rose from the floor of the ordering area and extended above the roof. When a thin glass-and-metal storm front was added to the building, the angles were reproduced in its frame. The angles gave Burger Chef a visual tension, a sense of upward and outward thrust restrained only by the strength of the frame, and the tension made the building more compelling. "When you're starting out, you need to draw attention to yourself. You want mind impression," said Grate. "Before you get mind impression, you've got to stomp on 'em, hit 'em in the eye."

But "hitting 'em in the eye" was, as we have seen, not strictly the province of roadside restaurants. Many "high-art" designers reveled in their ability to produce buildings that not only explored new structural techniques but advertised their advanced nature visually and flamboyantly. A writer in a 1943 issue of *Pencil Points* (soon renamed *Progressive Architecture*) had proclaimed: "The time is not far distant when concrete will begin to move freely in space instead of straight up and straight over; stairways will be replaced by gracefully spiraling ramps; and walls and roofs will follow the sweep of the sun and the stars." Such new forms, the writer declared, "may so revolutionize architectural design that masses of four plumbed wall-units will no longer represent a building to anyone." Heady words, yet it seemed in the postwar years as if a substantial part of the architectural profession was intent on making the forecast come true, not only with parabolic arches but with other dynamic forms devoid of traditional applied ornament. The fast-food restaurants of the fifties and the sixties—often looked back on today as unrelievedly garish—had much in common with this "serious" architecture. The boomerangs and kites paralleled, at a crude level, the architectural profession's emphasis on originality of form rather than continuity of surroundings.

Some roadside eating places were calm exceptions to the parade of ostentation, if only because they hadn't yet invested much money or attention in their exterior images. When George W. Church, Sr. retired from running a hatchery and selling incubators in 1952 and started Church's Fried Chicken in San Antonio, he worked from a boxy little metal-and-concrete building with a simple rectangular sign above. Dunkin' Donuts, started in Quincy, Massachusetts, in 1950 by William Rosenberg, used ordinary rectangular buildings with the company name mounted in large letters

Burger Chef in Indianapolis, 1958. After rapid growth followed by retrenchment, the company was sold to Hardee's in 1982, and most outlets soon adopted the Hardee's name.

overhead. So did Mister Donut, founded five years later in Revere, Massachusetts, by Rosenberg's brother-in-law, Harry Winokur.

Attempts had been made to persuade segments of the restaurant industry that the fascination with new design possibilities was unrealistic. In *Soda Fountain Service* magazine in 1944, an executive of Liquid Carbonic Corporation, a leading manufacturer of soda fountains, tried to convince his customers that opportunities for "daring design" would be sharply limited, that "the post-war fountain will serve the public with much the same tastes as today." The argument was futile; Liquid Carbonic's was the voice of an industry at odds with the prevailing currents and ill-prepared for what was coming. Within a dozen years, *Soda Fountain Service* would change its name and its orientation to *Fast Food,* and much of the public that had once gone to drugstore counters for refreshments and quick meals would move onto the highways, where opportunities for daring design abounded.

As chain operations proliferated, as competition intensified, and as highway traffic gathered speed, the majority of franchisers moved toward highly visible "image buildings" almost of necessity. Bold structural or pseudo-structural elements showed up even in restaurants that had first gotten along without them. This shift of style was evident at Burger King, a chain founded in Florida in 1953. In 1952 Matthew Burns in Long Beach, California, had invited his stepson, Keith G. Cramer—owner of Keith's Drive-in, a carhop operation in Daytona Beach, Florida—to fly to California and witness the enormous success of the McDonald brothers' self-service drive-in. Cramer acted on the suggestion, first observing the San Bernardino stand and then joining with his stepfather to acquire the right to use the Insta automatic broiler and Insta automatic milkshake machine recently produced by an inventor in Hollywood, California. Cramer and Burns went to Jacksonville and in the summer of 1953 built the first Burger King, a self-service drive-in on Beach Boulevard.

"When we came to Jacksonville," Cramer said years later, "there were a lot of sign restrictions by the city. We just made the sign an integral part of the building to get around the restrictions." This was not, of course, an unusual advertising technique. A variety of businesses across the country, including A & W Root Beer, had already achieved the same integration of sign and structure by having a rectangular pylon grow out of a rectangular building. Burger King's pylon tapered, growing wider as it rose through the slightly slanted roof. Emblazoned on it was the company's advertising—"BURGERS," "SHAKES," and a circle nearly five feet tall around the price, "18¢." Within a year Cramer and Burns built a second unit on Main Street in Jacksonville. There the top of the pylon carried a sign bearing the company's new symbol, a king sitting on a hamburger and holding a milkshake. Similar designs were adopted by other Burger King units, which were rapidly opened by Cramer and Burns in northern Florida and by franchisees in other regions.

To Cramer and Burns, who had formulated their plans while looking at the original low-roofed McDonald's in San Bernardino, not at its exuberant arched successor, this seemed satisfactory enough. But in Miami, David R. Edgerton, Jr., one of the earliest franchisees of Burger King—or Insta-Burger-King, as it was also known in the mid-fifties—became dissatisfied. The expense of reinforcing the pylon well enough to satisfy South Florida's hurricane-resistance standards, along with the refusal of some municipalities to allow a business to erect both a roadside sign and an advertising pylon, gave Edgerton an excuse to do away with the pylon and introduce elements much more graphic. In 1957 Edgerton erected a large sign at the front of a new Burger King's property, eliminated the pylon and, for the first time, installed on the rooftop a pair of garish metal "handlebars." Had metal elements like these "handlebars" appeared on top of a large building designed by a modern architect, they undoubtedly would have been structural, helping to hold the building together. Burger King, occupying a concrete block building of little more than 500 square feet, had no need for out-of-the-ordinary structural support, but it did need a strong, memorable image, and this the company achieved by putting the two angular appendages on the roof and painting them red. Like McDonald's, Burger Chef, and Carrols, Burger King realized that modernism—the kind of modernism that glorified exotic engineering techniques—could be exploited for its advertising potential. Edgerton

Burger King in Jacksonville, Fla., in 1956, when "self-service" still had to be announced on the building.

and his partner, James W. McLamore, installed glowing red neon in the handlebars, later replacing the neon with backlighted red plastic. In 1961 Edgerton and Mc-Lamore acquired national franchise rights to the company, then active primarily in Florida and a few other parts of the Southeast, and they began putting hamburger stands with radiant rooftop appendages along highways throughout America.

This penchant for treating modernism as a cosmetic device would have been disapproved by most architects—it was a matter of form faking function. Nonetheless, flamboyant restaurants did constitute a tribute to the remarkable acceptance that a gymnastic brand of modernism had achieved. Fast-food businesses would have found other, most likely nonmodernist ways to make their buildings stand out if the public mood had been unreceptive to this kind of architectural statement. The fifties was a time for brashness at most levels of design. Certainly those who set the tone for serious discussion within the architectural profession indulged in their own celebration of the bold and bright. The same year that Burger King raised its red handlebars, *Progressive Architecture* approvingly featured a motel that the magazine said was "planned with the conviction that a colorful, well-illuminated building is worth more than any sign!"

By the beginning of the 1960s, the architectural profession became briefly fascinated with yet two more novelties: the A-frame and the folded-plate roof—a roof composed of alternating slopes creating a busy zigzag effect on the horizon. Mister Donut put folded-plate canopies above the entrances to the rectangular orange-and-white-striped buildings it made in a New Jersey factory. The Vendo Company in Kansas City, Missouri, started Stop 'n Treat, the first highway restaurant relying entirely

Burger King in Miami with rooftop "handlebars," early 1960s.

on vending machines (somewhat like a roadside version of an Automat), and used steel folded-plate construction for its roof and its attached canopy. The two forms—A-frame and folded plate—could also be combined to accentuate the architectural effect. In California, folded-plate canopies were attached to the sides of Wigwam Wieners' A-frames, and in the Midwest they were joined to the front of A-frame buildings erected by Griff's Burger Bar.

A-frame and folded-plate construction were both adaptable to prefabrication in metal. Not only could the building be assembled quickly on its site. It could also, at least in theory, be easily taken apart and re-erected at another location—a form of flexibility that aroused considerable interest in the early 1960s, when new limited-access highways siphoned traffic away from many commercially established older roads. More important, however, were the visual advantages of A-frame and folded-plate design. When trusted firms like Reynolds Metals and Butler Manufacturing introduced multi-colored metal wall panels and roof shingles guaranteed to resist fading for twenty years, chains seized the opportunity to magnify their visual impact. In 1964 Dari-Delite, a division of the Good Humor Company of California, decided to employ steep roofs of shocking pink. In 1961 the Whataburger chain, founded in Corpus Christi, Texas, by Harmon A. Dobson in 1950, began to erect A-frames with orange-and-white stripes, a visual echo of the company plane that flew over towns in Texas, pulling a Whataburger banner and honking its specially mounted horn. This was no business for the reticent.

Like the arches at McDonald's, the A-frames did not necessarily serve a structural purpose. In a ten-year period beginning in 1964, Southern California's Der Wie-nerschnitzel chain built 190 false A-frame hot dog stands, all of them actually consisting of sloping roofs that slid down over a conventionally constructed rectangular kitchen at the front and a conventional, rectangular office and storage room at the rear. John Galardi had started Der Wienerschnitzel in 1961 with a flat-roofed building in Long Beach and he switched to the A-frame partly because he recognized its superior advertising value: "It doubled the exposure of the building. It looked like a billboard lowered to the street."

By the beginning of the 1960s, a public backlash was beginning to challenge the profusion of clashing modern forms. In January 1961 the prominent conservative political philosopher Russell Kirk told the nation's architects that "we have done more damage to our country's artificial and natural beauty since the Second World War than we were able to accomplish in the hundred years preceding." One of the nation's leading town planners, Catherine Bauer Wurster, pointed to "arbitrary forms and fascinating surfaces, competing for novelty," and said "their effect on less able designers and the commercial vernacular is horrible to contemplate." Jurors for *Progressive Architecture*'s 1961 design awards worried whether the architectural profession had descended into chaos. Indeed, the magazine sensed so profound an uneasiness that it began soliciting the thinking of fifty leading architects on where architecture was going and where it ought to be headed.

Aggressive experimentation with modern forms persisted in some quarters, but the buoyancy of a few years earlier began to dissipate. Flamboyant structural modernism no longer served as a symbol of unquestionably beneficial new possibilities. Some of this change of attitude stemmed from primarily architectural considerations; the bold structures had been around long enough to be appraised more coolly now. Thousands of gas stations, car washes, motels, and restaurants flaunting pseudo-structural elements also helped to generate the more critical atmosphere. But in addition, the country simply was not in the same mood by the early 1960s. The election of President Kennedy indicated a degree of dissatisfaction with existing conditions, and it was only a short time before concern about the country's faults and inequities manifested itself in books like Michael Harrington's *The Other America* and in the burgeoning of the civil-rights movement. Architecture—particularly popular architecture—responds to shifts in the emotional climate, and during the early 1960s it became evident that designs imbued with a brash futurism no longer fit as well as they had. When that happened, restauranteurs started drifting to other kinds of images—strong, immediately recognizable images, but less technological, less like the hardware of tomorrow.

Whataburger in the 1960s attached an open canopy to the front of its A-frame buildings to accommodate cars, and later replaced the canopies with enclosed dining areas. Photo 1983, Naco-Perrin Boulevard, San Antonio.

Red Barn, founded in Springfield, Ohio, in 1960, built its restaurants in the shape of a barn with a glass front and polished red brick walls, and it became one of the most successful chains of the decade. Incidentally, Red Barn found a new answer to a question that had cropped up ever since the early days of Howard Johnson's: Could some use be found for second-story space that was being built for primarily visual reasons? At Red Barn, the barn loft stored potatoes and held a peeling machine that sent freshly skinned spuds sliding down a chute into the kitchen.

Chock Full o'Nuts Corporation, which had operated New York City coffee shops since the 1920s, decided in 1960 to test the suburban market with a series of roadside stands on Long Island and in New Jersey. Jules Kabat, who for twenty-six years had designed Chock Full o'Nuts storefronts in a handsome Art Deco and then a disciplined modernism with smooth surfaces and glass façades, now produced a glass-walled roadside restaurant with a warped roof, a bloated chimney, swollen eaves, and an upper window like a cartoon version of work by the great Spanish eccentric architect Antonio Gaudi. It was a "crazy house," a throwback to the distorted designs the company had used in the 1920s, before Kabat's hiring, when Chock Full o'Nuts was still a nut store, or, as the original façades on Broadway suggested, a "nut house."

When Harland Sanders of Corbin, Kentucky, sold his Kentucky Fried Chicken recipe to independent restauranteurs, beginning with Pete Harman in Salt Lake City in 1952, the restauranteurs served the product in their existing buildings, merely adding Kentucky Fried Chicken signs and a likeness of the honorary Kentucky colonel. It wasn't until 1963 that architects Morris Hall and Peter Norris in Atlanta designed a red-and-white-striped pagoda roof, first placed on the rear of a Davis House Cafeteria on Peachtree Road in Atlanta, then used on a freestanding Kentucky Fried Chicken restaurant in Greenville, South Carolina. In 1966 it was adopted as the company's standard "image building" nationwide.

In 1958 Frank Carney, a nineteen-year-old engineering student at the University of Wichita, joined with his older brother Dan to open a Wichita pizza parlor, which they called Pizza Hut because the building they rented looked somewhat like a hut and because the sign mounted on the building had room only for eight letters and one space. In 1963 Carney decided to design a building that would be standard throughout the chain. He realized, he later said, that restauranteurs who resorted to "wilder designs would have trouble getting these things approved" by municipalities. Consequently, the prototype for Pizza Hut, designed by Wichita architect Richard D. Burke and first constructed in 1964, was a restaurant with a hatlike two-tier roof, the top rising high enough for the name to be mounted against it.

A vaulted yellow roof vaguely reminiscent of the chuck wagons of the Old West was adopted by Arby's, a chain of roast-beef restaurants begun in Boardman, Ohio, in 1964 by two restaurant designers and equippers, Forrest Raffel and Leroy Raffel of nearby Youngstown. Arby's—its name formed from the initials of "Raffel Brothers" after the Raffels failed to persuade an Akron restauranteur to let them use the name they wanted, "Big Tex"—differed from many fast-food chains in that its buildings

Left: A Whopper Burger erected by the San Antonio chain about 1967 at Blanco Road and the city's I-410 Northwest Loop; photo 1983. Below: 1960s design of Red Barn, which became a chain of some 500 restaurants before falling to about 50 in the early 1980s.

Roadside Chock Full o'Nuts, Route 22, Union, N.J., 1961. Within a few years, the chain retreated to its traditional urban base.

emphasized more expensive natural materials (primarily walls of stone) and had lighting recessed in the ceiling for a more pleasant atmosphere. The Raffels wanted to attract a more discriminating customer—consistent with their prices, which were higher than the hamburger outlets'—and they believed a building deliberately free of exposed chrome, neon, and stainless steel would help them do that.

But Arby's represented more than an attempt to reach a different caliber of customer. In conjunction with Red Barn, Pizza Hut, Chock Full o'Nuts, and Kentucky Fried Chicken, it reflected an altered approach to restaurant imagery. This early- and mid-sixties generation of roadside restaurants shunned the prime source of 1950s fast-food imagery—futuristic structural modernism. The new chains chose from a variety of sources—rural buildings, quasi-Old West buildings, exotic or eccentric buildings prominent among them. Together they made it clear that the era of buildings that flexed their structural muscles was ending.

While changes like these were taking place on restaurant exteriors, another form of evolution was proceeding on the inside. Initially the fast-food industry single-mindedly pursued a goal of delivering food as fast and efficiently as possible. "Our idea of a perfect building," Whataburger's Harmon Dobson told an interviewer in 1957, "is one in which three people can stand with their feet nailed to the floor and serve a thousand customers." The McDonald brothers insisted so strenuously on eliminating any unnecessary movement by the personnel that they carefully worked out the placement of windows and equipment and then had their employees draw the

1963 sketch that became the basis of Kentucky Fried Chicken's pagoda-roof design. At some outlets, the bucket revolved.

Arby's 1964–1975 standard building, designed by W. C. Riedel of Alliance, Ohio, brought a hint of the western chuck wagon to the shopping center parking lot.

floor plan of the restaurant in actual size, 44 feet wide and 30 feet deep, in chalk on the tennis court behind the McDonald home; the architect was to reproduce it with utmost precision. The McDonalds shortened the spindles on their Multi-Mixers so shakes and malts could be made directly in paper cups; there would be no metal mixing containers to wash, no wasted ingredients, no wasted motion, no wasted time. They developed dispensers that put the exact same amount of ketchup or mustard on every bun. They installed a bank of infrared lamps to keep the waiting French fries hot. They used disposable paper goods instead of glassware and china. Having done all those things, in 1952 the McDonald brothers installed a microphone at the front window to amplify the customer's voice and reduce misunderstanding about orders. Such attention to detail enabled even the early fast-food restaurants to turn out an enormous quantity of food in a tiny area. Burger Kings in the mid-1950s measured 22 by 25 feet, and Kroc's first McDonald's in Des Plaines—slightly reduced from the California version—was 30 by 32.

The McDonald brothers' employees, all men dressed neatly in white, were said to be capable in 1952 of serving the customer a hamburger, beverage, French fries, and ice cream in twenty seconds. Kroc later established the standard delivery time

Pizza Hut in the early 1970s, before the dough-tossing Italian chef was banished. The basic building shape, usually with the roof a bright red, has had a remarkable longevity, serving for more than two decades as the company standard.

for a burger, fries, and shake at fifty seconds. Burger King pushed for fifteen-second service. "There was a hole in the counter to push the cash into, and we had a change machine to give the customer his change," David Edgerton recalled. "Throwing the money in the hole was faster than opening a cash register and putting money in a drawer."

Such quickness mattered to people on brief lunch periods and work breaks, and it enjoyed a widespread appeal even among people who weren't at the mercy of a tight schedule; Americans loved to "save" time even when they had time to spare. Most people really didn't need to receive food or drinks in less than sixty seconds. They routinely waited much longer in the comfort of a sit-down restaurant or at a carhop drive-in, where they could stay in their automobiles. Speed was a necessity at self-service establishments primarily because the customers had to get out of their cars—leaving friends, dates, spouses, or children—and stand in line, sometimes paying for their food before the order was handed to them. The remarkable speed simply reduced the inconvenience inherent in such a system, and it also enabled the restaurants to sell more food.

Efficiency extended beyond the kitchen and out into the rest of the restaurant's premises. Few if any flowers, shrubs, or trees were planted; they would have demanded time and attention from employees, time that could better be spent behind the counter. Ray Kroc decided to construct built-in benches alongside the kitchen windows of some McDonald's units, beginning in Des Plaines. The benches were tiled like the exterior walls so that they could be hosed down easily, but even so, Richard McDonald had misgivings, since he knew that some customers would litter the benches with cups, wrappers, napkins, and other leavings—all of which would increase the restaurant crew's clean-up duties. Employees were sent out frequently to remove trash from the lot; indeed, the spotlessness of the McDonald's Drive-in property in San Bernardino had impressed Kroc from the start. But restauranteurs generally tried to avoid creating situations in which employees would have to spend much time outside the kitchen.

The efficiency and organization of fast-food restaurants were put to effective visual advantage in their ordering areas. A customer placing an order at Burger King could see the ceaseless production of the Insta broiler, which automatically cooked as many as 400 hamburgers an hour, expelling patties into a receiving pan of warm sauce and depositing toasted buns in a separate pan. Customers at McDonald's— standing outside on concrete that had been painted green to seem cooler—observed a counter and kitchen outfitted in sparkling stainless steel and watched the quickness of a kitchen crew made up in the Kroc years primarily of clean-cut teenage boys who didn't keep their jobs long but who nonetheless gave an impression of being organized and purposeful. As late as 1968, Kroc was still advising franchisees not to hire girls because they attracted boyfriends, whose presence, he believed, distracted the girls from efficient performance of their work. The open view of the kitchen also prodded employees to perform better. In addition, it helped customers feel more confident about the food.

A recurring issue in the fast-food business has been: Which forms of efficiency

A Burger King dining area about 1964, when glass was all that separated indoors from out.

Gino's dining area in 1966. Gino's was later merged into Marriott's Roy Rogers chain.

would win public acceptance and which would turn customers away? Early in the decade, "automatic restaurants" seemed to promise yet another jump toward the ultimate in efficiency. Stop 'n Treat, Buy-O-Mat, Pat Boone Dine-O-Mat, White Tower's Tower-O-Matic, and other automatic restaurants appeared throughout the country, most of them roadside structures dispensing a wide variety of foods, from sandwiches to casseroles, in coin-operated vending machines. Customers were expected to heat the food themselves in microwave ovens, although some automatic restaurants, like the thirty-six-seat Tower-O-Matic, employed a hostess to help customers figure out how to use the ovens. Despite an initial burst of enthusiasm, roadside automatic restaurants met the same fate the Automat had encountered when Horn & Hardart tried to get people in cities other than New York and Philadelphia to patronize its coin-operated restaurant system more than forty years earlier. The failure of the automatic restaurants appeared to stem from a number of causes: instructions too complicated for the average customer, unappetizing microwave-heated food, speed no better than that of a conventional fast-food outlet, and prices no lower than conventional competitors. By the late sixties, the automatic restaurants had been largely forgotten, except as adjuncts to factories and other places where people worked; as independent enterprises they could not survive.

An innovation that fared better—though not spectacularly in the 1960s—was the drive-thru window. As early as the 1920s, some Pig Stand drive-ins had handed food directly out a window to customers in their cars. Before World War II, the old nickel-hamburger chains, White Castle and White Tower, had also offered drive-up window service as an adjunct to regular counter service at some of their units. Not until 1951, however, when Robert O. Peterson started Jack in the Box in San Diego, did a sizable chain make drive-thru windows the keynote of its operation. At Jack in the Box restaurants, one window served walk-up customers and another window took care of drive-thru orders. Generally, the restaurants required three minutes to handle a line of four cars. To maintain the kitchen's speed, a menuboard and a microphone for calling in orders were placed three car-lengths back from the window. In busy periods during the early sixties, Jack in the Box experimented with having an employee go out with a microphone on an extension cord and take orders from cars farther back. The experimentation raised anew the question of where was the ideal location for the stationary microphone. The more distant the mike, the more time the kitchen had, but the more impersonal the service seemed to customers. The chain concluded that the efficiency was outweighed by customer dissatisfaction if the mike was located more than four car-lengths back.

The drive-thru idea was taken literally by one of Jack in the Box's imitators, Der

Jack in the Box in San Diego, designed in early 1950s by Russell Forester. A structure shielding rooftop equipment was disguised as a jack in the box, and this, according to the founder, prompted the name.

Wienerschnitzel's John Galardi, who first erected flat-roofed buildings with an opening in the middle, then switched to the A-frame with an automobile-sized hole in the center, effectively indicating where the customers should steer their cars at a time when the drive-thru was an unfamiliar form of service.

Der Wienerschnitzel initially settled on the drive-thru because it solved the problem of how to operate a fast-food restaurant on a property too small to offer much parking; the car-borne customer, upon receiving his food, immediately drove forward and was off the premises. This could also amount to a sly way of selling to teenagers, yet discouraging them from turning the parking lot into a gathering place. "My idea," said Galardi, "was to put the drive-thru in and dump 'em in the street. It was a real hassle for them to get back on the lot."

Burger King equipped some of its outlets with drive-thru windows and discovered to its dismay that a car waiting at the window invariably conveys more urgency than a customer standing at a counter. The reaction of the kitchen crew was to turn away from the standing customer and rush to fill the drive-thru order, thus slowing regular service and antagonizing customers. Rather than install and adequately staff a separate drive-thru operation, Burger King in the 1960s removed all its existing drive-thru windows and concentrated on customers willing to get out of their cars. Underlying Burger King's frustration with the drive-thru was the fact that it was not a service in great demand, perhaps because it constituted such an abrupt departure from the drive-ins' practice of encouraging people to eat in their cars on the restaurants' lots.

Actually, the fast-food industry would have been happy if *all* the customers had been willing to line up at the drive-thru, make their purchases, and be gone. Any social contact beyond a cheerful greeting and farewell was viewed in negative terms, as an impediment to maximum turnover. In 1962, *American Restaurant* magazine changed its name to *American Restaurant Hospitality* and stopped publishing articles about fast-food companies—the implication being that hospitality was one quality the fast-food outlets lacked. Companies like McDonald's and Burger King were geared to efficient feeding, not graciousness.

Comforts were so few at early fast-food restaurants that even the McDonald brothers doubted their concept would succeed in climates harsher than San Bernardino's, and Kroc wasn't sure whether his first outlet in Illinois would be able to stay open in the winter. It did, of course, and customers put up with the cold in many other northern locales as McDonald's expanded, but it wasn't long before glass-and-metal enclosures were added to the restaurants to offer a modicum of protection.

A different climate problem confronted fast-food operators in the South. Eating in an automobile on a sunny day was a hot and sweaty experience, so fast-food operators like Whataburger erected canopies for shade. Many restaurants added patios for outdoor eating, with umbrellas or a broad overhang over the tables. Burger King often put wooden picnic tables on a covered patio extending from one side of the restaurant. In California, where people were accustomed to spending much of their leisure time outdoors, patios were also commonplace. By contrast, in the North, patios remained fewer and more primitive, often with indestructible concrete slab seats and tables, and with metal saucers acting as umbrellas.

Another problem also emerged in warm weather, especially in the South. "You'd go there on a warm summer evening," former Burger King Corporation Chairman McLamore recalls of the early Burger Kings in Miami, "and the bugs—hard beetles

Der Wienerschnitzel's drive-thru possessed one disadvantage: employees had to dodge traffic just to go from the kitchen at the front to the storage room at the rear. Photo 1983, Brea, Calif.

and flying bugs—they'd be all over the screen. The operator inside this building would slide a screen out and say, 'What do you want?' and slide the screen back, 'cause all the bugs were crawling, trying to get in there." To combat the insect problem, Burger King began putting screens on its covered patios, and after doing that for some time, started replacing the screens with walls of glass around the eating and ordering areas and installing air-conditioning. The patio evolved into a rudimentary quasi-indoor dining area. Meanwhile, in the North, McDonald's began setting molded plastic chairs in the outer sections of the order areas for customers who didn't have cars or didn't want to eat in their cars. They sat in a fishbowl environment, next to floor-to-ceiling glass walls, exposed to the crush of the crowds during busy periods of the day.

Ray Kroc had always been leery of making his outlets too comfortable. He wanted to attract people, but he didn't want them to stay for more than a few minutes. He was proud to have prohibited such public services as newspaper boxes and telephone booths, to have banned such entertainment as pinball, to have done without candy and cigarette machines, to have made McDonald's a jukeboxless place. To a large extent, his policies were aimed at combatting his most enthusiastic yet dreaded customers—teenagers. Kroc wanted the teenage trade, yet he hoped to keep the transaction quick and limited; the objective was to prevent adolescents and others from turning his restaurants into social institutions as opposed to mere feeding stations.

Nonetheless, his attempts to eliminate social contact fell far short of the mark. With the resilience of youth, teenagers insisted on hanging out at McDonald's despite the absence of comforts and services other than inexpensive food and clean lavatories. In the sixties it was common knowledge that boisterous gatherings of the young had harmed some drive-ins financially, including some McDonald's outlets. McDonald's had reason for making its design and furnishings relatively antisocial.

Yet McDonald's attempts to discourage loitering were also representative of a broader phenomenon—the business community's narrow conception of its responsibilities, particularly in the booming suburbs. The typical shopping center in the early 1960s was just as unsocial as McDonald's, offering no sheltered arcades, little planting, and few places to sit comfortably. Retailers, whether in the fast-food business or some other endeavor, focused on delivering their products with utmost efficiency, to the exclusion of any broader vision having to do with encouragement of a more satisfying daily life. Kroc's dream was the typical capitalist's dream: to make himself and his associates rich without concerning themselves about whether their restaurants directly enriched the everyday environment.

McDonald's built in 1963 on Fillmore Avenue near Broadway, Buffalo; abandoned in 1985. Many old-style McDonald's were razed when their twenty-year leases expired.

Gradually, however, McDonald's and other fast-food operators had to adapt to new conditions. In 1964 McDonald's opened its first outlet in downtown Washington, D.C., and found it necessary to install a counter, tables, and chairs for the customers. The following year a restaurant in Huntsville, Alabama, used a similar arrangement. McDonald's competitors went further. Gino's, a chain founded in Baltimore in 1957 by Baltimore Colts captain Gino Marchetti and three other professional football players, remodeled eighteen of its restaurants by July 1966, installing eighty seats in each of them. "We believe that few fathers liked buying food at a window, then carrying it back to a car crawling with kids," the company explained. Red Barn by mid-1966 had put seating for sixty-four to seventy customers in many of its outlets and had made that a requirement for all its new units. Said a Red Barn executive: "People are tired of spilling their milkshakes in the back of their cars."

By the mid-sixties, the automobile and its effects on the landscape were the subject of widespread criticism. The desire to do everything in the car was wearing off, and eating was moving indoors. In 1967 Burger King made the dining area an integral part of the design of its new restaurants. In 1968 McDonald's, catching up to its competition, produced a new prototype containing an eating area at one side of the building. The enclosed eating areas of fast-food chains were a long way from formal dining, of course. Gino's provided ten long metal tables, each outfitted with eight hard, immovable seats. In what might have been the place of honor at the head of each table was a projectile-like trash container, hard and shiny like nearly every other surface in the room. Burger King installed a counter and stools along the front window and plywood seats in the rest of a room devoid of decoration. It was simply a clean, fluorescent-lighted place—one that, as a Gino's spokesman said about his own chain's dining areas, would "not encourage marathon sit-downs."

Thus, in a little more than a decade and a half, the fast-food industry underwent a major change—from bright, buoyant outdoor environments to eating places with calmer and climate-controlled, though austere, indoor surroundings. With the shift, the parking lot lost most of its role as a kind of extended eating area. Restaurants were able to reduce the congregating and commotion outdoors and bring most of the activity inside, where behavior could be more easily controlled. By making the change at the precise moment when carhop-service drive-ins, under public attack, were going out of business across the nation, fast-food chains signaled their own ability to accommodate themselves to a variety of conditions. There was nothing fragile about the fast-food concept; it could thrive even if the automobile and the consequences of the automobile were no longer considered worthy of much celebration. It could do so because the concept of "fast food" was not new at all. The urban lunchrooms of the late nineteenth and early twentieth centuries had shown that many people were willing to walk up to a counter, order their food, and then carry it to where they would consume it. Companies like McDonald's and Burger King transplanted that old idea to the roadside, installing it in freestanding buildings with parking on the premises. Like the lunchrooms, fast-food restaurants prospered by systematizing the act of feeding large numbers of people fast and inexpensively. But in one important respect, fast-food outlets surpassed their turn-of-the-century counterparts: not only did they systematize but they showcased their system—elevated it into an impressive display of the coordination of man and machine. In fast-food restaurants, the longstanding American admiration for efficient and systematic ways of satisfying basic needs reached its twentieth-century culmination.

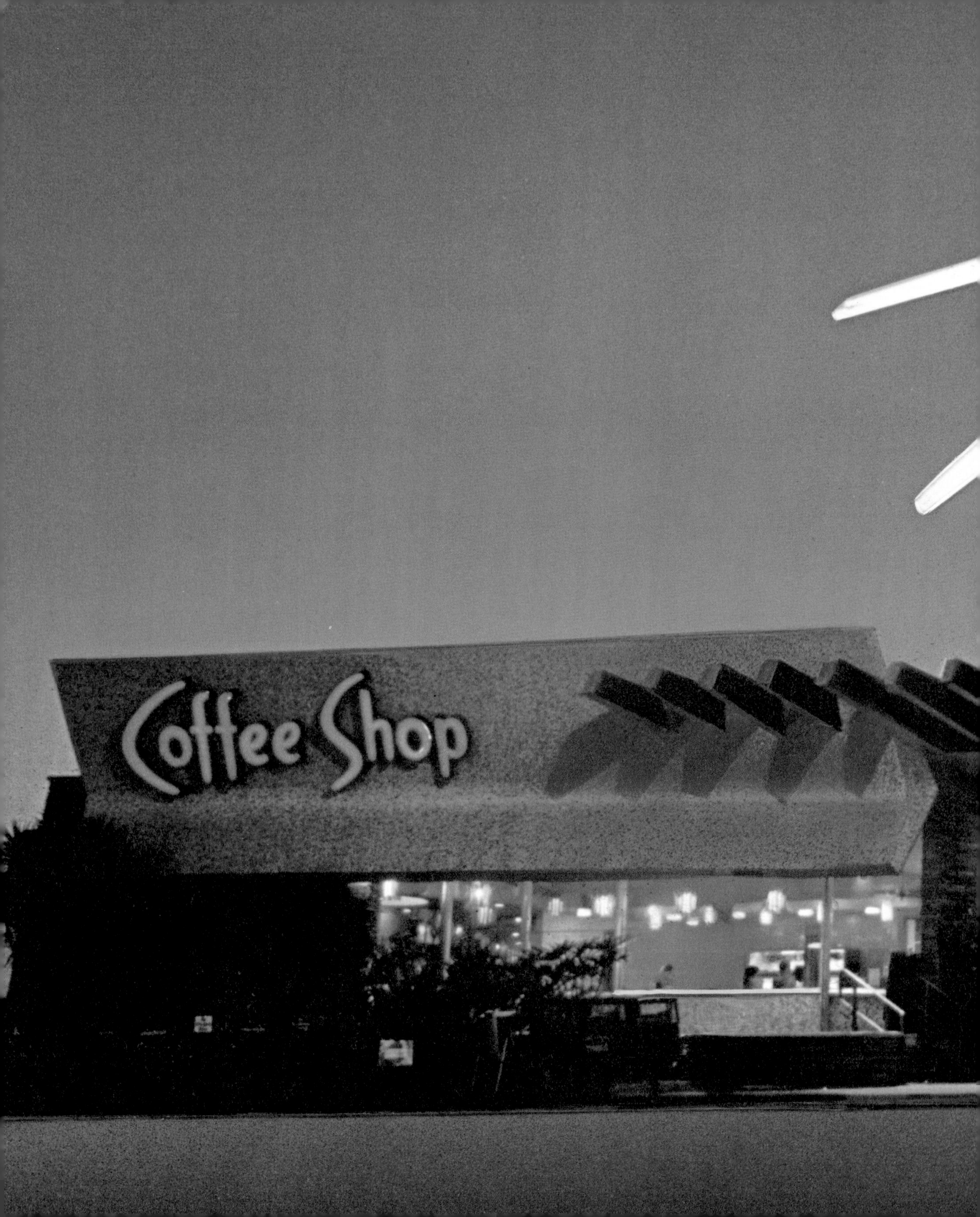
Coffee Shop

CHAPTER FIVE

"Googie": The California Coffee Shop

Overleaf: *Ship's Coffee Shop designed in 1958 by Martin Stern, at Wilshire Boulevard and Glendon, Westwood, Los Angeles, just before its demolition in 1984. This was one of three Ship's established by Matthew and Emmett Shipman.*

JOHN LAUTNER WAS A TALENTED LOS ANGELES ARCHITECT who had worked under Frank Lloyd Wright at Taliesin and had begun by the late 1940s to earn a reputation for unusual flair, especially in designing houses and apartments. A house by Lautner might have a winding ramp for an entry, a hinged wall that rolled out on casters, or a structural system that made the house look as if it were hovering above its dramatic hillside vista.

Lautner also occasionally designed restaurants, and in 1949 he received a commission to do the restaurant that would become the most controversial building of his career. It was a little coffee shop jammed onto a narrow lot on Sunset Boulevard in West Hollywood, next door to Schwab's, the famous pharmacy where movie stars were discovered.

"I just started from scratch with no preconceived idea," Lautner later recalled. For the roof and ceiling, he decided on a vivid red metal structure that would angle upward at one end, capturing a view of the Hollywood Hills for the customers sitting inside while at the same time providing support for an elevated outdoor sign.

The restaurant was to be called "Googie's," a name that suggested googley, bulging eyes like those of the cartoon character Barney Google. Lautner probably should have recognized it as an omen of the criticism to come. If people passing by had doubts about whether the restaurant's unusual shape was anything more than an attention-getter, the name would usually settle the question for them.

Then Douglas Haskell saw it. Haskell was an architectural editor committed to modernism, but to a modernism that acknowledged certain limits. Lautner's exuberant mixing of novel shapes, diverse building materials, and extraordinary engineering techniques struck him as originality carried to excess. Unfortunately for Lautner, Haskell also happened to be one of the few architectural journalists with a gift for

John Lautner's controversial Googie's, Sunset Boulevard and Crescent Heights, West Hollywood, soon after its 1949 opening.

satire, and so Lautner found himself the target of three pages of mockery in the February 1952 *House & Home.* The article was titled "Googie Architecture," and it began with a fictitious "Professor Thrugg" describing Googie's this way: "It starts off on the level like any other building. But suddenly it breaks for the sky. The bright red roof of cellular steel decking suddenly tilts upward as if swung on a hinge, and the whole building goes up with it like a rocket ramp. But there is another building next door. So the flight stops as suddenly as it began."

Was the building simply an effort to attract attention? "No," replied the scholarly Professor Thrugg. "You underestimate the seriousness of Googie. Think of it!—Googie is produced by architects, not by ambitious mechanics, and some of these architects starve for it. After all, they are working in Hollywood, and Hollywood has let them know what it expects of them."

The criticism stung Lautner, and he was still smarting when questioned about it in 1983, for Haskell succeeded in making "Googie" a term of condescension in the architectural world. From 1952 on, whenever critics wanted to sum up an architectural style epitomized by arbitrary, offbeat shapes, all they had to say was "Googie."

Lautner went on defending the original Googie's as a design with discipline, a design in which the roof and the ceiling were a single, economical structure, "all exposed, all real," nothing faked or suspended or covered over. But the restaurant industry, much like Douglas Haskell, naturally was struck not by the supposed discipline of Googie's but by its visual wildness. And where Haskell abhorred the wildness, restaurant owners learned to appreciate it, for they noticed that the coffee shop on Sunset Boulevard was reaping substantial profits.

There were other reasons for Googie's success. Probably any reasonably priced coffee shop blessed with a corner location on Sunset Boulevard next to Schwab's would have done well. But certainly Lautner's design contributed to its success. The unusual exterior called out to approaching motorists, giving them time to decide to stop and eat at Googie's. And the jutting roofline, besides serving as an effective advertisement, helped the interior open up to the pleasant Southern California outdoors and gain a sense of spaciousness. Moreover, the design of Googie's was no fluke. It was an outgrowth of the ideas Lautner had begun exploring in a few Coffee Dan's restaurants in Los Angeles and in a Henry's Drive-in in Glendale. Other Southern California architects were also beginning to gravitate toward energetic building forms that captured attention and visually connected the interior to the surroundings outside. Consequently, buildings with dynamic, startling shapes came to be demanded by a growing number of coffee-shop operators—businesspeople who didn't worry about such esoteric matters as whether the appearance was a direct expression of the structure. Googie's, partly understood, partly not, became a model for modern coffee-shop design, first in California, then throughout the United States.

Who would supply startling shapes for legions of coffee shops? Not Lautner. He wasn't about to base his whole career on catering to restaurant owners whose only concern about architecture was whether it would make money. No, the visual effects, even at one of the future Googie's outlets, would be delivered on a regular basis by others, especially by the prolific Los Angeles architectural firm of Armet & Davis.

From the time two University of Southern California alumni, Louis L. Armet and Eldon C. Davis, completed their military service and became partners in 1947, they saw freedom of form as a generator of commerce—"cash register architecture," the restaurant magazines approvingly called their coffee-shop designs. By the late 1950s, the restaurant industry showered the firm with praise, publicity, and commissions. Armet & Davis designed buildings for a number of Los Angeles chains—Norm's, Ship's, Clock's, Carnation, Tiny Naylor's. The firm worked for chains in other places—Lyon's in the San Francisco Bay Area, White Spot in Denver, La Marie Antoinette in Quebec—and it did coffee shops from 1958 to 1966 for Denny's, an expansion-minded chain run from the Los Angeles suburb of Buena Park. Most important, in 1957 Armet & Davis established a long-lasting relationship with Bob's Big Boy of nearby Glendale. The owner of Bob's, Robert C. Wian, achieved fabulous success in franchising the "Big Boy" name and menu specialties like double-decker hamburgers and strawberry pie to other operators. As he did so, Armet & Davis supplied the basic architectural concepts and often the actual designs that would spell "coffee shop" to much of America. By the 1960s, Googie restaurant architecture became a nationwide phenomenon.

The California-style coffee shops built their success on a series of practical advantages: obvious and adequate parking areas, moderate prices, quick, friendly service, and a varied but familiar menu, usually including breakfast items twenty-four hours a day. By definition, coffee shops offered service at a counter, but the California-style coffee shops made the counter more comfortable than before. The customer got a padded seat with an upholstered back rather than a spartan stool, and there were tables or booths for people who didn't like to sit at counters. These factors ensured that chain coffee shops would compete strongly against independent restaurants; but what set them apart visually was their powerful image. The California coffee-shop style prevailed in part because it so effectively distinguished coffee shops from other kinds of buildings and because it was fully the master of the roadside environment, commanding attention whether seen amid a jumble of buildings on a commercial strip or from the approach to an expressway interchange.

California, unlike eastern and midwestern states, did not build toll roads and make travelers captive to restaurants that had been commissioned to operate at designated rest stops. California was the land of the freeway, with free choice to eat at

Clock coffee shop built in 1951 at La Tijera Boulevard and Centinela Avenue, Los Angeles; demolished 1962. Armet & Davis designed a triangular sign pylon and insisted on triangular windows despite the worries of glass-installers. Said Eldon Davis: "It was dull to work with squares."

competing restaurants at one interchange after another, so the restaurants' need for a conspicuous profile was especially intense. The question confronting restaurant operators by the late fifties was: What would catch the eye of fast-moving motorists?

"The answer," said a restaurant magazine, "was roofs." So, the magazine said, "Armet and Davis began laying out roofs whose planes, angles, juttings, textures, and colors couldn't possibly coincide or blend with anything else around them; and which would dominate the skyline and beckon to a customer. The end result of these shapes is extreme long-range visibility and patterns that arrest people's attention and then draw it to the beckoning interior, perfectly visible through plate-glass walls."

An article in another magazine explaining the ABC's of good design—"**A**lways **B**eckoning **C**ustomers"—noted in a quasi-aeronautical prose style that "some of these roofs resemble the negative dihedral of a B-47 wing, others the positive dihedral of a DC-7, some are diamond-shaped, some undulate like an ocean swell, some are serrated or saw-toothed, and others just don't fit within one or two geometrically descriptive words." From 1957 to 1959 a long series of enthusiastic reports like these appeared in restaurant magazines, all without bylines, all the unattributed work of Jack Lincke, a writer who was paid by Armet & Davis to prepare articles that would drum up more business for the firm. John Lautner, in arguing for the eye-catching articulation of structural elements, had relied to a considerable extent on abstruse theoretical principles that held meaning for few people outside art-and-architecture circles. Lincke, by contrast, presented the case for expression and exaggeration of a building's structure in terms of a higher business volume and bigger profits that would result. Thus was the Googie brand of restaurant design promoted for a national market.

One of the businessmen most enthusiastic about the Googie style was Harold Butler. In 1953 Butler started a small shop called Danny's Donuts in Lakewood, California. The following year, he opened a second doughnut shop in the nearby town of Garden Grove, and when it didn't do well, he added a grill, expanded the offerings, and changed the name to Danny's Coffee Shop. The growing chain of Danny's Coffee Shops, however, was often confused with another Southern California chain, Coffee Dan's, so Butler changed the name again, this time to Denny's Coffee Shop. In 1958 he started going to Armet & Davis for designs for new shops.

Denny's outlets were built immediately adjacent to freeway interchanges, and Armet & Davis accentuated their conspicuousness by forming the roof's thick sides into boomerangs and covering the rooftop with gravel, striped in alternating colors. Armet & Davis would do almost anything to make a roof stand out. For Norm's, a chain that Norman Roybark had founded in Los Angeles in 1949, Armet & Davis

Armet & Davis sketches for Lyon's Coffee Shop, San Bruno, Calif., 1962, and Danny's (later Denny's) Coffee Shop, Riverside, Calif., 1958.

sometimes mixed brilliants into the stucco used on the roof so that the roof sparkled in the sunshine and under night illumination.

A few coffee shops with exaggerated roofs did appear in other parts of the country in the 1950s. Peter Pan Snack Shops, which Chris Carson founded in Chicago in 1942, hired William Riseman Associates of Boston in 1956 to design a Peter Pan unit on Boston's Commonwealth Avenue, and the result was an octagonal coffee shop with a busily zigzagging roof. Energetic roof forms began to influence the design of diners, drive-ins, and fast-food restaurants as well. Nonetheless, in coffee shops Southern California unquestionably remained the heartland of the boisterous new style. A zig-zag roof might seem bold back east, but in California its unrelenting up-and-down geometry would appear overly rigid, lacking the flow and the imagination of West Coast buildings, which had roofs that curved, swelled, pointed, and gestured in a more emotional manner.

Lights were set into the overhang of Norm's in Long Beach, Calif., to direct motorists' attention toward the interior at night. Armet & Davis, 1963.

Those who started new chains of coffee shops in California quickly learned they would have to build dynamic structures. In 1957 in Santa Barbara, Sam Battistone and Newell Bohnett formed a new restaurant, combining the "Sam" and "Bo" of their names to come up with Sambo's (a name that was later attacked as racially insulting, especially since the restaurants usually featured "little black Sambo" illustrations on the interior). The first Sambo's, along the ocean near downtown Santa Barbara, didn't indulge in theatrics, but the later, more highway-oriented Sambo's units used arresting roof shapes. In one 1960s Sambo's design, a roof punctuated with ridges sloped toward the street, then shot upward in the form of a thick fascia with semicircular bites taken out of its upper edges. In another 1960s design, the name s-a-m-b-o-'s was hoisted, letter by letter, on spears at the roof's forward edge, and the spears were topped by pennants.

The California coffee shop was an architecture of superabundance. From its extravagant gestures and its lack of inhibition sprang a sense of exhilaration, especially at some of the Ship's, Norm's, and Bob's Big Boy units. Unlike fast-food outlets, coffee

Sambo's coffee shops in the 1960s were designed in-house, but with an eye on Armet & Davis techniques.

shops made their flamboyance convincing. Fast-food restaurants suffered from the Mickey Rooney effect—their smallness was compensated for with a loudness and energy that all too often became shrill and grating. The typical coffee shop was much larger, containing a sizable dining area as well as a kitchen, and its construction budget was more generous. With its size and money, a coffee shop could establish a visual theme on the exterior and continue it inside, amplifying the theme by coordinating the treatment of ceilings, walls, lighting, and other elements. The consistency between inside and outside added strength to the design. At a Norm's on La Cienega Boulevard in Los Angeles, a half-dozen protruding panels containing the air-conditioning ducts extended across the dining room ceiling from the kitchen wall to the perimeter windows and continued outside (without ductwork) to the edge of the deep roof overhang. At a Tiny Naylor's in Los Angeles, the diamond pattern of the roof not only flowed into the diamond pattern of the ceiling but found an echo in lighting fixtures of the same shape.

Interiors designed by Armet & Davis possessed drama. Walking into some of their coffee shops meant entering under a low canopy and then finding the space exploding upward to a high sloped ceiling and then back down to a lower scale at the counter area, where a canopy was suspended in any of a number of shapes—rectangular, hooded, serrated, free-form. Rather than produce predictable, right-angled floor plans, Armet & Davis sometimes turned the layout into a series of thirty- and sixty-degree angles or made the aisles meander slightly. Exhibition-style cooking added to the liveliness of the interior. Seated customers could often watch the cook working in the open behind the counter. Chains that expanded rapidly, like the Big Boy organization, couldn't routinely attract employees polished enough to put on a good show, but Armet & Davis dealt with that problem by arranging for semi-exhibition-style cooking, with the cook visible—from the chest up—through a cutout in the kitchen wall. Activity would be seen, but sloppy technique wouldn't.

To position the cook facing the dining area, unobscured by smoke, the grill had to be designed so that the smoke was carried downward, out of sight. This was the sort of technical challenge that Armet & Davis was adept at meeting. "We always had a rule that with each new job we had, we'd develop at least one new idea," said Davis. To create an uncluttered appearance and make cleaning easier, Armet & Davis anchored stools to the counter base instead of attaching them to the floor. Equipment in the kitchen was hung on the walls or placed on islands. Ranges at Bob's were put on wheels so they could be pulled out from the wall for scrubbing every night. To discourage insects and rodents, kitchens were equipped with machinery to wash and brush out empty metal food containers, press them flat, and keep the trash refrigerated until the refuse could be taken away. A downdraft fan above the restaurant's entrance helped keep flying insects out.

Such technical prowess, along with an uninhibited approach to esthetics, helped create a feeling within the restaurant industry that California was years ahead of the rest of the country. By 1957 Armet & Davis had bonded Formica veneers to the fronts of stainless steel cabinets on view behind the counters. Formica had color, which was something the coffee shops loved. Color was not to be tranquil. Larry Ray, an architect who left Armet & Davis to establish Colwell & Ray, which designed many Denny's units in the mid- and late sixties, observed that "it was against the unwritten law to ever use a blue or green or anything like that in a coffee shop. Those were restful, peaceful colors." In favor were oranges and pinks, hot colors, which were believed to stimulate the appetite and make people move faster. The more rapid the turnover, the bigger the profit. Norman Roybark of the Norm's chain is remembered by Eldon Davis as having said he "would like to have seats with wires so that after the first cup of coffee, you could give them a shock to get them out."

Peter Pan Snack Shop, Commonwealth Avenue, Boston, designed by William Riseman Associates, 1956.

There might appear to be nothing soothing about sitting at a pink-striped table or counter with a soaring ceiling above, a hard terrazzo floor below, and bright plastic on many of the other surfaces, yet the setting was not as jangling as it may seem. The counter stools, with their thickly padded and often contoured backs, were set farther apart than the stools in older urban coffee shops like Chock Full o'Nuts, providing both more physical and psychological comfort. Some counters had notches and inlays of Formica in contrasting color to give each customer the sense of having his own defined space. The California-style coffee shops increased the use of booths, straight or U-shaped. Just as bowling alleys adopted horseshoe-shaped seating areas, providing each group of bowlers with something of a sense of shelter from the visual and acoustic commotion all around them, coffee shops with U-shaped booths gave each group of diners a sense of possessing its own strongly demarcated territory, unlikely to be intruded upon. From the comfort of a well-upholstered booth, customers could appreciate the stimulating, stirred-up atmosphere without being overwhelmed by it. The brightness and energy were cheery, the interior refreshingly unconfined.

The impact of the architectural theatrics was offset, too, by greenery that grew outside the windows and sometimes inside as well. Artificial surfaces of Formica and plastic were relieved by a wall of natural material, usually brick or stone. At Big Boy restaurants, the stone consisted of irregularly shaped boulders laid in a random pattern, offering solidity and permanence while reinforcing the characteristic Big Boy air of boldness and informality. Coffee shops assiduously avoided giving the impression that they had been labored over; their appeal lay in their spontaneity. Because, unlike so many works of architecture, they had not had effervescence refined out of them, coffee shops were places where people did not feel the weight of sobriety pressing down.

There is no denying that the brash individualism of the Googie-style coffee shops aggravated the chaotic look of the roadside strip; aggressive performers do not make good neighbors. The fact is, however, that in the 1950s the architectural profession as

Interior of Peter Pan Snack Shop, Commonwealth Avenue, Boston.

a whole was insensitive to the need for harmonious surroundings. If a commercial district was predominantly constructed of rough-textured brick, an architect would insert a new building of smooth, metal curtain walls and claim, if questioned about the clash, that it made an invigorating contrast. Moreover, since most architects received their commissions one at a time from individual clients, not from neighborhoods or entire communities, they had little incentive to think in terms of broader environmental responsibilities. The profession's esthetic vision was inextricably linked to the demands of self-centered competitive enterprise.

The coffee shops' excesses—infatuation with unusual forms, vivid colors, and futuristic structural ornament—were shared not only by the works of some leading architects but also by a wide range of objects designed for popular use, most notably automobiles. A spirit of originality uncontrolled by discipline increasingly permeated the design world as the 1950s progressed. While coffee-shop design took its direction from architects within a ten-minute drive of Hollywood, American automobile design reflected the instincts of Harley Earl, General Motors' chief of styling, who appropriately enough had begun his career in Hollywood, customizing cars for movie stars.

The key element in this Hollywood spirit was the ability, through style, to incite the emotions. By the late fifties, money was getting easier to come by, and there was practically an entire leisure environment suffused with the impulse toward ever more intense stylizing—fantastic cars, Googie restaurants, and other expressive roadside buildings, even a new form of music featuring highly stylized voices: rock 'n' roll, the suspect rhythm of an emerging segment of consumers, teenagers. With so much prosperity, stylizing was immensely profitable, and there were no firm rules to limit the esthetic exploration.

The coffee shops, the cars, and the music all helped lift daily life above the mundane and merely utilitarian. Driving a car or having an inexpensive lunch took on an aspect of excitement. Those who detested the period's cars, like John Keats, author of *The Insolent Chariots,* might well have called these "the insolent coffee shops." Some coffee shops were as tortured-looking as the '58 Oldsmobile or the '59 Cadillac. Denny's, in particular, was usually overdone. Canopies intended to reduce the scale at the counter area were often designed crudely, and although the boomerang profile of the roof packed energy into the exterior, a series of blocky ornaments jutting up along the roof's front edge amounted to nothing more than jabs in the eye. Armet & Davis sometimes started with an appealing design and then piled ornamental clutter on it, much the way car designers in the 1950s slathered chrome onto automobile bodies that would have looked better clean and unadorned. Armet & Davis's first Big Boy prototype, designed in 1957 for a site in Garden Grove, had a curving roof that grad-

Garden Grove, Calif., 1957: the auspicious beginning of Armet & Davis's work for Bob's Big Boy.

ually and gracefully rose toward the road. But the architects chose to stir up the design so that the roof's front edge was punctuated with a succession of dark indentations—the architectural equivalent of exclamation points, making the building more noticeable but at the same time disrupting its composure. Chunky elements along the roof edges came to be the most characteristic Googie decoration, pounding out a bass-drum rhythm that made the buildings a more forceful presence. And although coffee-shop designers tried to make the restaurant become its own best advertisement—in effect, a three-dimensional billboard that customers could walk into—restauranteurs still demanded signs, and the signs rose to great heights. Some tapered to a point, so that they looked disturbingly like skewers piercing the sky. Norm's erected a tall pole with each letter—N-O-R-M-S—mounted individually on a sort of electrified pennant, a display that was invigorating during the daytime and even more rousing when illuminated at night. Other signs, with exceptions like Ship's dynamic rocket-piercing-a-circle logo, were merely loud. Denny's signs, featuring dancing letters on a pentagonal background, often had tapered signpoles holding other objects—one of the stranger ones looking like a prickly golf ball impaled on a spear. Armet & Davis preferred to integrate the sign into the building, so that it wouldn't be too garish; but, as Davis acknowledged, "mostly they were garish."

Despite the excesses in ornament, structure, and sign, the California-style coffee shops delivered a substantial amount of visual and kinetic pleasure. If you went into a chain coffee shop of the kind that Bill Knapp was building in Michigan in the early

Denny's in the 1960s. Note the attempt to define each customer's counter domain.

1950s, you found a flat, acoustic-tile ceiling at a single monotonous height. The atmosphere was dull. Bill Knapp's was the coffee-shop equivalent of a dowdy 1950 Plymouth—serviceable but uninspiring—while the coffee-shop designs that came eastward from California in the late fifties were like the "Forward Look" '58 Plymouth with its free-flowing fins; they had a sense of energy, of motion, of thrust. They gave a sensation of spontaneous enjoyment—a quality to be valued in the daily environment.

California coffee shops operated on the show-business principle that gusto and enthusiasm, power and confidence, win the audience. On Broadway, Ethel Merman recalled that she burst into stardom when she held a high C "for 16 bars while the orchestra played the melodic line—a big, tooty thing—against the note." "It seemed to do something to them," she observed. "Not because it was sweet or beautiful, but because it was exciting. Few people have the ability to project a big note and hold it." Indeed, few coffee shops demonstrated that ability prior to the 1950s. But with Googie architects, there was a new kind of coffee shop, one that projected a big note from the dining room right out into the freeway traveler's line of vision and held it twenty-four hours a day. The nation applauded.

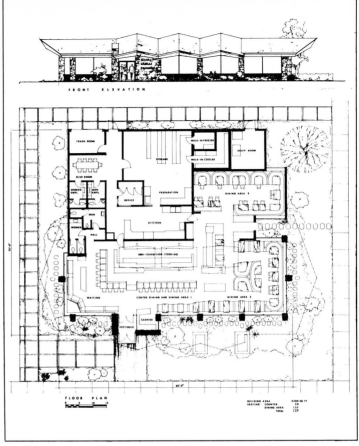

Above: *A ten-coffeepot salute from the Southern California–based International House of Pancakes, which used an unusual blue-and-persimmon color scheme from 1963 to 1975.* Right: *Plan of Big Boy "Prototype 600," 1970, showing its varied seating.*

By the mid-sixties, flamboyant California-style restaurants triumphed almost everywhere. An Azar's Big Boy designed by Armet & Davis flexed its folded-plate roof amid the sober brick buildings of downtown Fort Wayne, Indiana. Frisch's experimented with warped-roof restaurants in Cincinnati and introduced chunky Big Boy designs with thick roofs and tapered stone walls in southern cities like Tallahassee and Winter Park, Florida.

There were holdouts, of course, with some of them, like the Bill Knapp organization in Michigan, sticking to a calm Colonial. By far the most prominent exception to no-holds-barred California modernism was Howard Johnson's, which had made a cupola-topped Georgian its original trademark and had evolved by the mid-fifties into a simplified, one-story contemporary design with a gently pitched roof. Howard Johnson's did install large plate-glass windows, accepting the western and southern dictum that motorists must be able to see straight into the restaurant interior. In some HoJo's in the sixties, ceilings angled upward, matching the roof configuration, and beams were exposed. Still, the roof and ceiling at least maintained a center ridge; the space was anchored on the center of the interior, not exploding outward as in the dynamic California-style restaurant chains. HoJo's took its modernism in moderation.

By about 1964, the Googie esthetic began to encounter trouble. Many of the California coffee shops had consisted essentially of a boxy kitchen area at the rear, out of which rose a big, sculpted roof shape that sat poised above the dining area's walls of glass. As more air-conditioning and other equipment was added, it was positioned on top of the kitchen, and the rectangular rearward walls extended upward to some 16 feet, practically as high as a two-story building. It was hard to prevent such a bulky shape from interfering with the visual effect of the restaurant's main roof.

At the same time, neighbors were beginning to complain about the unattractive restaurant backs, which were often set smack up against asphalt that was greasy from washing down the cooking equipment. There had been a problem from the start with coffee shops like Denny's that had their fronts beckoning to the freeway: once the

Frisch's, Reading Road, Cincinnati, built 1960, with a swoop borrowed from Eero Saarinen.

Remodeling at Azar's Big Boy brought West Coast rhythm to downtown Ft. Wayne, Ind., in 1961.

customers exited from the limited-access highway onto local roads and approached the restaurant, an awkward transition took place as they found themselves coming toward the restaurant's *rear*. This flaw might have continued, except that Denny's and its competitors were using the same freeway-oriented designs for sites on shopping center parking lots, and the centers' tenants didn't want their customers to see the ugly back of a restaurant. If coffee shops were going to occupy such conspicuous locations, they would have to develop new designs with four presentable sides.

In 1965 Denny's introduced an Armet & Davis design—variously called a "carousel," "caterpillar," or "cupcake" building—that seemed to solve the problem. It had four acceptable, relatively equal sides, each with a folded-plate roof that zigged and zagged, up and down, all the way around the building. The equipment was hidden in a center well, behind the zigzagging parapet at the top of the zigzagging roof.

The problem of exterior appearance was thus taken care of, but not for long. The critical attitude that required this modification in coffee-shop design reflected a much deeper shift in the national mood. As if to signal the declining fortunes of futuristic design, automobiles had suddenly given up their soaring tailfins in the early sixties and turned blocky and regular. In a transformed emotional climate, even Denny's modified "cupcake" would soon seem gaudily out of place. The days of unlimited design freedom were coming to an end.

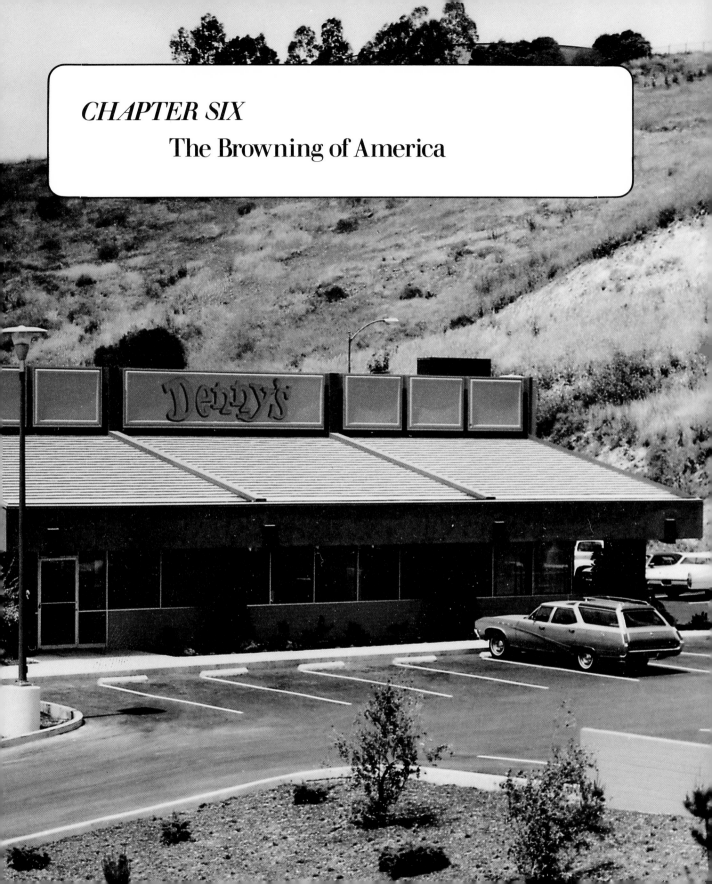

CHAPTER SIX
The Browning of America

Overleaf: *Denny's "Model 106" restaurant, introduced in the late 1960s.*

On a Saturday morning in 1964, Thomas Wells was working in his architectural office in Honolulu when he got a phone call from a California restaurant executive, John Reuben McIntosh. McIntosh had opened a twelve-stool restaurant in Corona del Mar, California, in 1948 and gradually expanded it into a series of Snack Shops. Now he had an idea for a future restaurant, an idea he'd thought about so briefly that he still had no name for the new enterprise and called it simply the "Podunk restaurant." The idea was to establish a coffee shop—eventually a chain of coffee shops— that would serve hamburgers, malts, and a few other uncomplicated menu items, but would maintain a noticeably higher quality than competitors. He wanted Wells to think about what sort of architecture would fit the concept.

Wells had strong feelings about what should and should not be done. He didn't want to produce anything in the usual "Googie" coffee-shop style—"weird plaster shapes meaning absolutely nothing," as he put it. To Wells, the aggressively conspicuous coffee shops of chains like Denny's and Sambo's represented "just a cheap Las Vegas approach to architecture," an attitude of "anything goes."

"Everybody that started to do a coffee shop thought they had to look weird," Wells recalled years later. "I told John McIntosh, 'If you want to be different, let's just do a nice, quiet, well-landscaped building.' "

Wells had already earned McIntosh's trust. His first project after moving from California to Hawaii in 1957 and joining the well-regarded architectural firm of Vladimir Ossipoff & Associates had been to design Snack Shop #7 on Kalakaua Avenue in Waikiki. The Waikiki Snack Shop prospered at least partly because it gave customers an atmosphere of tranquillity, in harmony with a beautiful natural setting. It had a low-slung cedar-shake roof which caught shadows from the palm trees above, and lush plantings grew at the base of lava-rock walls. In contrast to the hyperactive restaurants designed by Los Angeles's Armet & Davis, the Snack Shop was soothing. It emphasized natural materials like redwood and lava rock on the interior, and on sunny days its wooden doors could be folded back to let the dining area expand outward onto a comfortable patio. An absence of corner columns further accentuated the sense of uninterrupted space flowing from the interior of the restaurant to the adjoining gardens of the Royal Hawaiian Hotel.

In 1961 Wells had established his own firm, and his first job in independent practice was the designing of a Reuben's steak-and-lobster restaurant for McIntosh in Santa Ana, California. It, too, made extensive use of wood and lava rock, though with

Snack Shop #7, Honolulu, built in 1958. Architect, Thomas Wells.

a heavier feeling. Thick beams supported the ceiling, which had sloping areas in redwood and flat expanses in dark cork. The dining room was dimly lighted, with candles on the tables, spotlights accenting the plants and paintings, and logs burning in the fireplace. Reuben's aimed for a homelike atmosphere. Couches, a coffee table, and the kind of lamps that might be found in an upper-middle-class living room served as furnishings for Reuben's waiting area. Outside, a timbered trellis sheltered the entrance, and eucalyptus trees were planted around the grounds.

The "Podunk restaurant," McIntosh thought, should be the kind of place where Reuben's customers could go on occasions when they wanted relatively simple food in a comfortable, informal atmosphere. In fact, the first of the new coffee shops would be built on well-traveled Seventeenth Street within sight of the Santa Ana Reuben's and would bring the spirit of the Honolulu Snack Shop to the mainland. Wells designed a dining room that had leather-like upholstered booths under a cork ceiling coffered in 3-foot squares, with indirect lighting. Wood columns framed the windows, which came together at the corners with mitered glass, just as they had in Honolulu. The floor of the entrance and counter area was covered in squares of textured brown tile; the dining room had earth-toned carpeting instead of the terrazzo floors found in most coffee shops. Because there was nothing to obstruct the view, the dining room felt spacious, yet it also felt calm. The difference between the climates of Hawaii and California ruled out the possibility of literally opening the building to the outside, but Wells nonetheless created a sense of harmony with the surrounding environment. He bermed the earth up to the bottom of the windows and gave the building broad overhangs. The roof rose at a gentle, even pitch, then curved upward at the top, hiding the air-handling equipment in a center roofwell. The restaurant opened in January 1966. Months before that, McIntosh had stopped talking of "Podunk" and had given the coffee-shop concept the name under which it would operate—Coco's. In May 1966 a second Coco's designed by Wells opened in Scottsdale, Arizona. Eventually Coco's would grow into a chain of more than 200 coffee shops distinguished by a soft, somewhat residential flavor.

Wells's work had a major impact on other chains and other architects, particularly on Robert Colwell and Larry Ray, two architects who quit Armet & Davis in 1962 to start their own firm. In 1964 Colwell & Ray moved from Los Angeles to Orange County, not far from the sites of Reuben's and Coco's. Ray, the firm's principal designer, often produced coffee shops in a style similar to Armet & Davis's, with whipped-up interiors of hot pink and orange and with emphatic roofs covered by colored stripes of gravel. This was the style expected by the majority of coffee-shop owners, including his firm's most important client, Harold Butler, who developed Denny's into a publicly traded company, with coffee shops throughout the nation.

But Ray had qualms about the Googie approach. He displayed his preference for a more tranquil appearance when in 1964 he began designing Marie Callender's, a chain of pie-and-coffee shops, in an Old English style. In 1967, emboldened by the successful example of Coco's, Ray and Colwell decided to push Butler toward using a more subdued, residential design for Denny's units in non-freeway locations. By that time, it had become evident that Denny's couldn't endlessly continue to acquire restaurant property overlooking freeway interchanges; even in California there were limits to freeway expansion. In fact, the company had already started putting some of its restaurants in established communities, and Ray was the one who had to defend the flamboyant designs to not-always-friendly municipal planning boards. Consequently, on their own time and without pay, Ray and Colwell developed a design for a more composed, restrained "neighborhood Denny's" and presented it to Butler, hoping he'd buy it and build it. According to Ray, Butler's initial reaction was "we're not in that kind of business," but the architects kept after him until eventually he agreed to give the new design a try.

Inside the experimental Denny's were wood beams, wood trim, a working fireplace, tables whose plastic-laminate tops were decorated in wood patterns, and a floor that was carpeted rather than surfaced in terrazzo. Outside, the walls were covered with oversize reddish-brown bricks. The roof of charcoal-gray barrel tiles had deep overhangs, and it ascended gently from all four sides, like a low pyramid that had been truncated at the top. It climbed just high enough for air-handling equipment to sit out of sight in a center roofwell. A rough-sawn fascia board rose from the edges of the roofwell; at some Denny's units, it would provide a natural-looking horizontal backing for the restaurant's sign. The company called this mellow building its "Intowner" model and initially used it where more flamboyant Denny's designs would have run into community resistance. In a few years, the "Intowner" and models like it would become a major part of Denny's operation.

Even the king of coffee-shop architecture, Armet & Davis, began edging away from boisterous buildings with free-flowing roofs. In 1968 the firm produced an enlarged version of a California ranch house for Bob's Big Boy restaurants. It featured a regular, pitched roof of clay tile and exterior walls surfaced in small beige blocks of slumpstone, a southwestern building product made of concrete with plump sides, intended to resemble blocks of adobe. The new design emphasized a ceiling of wood with exposed timbers, and floors covered with a mix of quarry tile and carpeting. This design—adopted with modifications by JB's, Elby's, and other members of the far-flung Big Boy network—brought Armet & Davis into the realm of residential imagery, but without becoming entirely sedate. The design often included a tall gable-wall of glass, and the interiors retained some of the cheery energy of the earlier Big Boys.

The impact of Coco's continued to penetrate the restaurant industry. In 1971 Harold Butler left Denny's and started a new chain. Its name: Jojo's. The prominent features of its buildings: natural-finished woods, deep overhangs, and earth bermed up to the windows. Jojo's was designed by Colwell & Ray, and it displayed a subdued demeanor except for having big numbers painted on the ends of booths—a decorating element borrowed from the brief "supergraphics" fad which involved placing exaggerated graphic elements on walls and other surfaces. Finally, in 1975, spurred partly by Northern California communities' resistance to brash-looking restaurants, Denny's adopted as its main prototype a brick-veneered building, its base embedded in the earth, with an overhanging brown metal roof and an interior divided into three separate dining areas. Out went the pink and orange, the plastic and fiberglass. In came wood and fabrics in browns and greens.

Tom Wells, as he looked at the changed landscape in the 1980s, remarked, "I feel like I designed the whole country." Indeed, some architects, like Larry Ray, were

Denny's "Intowner," late 1960s, designed by Colwell & Ray.

Bob's Jr. Big Boy, a smaller version of Big Boy's California ranch design, was introduced in 1971. The junior's menu was also pared down.

grateful for the influence that Wells, through Coco's, had exerted on the restaurant industry. Ray had wanted to bring his work in line with his sense of responsibility for the environment. He was uncomfortably aware of the impact that restaurant architecture made on the American landscape. "You drove into any town," he observed, "and the first corners you came to had either coffee shops or service stations. All the low-end kinds of commercial things are always in very important places in towns, and I felt strongly about it. I thought it could be better."

Wells was correct in believing that Coco's success helped the softer coffee-shop esthetic blossom throughout the nation; restaurant owners pay attention to designs associated with profits. But the critical factor was that Wells captured the emerging spirit of the times. The public's mood was shifting, and Wells offered—in an attractive way—the subdued sensibility that people were increasingly inclined to embrace.

The shift in image and atmosphere appeared not only in the coffee-shop segment of the industry but also in fast-food restaurants, whose flamboyant 1950s-style designs were running up against increasing community resistance. In 1963 McDonald's began yielding to public pressure for a less brash appearance by putting brown brick on sidewalls that had previously been sheathed in gleaming red-and-white tile. The sides of the roof-wedge were given an inoffensive covering of shingles. Instead of thrusting skyward, the front of the roof-wedge tapered downward, wrapped in brown shingles.

Some municipalities continued to object to McDonald's because arches still burst through its roof. Even within the company, Ray Kroc heard complaints that the slant-roofed, arched buildings were eyesores, and he couldn't help noticing that his competitors were moving to make their buildings less garish. In 1967 Burger King took the red handlebars off its roof. In March 1968 Carrols adopted a new prototype with a flat roof and no boomerang appendages. Finally, in April 1968, after a shakeup of the McDonald's organization put Kroc once more in firm control, Donald E. Miller was hired as chief architect. Miller, who had designed truck and tractor showrooms

Bob's Big Boy design by Armet & Davis, introduced in Chula Vista, Calif., in 1968.

and service centers, was given the job of designing a new prototype, one that would have an indoor dining area and would be acceptable to cities and towns throughout the country.

Miller developed four alternatives to the arched building and laid his sketches on the desk in Kroc's office for President Fred Turner and Chairman Kroc to review. They examined them, then Kroc slapped the desk: "'That's what I want. When can we have the drawings?' It hit him right away," Miller recalls. The understanding within the company's upper echelon, according to Miller, had been that "they had to use brick on the walls; they had to dress their building up to fit the community." In many municipalities, he noted, "it was the only way you could pull building permits and obtain zoning."

The first of the new buildings, thirty-four feet wide, with a fourteen-foot side extension seating about sixty customers, opened in January 1969 in the Chicago suburb of Matteson. Above its walls of beige and brown brick was an overhanging roof—surfaced in slate for a more dignified appearance and illuminated at night by metal ribs. The double-hip parapet roof, or "double mansard," as Miller called it, sloped at a thirty-degree angle along the perimeter and then rose at sixty degrees to form a parapet. Soon there was a new double-arched sign to perpetuate the McDonald's symbol now that the arches had been removed from the roof. Other companies would be tempted to duplicate McDonald's new building, the executives realized. White Castle had to take White Tower to court in the 1920s and 1930s to end blatant copying, and in 1960, Howard Johnson's had to resort to a lawsuit to stop a businessman in New Johnsonville, Tennessee, from naming his restaurant "Johnson's" and adopting the cupola-topped roof and the orange and blue-green color combination. McDonald's acted to protect itself in advance; the company patented the roof configuration.

The parapet of the new roof hid the heating, ventilating, and air-conditioning equipment, which had sat exposed on top of earlier McDonald's outlets. Equally important, the weighty roof gave the building a relatively calm, horizontal profile, a feeling of shelter on a lower and more human scale. It seemed to pull the building toward the earth rather than propelling it upward and outward, as the earlier wedge roof had done. The exact configuration of McDonald's new roof may have been protected from infringement, but its general character became virtually standard for fast-food architecture. Burger King had moved in the same direction as McDonald's in 1967 by adopting a nearly vertical roof perimeter, which it called a "mansard"; genuine mansard roofs, popular in the United States in the nineteenth century, contained windows and enclosed habitable space, but restaurant companies applied the term to any sharply sloped area of roofing material around the upper edges of the building. The "mansard" was the least expensive means of displaying a somewhat traditional roof, yet creating plenty of space out-of-doors for restaurant equipment. Dunkin' Donuts adopted a mansard of brown metal with built-in signs. Burger King, having first employed a mansard painted bright red, decided in 1972 to cover the mansard in cedar shingles in natural shades. The only remaining red would be an illuminated plastic light-band above the mansard. Wood was used to trim Burger King's windows, and brick covered those portions of the exterior not made of wood or glass.

By the mid-seventies, there had been a change literally in the complexion of fast-food buildings. Der Wienerschnitzel in California shifted to a softer shade of orange for its roofs, then discontinued orange roofs entirely. The company had Colwell & Ray design a new building with a flat-topped brown roof and walls of dark brown wood or ivory-colored stucco. Jack in the Box, which had been picketed by citizens protesting "visual pollution," switched to a color scheme of blue with beige or brown. In 1977, Kentucky Fried Chicken, rebounding from a period of lax management, belatedly introduced a new prototype with tan walls and a terra-cotta-colored mansard. Above the mansard was a small red-and-white-striped pyramid—a vestige of the red-and-white stripes that in the 1960s had been used on top of the entire building. Red Barn introduced a lower, mansard-topped building with brownish-red brick walls, while older Red Barns turned into brown barns and beige barns. One of the best-selling books of 1970 was Charles A. Reich's prediction of the rise of a new form of consciousness; *The Greening of America* was the book's catchy title. In the realm of commercial buildings, what actually developed was the browning of America. Earth tones became the national colors.

The newly muted color schemes seemed mandatory in an era when millions of people exhibited an intense concern over degradation of the environment. One signal of the new civic attitude was the nationally publicized "Earth Day" observance on May 1, 1970, but there were many others, especially at the local level, where citizens' groups criticized businesses' treatment of the environment, and municipalities tightened their environmental regulations. Restaurant organizations learned they would have to adopt softer colors—colors that emphasized their connection to the land. They also decided it would be prudent to put lawns, shrubbery, and trees on portions of their properties that had until now been occupied by pavement and trash receptacles. The thoroughness of the landscaping varied in accordance with local requirements, the degree of community resistance to fast-food outlets, the physical and socioeconomic character of the surrounding area, and, to some extent, the clientele. Generous landscaping in some affluent California suburbs contrasted sharply with

Above: *Mansardized Kentucky Fried Chicken design introduced in 1977. Photo, Whalley Avenue, New Haven, Conn., 1983.* Right: *Whereas advertising had stood boldly atop 1960s Burger Kings, by the early 1970s outlets like this one on Whalley Avenue in New Haven placed lettering against a background of soothing cedar shakes. Photo 1983.*

the minimal planting at urban fast-food restaurants in the Northeast. Most fast-food restaurants were not about to devote large numbers of man-hours to landscape maintenance; the emphasis on low labor costs ran as strong as ever. As a result, chains concluded that planting should generally be kept simple. A & W Root Beer mandated landscaping of at least 5 percent of each franchisee's site but advised: "Keep grass to a minimum; it needs cutting. Hedges need trimming and deciduous plants have a habit of dropping their leaves. Be smart and lazy by planting evergreens and covering the ground with crushed rock or redwood bark." One manufacturer merchandised "Carefree Shrubbery," "permanent shrubs made to look like the real ones." They

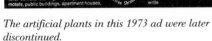

Carefree Shrubbery are permanent shrubs made to look like the real ones. But made to last. Easy to install, just plant them and forget them. No fertilizing. No watering. No spraying. No trimming. And no replacing. They just sit there month after month. Year after year. Making your place look attractive.

Ideal for residences, pool areas, service stations, fast food chains, shopping centers, cemeteries, highways, golf courses, motels, public buildings, apartment houses, parks, etc. Carefree Shrubbery can make your business a beautiful asset to the community.

All the time your maintenance costs go down, reducing your overhead. And all the while, you're writing off this landscaping investment. That's why in landscape maintenance we're known as Carefree Shrubbery. The cost killer. RESTAURANTS • FAST FOOD CHAINS • DEALERS • DISTRIBUTORS • AND LANDSCAPERS INQUIRIES INVITED. Call or write

The artificial plants in this 1973 ad were later discontinued.

Burger King logo in Tustin, Calif., landscape.

were, according to their maker, "Easy to install, just plant them and forget them. No fertilizing. No watering. No spraying. No trimming. And no replacing."

Despite such enticements, most chain restaurants chose plants that were alive, and there was an effort to make planting not simply a gesture to the community but also an effective advertising tool. In 1973 a Miami architect who had been Burger King's "director of architecture and ecological planning" (a title that would have been unthinkable in 1960) told restaurant operators: "By using landscaping as a backdrop or background for your attention-getting signs, they stand out far better than in a visual conglomeration of other signs. . . . Furthermore, landscaping provides a pleasant contrast to the stark, man-made environment of the surrounding business district and thereby separates the site from the neighborhood in a positive way."

This was no romantic Olmstedian landscape. Fast-food restaurants kept nature on a tight leash. Specialists recommended such plants as Chinese junipers, which stayed close to the ground. Few managers planted trees capable of overshadowing their restaurants. A policy of planting on a diminutive scale made sense not only from the standpoint of keeping maintenance chores minimal and of keeping the restaurant and its signs in plain view; it also created an aura of orderliness—an impression that served fast-food restaurants well. A full, luxuriant landscape would have suggested relaxation, and in an inexpensive restaurant, that could connote a loosening of discipline. It might suggest that the employees—and not just the atmosphere—were relaxed. It might also have encouraged customers to relax—to sit back and enjoy the surroundings instead of eating and hurrying on. Better to have a short-cropped landscape, one that signified the exercise of control.

The trend toward more nature-oriented, subdued designs did not win universal acceptance immediately. For a time, one notable exception to the parade of brown mansards was Wendy's, a chain specializing in chili and larger-than-usual hamburgers. R. David Thomas, who had been an executive with the Kentucky Fried Chicken and Arthur Treacher's chains, started Wendy's in a former automobile showroom in downtown Columbus, Ohio, in 1969, naming the restaurant for his third daughter. Two years later he opened a second Wendy's, a freestanding structure in Columbus with backlighted turquoise-and-white pinstriped plastic panels wrapped around the top of the building between the large plate-glass windows and the flat roof. After about 50 restaurants in that design had been built, the company produced nearly 2,000 more restaurants with plastic fascia panels that had red decorative scrollwork on a white or yellow background. Plastic panels were cheaper than mansard roofs, and more noticeable. For a restaurant organization starting out at a time when many business analysts thought the fast-food industry was already overcrowded, brashness could still be effective. Not until 1980 did Wendy's shift to a more subdued copper-like fascia.

Wendy's put a drive-thru window on the first freestanding building it opened—this in 1971, when no national chain routinely equipped its restaurants with drive-thrus. "I knew that there were more cars than ever out there," said Thomas. ". . . Those people in their cars don't fill up a table, they don't take up a parking space." The drive-thru was doubly rewarding. It gave customers a convenience they appreciated, and by enabling Wendy's to keep its buildings and parking lots smaller than competitors', it conserved capital. Wendy's claimed to earn more revenue per square foot than any other chain. By the end of the decade, the drive-thru window, equipped with its own cash register, crew, and food preparation area, generated 46 percent of the sales at a typical Wendy's unit. Watching the success of this upstart competitor, McDonald's, Burger King, and others belatedly knocked holes in the walls of their own restaurants and installed drive-thru windows.

While fast-food restaurants increased their accessibility to the automobile, they were not free to pare their buildings down to shapes that could be taken in with a

The scalloped edges on the fascia panels of a late 1970s Wendy's in Buffalo (left) were supposed to suggest historical ornament. Wendy's 1980 prototype (below) moved toward more thoroughly nostalgic styling.

quick glance from the road, like the simple forms of 1950s restaurants. Restaurants of the 1970s possessed much more detailing. Kentucky Fried Chicken's 1977 proto- type—part of the company's attempt to reverse years of deterioration in the company's food quality, service, and buildings—was, by earlier standards, intricate. White globes were held by black rectangular frames on each side of the front entrance. Placed around the exterior was a collection of planters, some round, some rectangu- lar, some tall, some short. A series of recesses and projections modulated the exterior walls, and wooden muntin inserts divided large windows into small squares. The Ken- tucky Fried Chicken design typified the industrywide trend toward more elaboration. Such complexity made chain restaurants seem more dignified, and the feeling was accentuated by symmetrical or nearly symmetrical façades.

The public's insistence on a measure of refinement was understandable, in light of how the roadside environment was being transformed in the quarter-century after World War II. Restaurant companies realized that customers were to be found on suburban thoroughfares, and they knew that the restaurants' drawing power would further increase when several eating places located near one another. The knowledge

Taco Boys celebrate a Taco Bell opening in Orange County, Calif., 1967. Two years later they were eliminated.

that McDonald's conducted reliable marketing surveys before selecting its sites also encouraged minor chains to pick locations close by, on the assumption that the demographics would favor their own operations as well. In the process, thousands of stretches of suburban highway became eyesores. All across the well-fed land, the chains coalesced into a garish new symbol of American life: the roadside restaurant strip—the place where the amber waves of grain, having been processed, provided sustenance to a nation of passengers. Burger Kings and Dairy Queens, farmless Red Barns and drydocked fish franchises all clamored for attention—clamored less stridently in the new earth tones and shingles, but insisted on capturing attention nonetheless. What they had given up in brashness of form, they compensated for with sheer repetition. By the end of 1970, for example, McDonald's had 1,592 outlets, and the number was growing fast. With so many outlets, each one of them could lower its voice slightly and yet continue to make its presence known.

To attract attention and give their restaurants more personality, many chains, especially in the 1950s, had devised cartoon-like characters and prominently displayed them near the road. McDonald's put Speedee on its single-arched sign; Burger King had its "little king"; and Pizza Hut showed an Italian chef tossing dough. Jack in the Box put a smiling Jack on a box high in the air, and Kentucky Fried Chicken liked Harland Sanders so much the company turned him into a weathervane, a beneficent expression on his grandfatherly face as he pointed his cane into the wild blue yonder. Even the Big Boy coffee shops had a plump, brown-pompadoured boy—more than adult-size—standing out front, dressed in red-and-white overalls and carrying aloft a double-decker hamburger. But in the almost industrywide refinement of corporate images, these human-like characters began to disappear. In 1962, after nine years of heavy promotion, McDonald's eliminated Speedee, ostensibly for a number of reasons, one of them being McDonald's desire to emphasize attributes other than speed, another being the resemblance of Speedee's name to the "Speedy Alka-Seltzer" character. A restaurant chain would understandably be disturbed by having a character that summoned up suggestions of indigestion, but in fact Miles Laboratories' little Speedy Alka-Seltzer, with his tablet-shaped abdomen and tablet-cap, had been used in magazine, drugstore, television, and radio advertising since 1952, the

Discarded Shoney's Big Boys await their fate in Nashville, Tenn. Painting by John Baeder, 1985.

year before McDonald's Speedee made his debut. The two "speedy" characters had coexisted well enough for nearly a decade. An important reason for the change was that by 1962, McDonald's wanted a different kind of representation, an abstract logo consisting of two crossed arches with an angled (roof) line through them. This logo would in turn be replaced in 1969 by an even simpler shape—a pair of linked arches that could also be read as an *M*. In 1963, to strengthen its appeal to children, McDonald's did introduce another character, the clown Ronald McDonald; but Ronald was reserved mainly for radio and TV and for personal appearances; the company tried to avoid making Ronald an integral part of the building exterior or placing him on signs out front.

Pillsbury, after purchasing Burger King in 1967, began maneuvering to abolish the little king. As Edgerton recalls the episode, the Pillsbury operatives produced some market surveys purportedly showing that the little king made adults think Burger King was a place strictly for children, while children themselves hardly noticed the little-king sign. Instead of the little king, Burger King chose to identify itself with a logo made up of nothing more than the name "Burger King" in rotund letters between the halves of a bun.

At the urging of the New York marketing, communications, and design firm of Lippincott & Margulies, Pizza Hut banished its Italian chef and began to represent itself solely through the profile of its roof, which was echoed in a roadside sign. Jack in the Box's Jack was exploded in TV commercials, never to rematerialize. Many of the Big Boys disappeared even before customers were invited to vote in 1984 and 1985 on whether the boy would stay or go. (They voted overwhelmingly to keep the Big Boy, a decision that left the company to ponder another question: Could a heavyset character in red and white checkered pants be somehow restyled to 1980s tastes?) Colonel Sanders was one of the few characters to remain on display, but he was, after all, a special case—a human being, not a made-up character, and he was so quaint, with his white suit, his white moustache and goatee, his black string tie, and his rags-to-riches history, that he made fried chicken come across as a product brought to perfection by an amiable if odd old gentleman. Still, in 1977 the colonel's likeness began to be reserved for uses more dignified than a weathervane.

The decline of restaurant characters was encouraged, in some instances, by a shift in sign technology. Backlighted plastic panels, which came into wide use in the 1960s, could not generate the sense of motion that a figure like Speedee had achieved through pulsing neon. In addition, a growing number of municipal regulations prohibited signs that pulsed, rippled, flashed, and blinked. A more significant factor, however, was the increasing professionalization of the process of designing and promoting chain restaurants. More and more chains that had once relied on signmakers' ideas now hired marketing, design, and communications specialists to guide their increasingly expensive design and marketing programs. The exuberant profusion of human-like restaurant symbols seemed hokey to the professionals, and unnecessary. Consultants found hazards in the existing characters; Lippincott & Margulies warned Pizza Hut that the Italian chef wasn't what Italians looked like and could incur resentment among Italian-Americans. The new cadre of image-makers was intent on clarifying the message that each company sent out—and that meant getting rid of such extraneous objects as human-like figures.

Graphic designers, most of them enamored of abstraction, reduced corporate symbols to the simplest of shapes. This was an approach that, under other circumstances, might have infused a sense of calm into the man-made environment. But in fact the results were otherwise. Designers made certain that each company's symbol differed strikingly from its competitors'—contrasted enough so that it would be conspicuous in busy commercial settings. The very simplicity helped the corporate signs and logos compel attention, especially when they were made as tall and large as local ordinances would allow. Thus, while the buildings became more subdued, their illuminated plastic signs insisted as much as ever on being noticed by everyone passing by. McDonald's removed the pair of arches from its building and made them into a sign nobody would miss—arches not in gold, which would have had a trace of tranquillity, but in bright yellow, a more aggressive color. Arby's erected a huge hat for a sign and Kentucky Fried Chicken sometimes had a giant illuminated bucket. Since the restaurants sat back from the highway, it was the collection of signs in competing shapes that formed much of the visual character of American roadside strips. Some communities combatted the conspicuousness of the signs by strictly limiting their size, requiring that they be made of wood, or ordering that they be placed close to the ground, but in most cities and towns, business owners possessed more political power than did environmental activists. Thus, despite the tendency toward toning down the buildings and eliminating neon, the overall impression along important thoroughfares remained a hodgepodge.

Some thought there might be another way of avoiding such gaudy lineups of roadside "image" buildings and signs. At the peak of the environmental movement in the late 1960s and early 1970s, critics suggested that restaurants organize themselves into clusters like shopping centers. Several restaurants, each with a different specialty or price range, could share a common parking lot and common outdoor seating area. Clusters appeared in such places as Columbus, Ohio, and Bellevue, Washington. But few of the large national chains cared for cooperative ventures; they could attract customers easily enough to their highway locations, and they didn't want to work with their competitors. In the absence of widespread government pressure to concentrate chain restaurants into smaller or less conspicuous development, this sort of clustering never became a common pattern.

Some chains did open units in shopping malls, but those served people who had already decided to visit the mall; restaurants in malls weren't meant to shift the industry's primary focus away from freestanding buildings. In fact, most chains preferred to put freestanding buildings on shopping center parking lots, where they could appeal both to shoppers and to people driving past on the highway. California cities and towns fared best at trying to force chain restaurants to blend in with their neighbors. There, the Spanish colonial architectural tradition helped communities to settle on stuccoed walls and tiled roofs as the common elements of future commercial construction. In rapidly growing California communities where the shopping center rather than the individual building was the basic unit of development, restaurants on the center's parking lot were often required to adopt the same materials and colors as the center and sometimes the same shapes as well.

Other sections of the country evolved fewer means of making restaurants harmonize with their neighbors. Even if a municipality desired a homogeneous appearance, it had trouble defining what that look should be. McDonald's devised a half-measure that exploited the communities' weakness. In municipalities that refused to accept a standard McDonald's, the company offered a choice of "Country French," "English Tudor," "Mediterranean," "Village Depot," and a dozen other stock façade alternatives, all of them like three-dimensional wallpaper pasted onto the standard mansard-roofed building. Generally, opposition had to be persistent before McDonald's would make a more meaningful response to a community's yearning for distinctiveness or to existing local architectural conditions.

One of the earliest architecturally effective protests took place in 1973 in Ann Arbor, Michigan, where 5,000 people signed petitions opposing McDonald's plans, which called for razing an old house of moderate historic importance on the edge of the University of Michigan's central campus and constructing a standard restaurant on its site. The demolition went forward, but the company, faced with determined and articulate opponents, hired a local architectural firm, Hobbs and Black Associates, to design a brick building with such imaginative features as a front courtyard built around old trees, a rose window containing the McDonald's logo, and another logo crafted in wrought iron. The additional costs of the unique design were quickly recovered through higher-than-anticipated sales volume. As McDonald's moved in-

Above: *Exterior and interior views of a shopping-mall McDonald's outlet, 1984, by Hamill & McKinney.*
Below: *Interior and exterior of McDonald's in Ann Arbor, Mich., designed 1974, known locally as "St. Mac's."*

creasingly into city and town centers in the 1970s, the chain made more use of old buildings and special designs.

Generally, however, chain restaurants—including McDonald's—preferred to put on urban sites the same one-story buildings that they erected near suburban highway interchanges. Large cities enjoyed no special dispensation. A typical freestanding McDonald's was built at Broadway and 125th Street in Manhattan. In the Main–Utica business district a mile north of downtown Buffalo, a standard Burger King with a sprawling parking lot went up in 1978 on the site of a partly vacant two-story commercial building that a few years earlier had contained a restaurant, a tavern, a furniture store, a pool hall, a bowling alley, a tire store, an appliance business, and more than a dozen offices. One of Burger King's closest neighbors, about a hundred yards to the south, was a McDonald's outlet built in 1965—it, too, standing off by itself behind an asphalt parking lot.

Fast-food restaurants were by no means a prime cause of the deterioration of urban areas. In most instances, they simply took advantage of the fact that there had already been a decline in the demand for dense urban development of the traditional kind—buildings standing shoulder to shoulder, hugging the sidewalks, strengthening the street patterns, and creating environments conducive to walking. But the chains showed few compunctions about suburbanizing the cities wherever the real-estate costs were low enough or the local regulations loose enough to permit it. Church's Fried Chicken sought locations in inner-city neighborhoods and almost invariably erected a standard new restaurant—in many instances, a building that had been manufactured on the company's construction yard across from Church's headquarters in San Antonio and then shipped in three sections to its destination. In troubled urban areas, the chains rarely had to worry that local people would demand a building custom-fitted to its surroundings.

Like exteriors, the interiors of fast-food restaurants changed appreciably from the late 1960s through the 1970s. The popular anthropologist Desmond Morris asserted in 1977 that the typical low-priced restaurant, intent on rapid turnover, sought eating areas as harsh as possible. "To make its eaters flee the eating-site, it uses intense strip-lighting, harsh, bright colours, clanking metallic trays, and hard, uncovered table surfaces." Much of this description fit fast-food restaurants in the late 1960s, but by the middle and late 1970s, it no longer applied to many of them. A continual upgrading took place during the seventies, generally increasing the level of comfort, but with notable differences from one chain to another. Kentucky Fried Chicken's "new image" prototype of 1977 featured hanging plants, decorative woodwork, earth-toned vinyl floors, wooden tables and chairs, booths with cushioned seats and cushioned backs, and a combination of recessed and ornamental lights. Customers had to be given moderately pleasant surroundings; the objective of most chains was to develop a dining area that would be agreeable for a brief duration without requiring a great deal of maintenance. Sitting down at a typical McDonald's, customers felt immediate relief in the cushioning of the seat backs. A few minutes later, however, they became restless because the seat bottom consisted of hard, uncushioned fiberglass. Tables and chairs presented a neat appearance, all lined up in uniform rows, but the order was achieved by permanently anchoring the tables to the floor and attaching the seats to the table bases. The customer was denied the possibility of making the minor adjustments that do much to determine whether a person will feel in control of his surroundings. Wendy's, from early on, provided small tables accompanied by what R. David Thomas referred to as "four not particularly comfortable chairs." What the fast-food industry learned was summarized by Dunkin' Donuts' chief architect, Abraham J. Goldberg: "You have to give comfort, but it's measured comfort."

Nearly every chain introduced softer tones and textures as the 1970s progressed. Wendy's installed a carpeted floor. A Hardee's prototype designed in 1976 by Lippincott & Margulies of New York featured an ordering area counter surfaced in three-inch-thick maple butcher block. Trash receptacles, once conspicuous, took on colors, materials, and shapes enabling them to merge quietly into the decor. Dining areas were placed away from the commotion of the ordering areas. Throughout the industry, illumination became softer and more sophisticated. The bright, exposed fluorescent lighting inside Dunkin' Donuts units in 1963 evolved, at Goldberg's direction, into skillfully recessed fixtures that cast light around the perimeter of the building and onto the food displays but not on the customers.

Ceilings, in most chains, remained the least handsome part of the interior. The dependence on mass-produced materials and rapid construction often resulted in acoustic-panel grids that collided gracelessly with the walls and provided an insubstantial surface from which to hang increasingly elaborate wooden decorations and lighting fixtures.

Overall, fast-food interiors advanced significantly from the rudimentary designs of a few years earlier. Hardee's 1976 prototype introduced a "cozy corner"—a windowless area removed from the main flow of restaurant traffic, to create a greater sense of privacy. Of the major fast-food chains, Burger King created probably the most pleasant atmosphere, from an adult point of view. Not only were the interiors given to

Dunkin' Donuts progressed from the late 1960s' bright, tiled interior (above) to a "brick oven" motif (top) in the late 1970s, and then to a wood-toned interior with plants (left) in the early 1980s. Along the way, seat backs appeared and then disappeared.

earth tones, plants, and subdued lighting; they often had comfortable booths along the perimeter, where people could sit without feeling pressured to be on their way. In one of the fastest-paced areas of Manhattan—Lexington Avenue just two blocks north of Grand Central Station—customers at a Burger King outlet could be seen sitting next to the windows in mid-morning, reading books, an activity that would have been anathema to any fast-food chain in the 1960s.

The fast-food chains discovered that their restaurants attracted more customers if the interiors were not all alike. Thus, in the 1970s the inside often provided individualization that was, by corporate policy, lacking on most of the exteriors. Often the dining-area walls displayed a collection of photos showing the community in earlier days. The McDonald's near the University of Michigan, for example, exhibited nearly a hundred photos of old Ann Arbor. All that was missing was a photo of the historic house it had replaced. Another McDonald's in Ann Arbor used translucent panels with etched depictions of University of Michigan landmarks. This was a localism-by-national-guideline. From the company's book of "decor packages," franchisees chose the style and color of the seating. Based on that initial choice, the book suggested coordinating draperies, wall coverings, picture frames, accent trim, and other accessories. From these, the franchisees made their selections, and from the national company also came the ideas for many of these themes. Genuinely different and imaginative interiors were reserved for affluent, sophisticated neighborhoods and for other unusual locations, such as resorts.

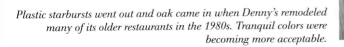

Plastic starbursts went out and oak came in when Denny's remodeled many of its older restaurants in the 1980s. Tranquil colors were becoming more acceptable.

In October 1972, in the San Diego suburb of Chula Vista, McDonald's opened its first McDonaldland Park, a fenced-in 7,000-square-foot playground containing large reproductions of Ronald McDonald and other characters used in the company's TV commercials. In a two-day inaugural celebration, hordes of children and parents—an estimated 10,000 people in all—visited the McDonaldland, adjacent to a McDonald's outlet that had opened two years earlier. Entertainment for children would prove to be one of McDonald's most successful promotions. A company that in the 1950s used amenity-stripped design to deter teenage loitering had evolved to the point that it encouraged people to come and spend some time, to have some fun, as long as the population having the fun consisted of young children accompanied by their paying parents.

The addition of a McDonaldland could establish a theme for a McDonald's unit, putting some character into what was otherwise a relatively bland restaurant. Many chains, however, established their theme through more architectural means—especially, as the 1960s wound down, through architecture that was old-fashioned. The small-town architectural flavor of a bygone era set the tone for Bob Evans Farms Restaurants, a chain that opened its first unit in Chillicothe, Ohio, in 1968. The company's founder, Robert L. Evans, a farmer from Gallipolis, Ohio, who had first become known as a sausage-maker, gave the restaurants brilliant red board-and-batten walls decorated with fanciful white Steamboat Gothic ornament—features he had seen on visits to Phoenix and Scottsdale, Arizona, and to Disneyland. Long John Silver's, started in 1969 by Jerrico, Inc., in Lexington, Kentucky, was dressed up as a wharf building to enhance its image as a fast-food restaurant specializing in seafood.

Throughout the restaurant industry, nostalgia was on the rise, appealing to a wide range of customers. In 1965 at First Avenue and Sixty-third Street in Manhattan, for example, Alan Stillman established the original TGI Friday's. One of TGIF's distinctions was that in the 1970s it blossomed into the first chain of singles bars, arranged usually with wide aisles and a tiered dining area around a four-sided bar to encourage observation and socializing. Another distinction was its revival of old-time saloon decor. Friday's served as a prototype "fern bar," containing plants, brass railings, oak floors, Tiffany-style lamps, a menu chalked on a slate, and a large quantity of unusual decorative items ranging from racing sculls to stuffed animal heads. Its decorators focused primarily on urban artifacts from prior to 1930. Eventually TGIF's appetite for eclectic decorations became so voracious that the company employed a full-time antiques buyer to attend estate sales and shop flea markets.

In Kansas City, Missouri, in 1972, the Gilbert/Robinson restaurant company started a similar establishment called Houlihan's Old Place. The goal was to assemble a collection of objects so varied and plentiful that the customer, on return visits, would always notice something different. Of the decorative scheme, one partner, Paul M. Robinson, said, "We just get a truckload of stuff from our warehouse, drive to the site, and put up what seems right."

The Howard Johnson Company embarked in 1969 on a similar if less elaborate approach for a new family-oriented restaurant, The Ground Round. The decor consisted of old merchandising memorabilia, framed pictures of early automobiles, flickering old-time movies, and other nostalgic items. At its cheapest—which is to say, at Wendy's—the nostalgic strategy degenerated into plastic pseudo-Victorian beads, horse-and-buggy wall murals, and tabletop reproductions of late-nineteenth-century newspaper advertisements.

Like Long John Silver's, budget-steak restaurants tried to tie architecture, decor, and food into a consistent theme. Bonanza Sirloin Pit, a chain begun in 1962 in Eastchester, New York, taking its name from the popular *Bonanza* television show, featured inexpensive steaks served in a building meant to evoke the rugged, informal flavor of the cattlemen's Old West. The ranch featured in the TV show was, of course, the Ponderosa, and three years later, in Kokomo, Indiana, another budget-steak restaurant chain appeared—Ponderosa Steak Barns. Ponderosa put up a board-and-batten false front with a covered front porch and, to the rear, a simple pitched roof with a massive broiler stack. Inside, a sign saying "That a way pardner" pointed toward the cafeteria line. As many as 186 people could sit at varnished picnic-style

Long John Silver's, operating in landlocked Lexington, Ky., found a wharfside image appropriate to its seafood menu.

Right: *Fabric and plants in a 1980s Denny's.*
Below: *Coco's on North Scottsdale Road, Scottsdale, Ariz., designed in 1966 by Thomas Wells; photo 1985.*

The old-building look in TGI Friday's in the Galleria area of Houston. Photo 1983.

tables in the main dining room, which in truth bore more resemblance to a mess hall than a Western barn. The ceiling was surfaced with indubitably modern acoustic panels; the "Western" atmosphere on the interior was to be established through decorative items like dark-stained beams and wagon-wheel lamps—and through semantics. Private parties of up to forty could meet in the "hayloft."

In San Francisco in 1969, three Cornell University graduates started a restaurant made up of five boxcars and two cabooses, with a menu featuring prime rib, steak, and shrimp. It was called Victoria Station, in honor of the great railroad station in London. By 1980 the company had 100 restaurants, each typically with its kitchen, waiting room, bar, and lavatories housed in new construction that was inserted between and behind the retired railroad cars. While dining in wall-to-wall-carpeted boxcars, customers gazed upon an assortment of authentic railroad articles, some from the British railway system of the 1890s. Old baggage carts were turned into salad bars. Tickets and schedules were inlaid in the tops of the bars and cocktail tables. Outside stood a red English phone booth and an English taxicab. Victoria Station's owners took pride in the restaurant's authenticity, in having avoided "plastic culture." The prime difference between the nostalgia of a dinnerhouse and the nostalgia of a fast-food outlet had come to lie in the quality and genuineness of the artifacts. By 1980, even Wendy's was trying to upgrade its authenticity quotient; plastic beads gave way to genuine stained glass dividers, a wooden "gazebo" salad bar, and sandblasted patterns on exterior windows.

Victoria Station was also part of another phenomenon: the emergence of informal chain dinnerhouses, first in the western United States, then throughout the nation. Unlike the white-tablecloth restaurants of the 1960s, which had extensive menus and traditional expectations about dressing for dinner, the emerging dinner-

Victoria Station's railroad-theme bar area and exterior in the 1970s.

house chains of that period operated more casual places, usually offering just a few entrees, mainly steaks and seafood, along with a salad bar where people served themselves. Probably the first such restaurant was The Embers, which Paul Livermore operated on Beachwalk in Waikiki in the 1950s. The Embers' building was converted in the mid-fifties into Buzz's Steak & Lobster, run by a former liquor salesman, Buzz Schneider. Buzz's, in turn, was admired by Charles G. Rolles, a recent graduate of Cornell's school of hotel and restaurant administration. In March 1959 Rolles opened a similar establishment, Chuck's Steak House, in the Edgewater Hotel in Waikiki. He and various partners eventually established more than fifty Chuck's Steak Houses throughout the United States. But before expanding under the Chuck's name, Rolles moved to Aspen and, with Peter Guy, opened the Steak Pit on July 4, 1960. The Aspen operation was apparently the first limited-menu steak, lobster, and salad-bar restaurant on the mainland. In Aspen in 1962, two of Rolles's Steak Pit employees, Joey Cabell and Buzzy Bent, started the first unit of what would become a chain of more than fifty Chart House restaurants. Two other men who saw the Steak Pit while in Aspen—Peter Greene and Tom Fleck—went to Scottsdale, Arizona, and founded the first of about thirty-five Cork 'n Cleaver restaurants in 1964. John McIntosh, who ultimately made his major impact on the restaurant industry by founding Coco's, had opened the first of his string of Reuben's steakhouses in Newport Beach, California, in November 1960. In 1966 Norman Brinker, former southwest regional manager for Jack in the Box, opened the first Steak & Ale in Dallas.

In Hawaii, where many of these restauranteurs had first become acquainted with one another, the limited-menu dinnerhouses often finished their interiors in bamboo, tapa cloth, coconut thatching, and other natural materials ranging in color from light to medium brown. In moving to the mainland, steak-and-lobster restaurants became darker, with interiors emphasizing stone or half-timbered walls, heavy beams, barnwood, and other aged materials. The most conspicuous lighting in the dining rooms emanated from candles on the tables and logs in the fireplaces. Steak & Ale divided its interiors into individual rooms, each with a fireplace. The movie *Tom Jones* was in Brinker's mind at the time he was developing the design concept; Steak & Ale adopted a heavy Old English appearance for the exterior as well.

Unlike Steak & Ale, many of the dinnerhouse chains concluded that although standardization of the menu was desirable, standardization of appearance was not. Many of the Chuck's Steak Houses opened in distinctive old houses, barns, or seaside buildings. Chart House wanted its buildings to be blessed with history (some were converted old houses), scenery, or imaginative new architecture, and the company didn't complain when the works of talented designers turned out to be expensive. By the end of the 1970s, Chart House spent as much as $2 million on the development of a single unit—the restaurant in Rancho Mirage, California, designed by Kendrick Kellogg of San Diego. Kellogg designed the restaurant so that it not only followed the irregular contours of the site but also made the land a principal attraction. By supporting the massive roof on 156 posts, the architect was able to free the walls from structural demands; a continuous expanse of glass could be inserted at the top of one long wall to give diners a view of ground squirrels, lizards, and other desert species in a natural setting. At night, the exterior was softly lighted to create a vista of native rock, sand, and plants.

A common thread running through most of the chain dinnerhouses was informality: the dress was looser, the service more relaxed, the decor far less traditional than in established white-tablecloth restaurants. Some of the dinnerhouses also downplayed the fact that they were part of a chain. They stressed their distinctiveness and tried to avoid being seen as a formula-bound operation. The emphasis on individuality was hardly surprising in restaurants whose prices put them in the special-occasion category. But the softpedaling of chain identity also reflected an awareness of a growing public reaction against chains—indeed, against many large organizations.

Restaurants felt the impact of an age of social protest. The entire industry adjusted to a series of broadly popular, interrelated trends: toward natural or natural-looking materials, toward textures seemingly free of machine-smoothing, toward calm horizontality, domestic imagery, landscaping, nostalgia, and earth tones. These constituted a new esthetic, one that emerged from an elaborate set of factors.

Some of the changes in restaurant design and decor reflected conditions specific to the restaurant industry. The industry had grown into a much more prominent national presence. Many low-priced restaurants that were small, local operations in the 1950s had expanded into large, well-established companies by the 1970s, and now faced higher expectations. They had national reputations to safeguard, and they became more amenable to making gestures of corporate responsibility. They wanted to avoid looking like bad citizens. If this meant discontinuing their most attention-getting architecture, the loss could be offset by the powerful advertising budgets that companies like McDonald's had come to wield. Radio and TV commercials could do what had once been accomplished through building design: create a widespread awareness of the restaurants.

The companies' customers had changed, too; they had matured. Teenagers who didn't mind eating hamburgers in their cars at drive-ins in the 1950s wanted at least a minimally comfortable indoor dining area twenty years later. Fast-food chains had to upgrade their design and decor if they were going to appeal to their maturing baby-boom clientele along with a new generation of youngsters. As the cost of land and buildings rose, the chains also needed to maximize the number of hours the restaurants made money. The lunch trade became as large as the restaurants could handle, and breakfast was added; but the dinner trade—a favorite path to continuing growth—required a more refined atmosphere. As the chief architect for Wendy's observed, "People will eat lunch in a dinner place, but they won't eat dinner in a lunch place." Fast-food restaurants decided that a more relaxed and comfortable atmosphere would help boost their daily revenues. A similar shift took place in coffee shops. Breakfast and lunch were always busy times in coffee shops, but these establishments decided to fight more aggressively for the most expensive meal of the day, and as they did so, they became mellower in the kind of surroundings they offered. Often they also changed their name to "family restaurant," although the term "coffee shop" remained accurate as long as they retained some counter seating.

Factors such as these, largely internal to the restaurant industry, probably made less of an impact than the social forces of the 1960s and 1970s. There was a growing public reaction against visual excesses. In 1964 the architectural critic Peter Blake directed an angry book-length assault against the commercialized landscape, calling it "God's Own Junkyard." Two years later, a writer in *Fortune* magazine expressed a widespread sentiment when he declared, "For sheer hideousness, America's thousands of miles of honky-tonk commercial-strip highways are unsurpassed in the industrialized world." Lady Bird Johnson used her prestige as First Lady to push a

Chart House restaurants in a remodeled farmhouse in Duxbury, Mass. (above), and in two renovated boathouses—in Coronado, Calif. (above, right), and in Annapolis, Md.

campaign for highway beautification. Increasingly, people recognized that the road-side strip had become a basic form of commercial development, one that required planning, often backed up by design review ordinances. Municipalities tried to capture control over a situation that had gotten out of hand. Since large chains wanted to build their standard designs almost everywhere, the opposition of even a minority of American towns could rule out the development of any loud prototype.

The demand for a less garish roadside strip, when combined with other currents in the culture—a growing awareness of the nation's faults and a fading away of the once-euphoric attitude toward futuristic technology—fostered a more subdued esthetic. When dynamic structural modernism lost its potency as symbolism in the 1960s, chains had to adopt an esthetic that connected their restaurants to the current state of mind. The change that ultimately unfolded, however, was nothing less than a transformation of American taste. Note, for example, that the explosive growth of restaurants—fast-food, coffee-shop, budget-steakhouse, dinnerhouse—bypassed the traditional white-tablecloth establishments. The maturing baby-boom shied away from such seemingly stuffy places. A generation accustomed to eating with its fingers was uncomfortable with stemware and linen; the new adult market, when it sought something more than fast food, gravitated to restaurants whose atmosphere was dim, informal and nostalgic, or "natural"—places where loosened manners brought no glares of disapproval. Refined manners came to seem artificial, and as the 1960s progressed toward its emotion-packed culmination, the artificial—in manners and in many other aspects of daily life—met with rejection. By the end of the decade, whatever was "natural" struck a responsive chord. New houses were built with unpainted wooden siding, the quicker to appear old and to harmonize with the land. Natural fibers began to make a comeback, and denim became the uniform of the young. This widespread restyling of elements of daily life initially manifested a sense of confidence that customs could be changed, attitudes could be altered, and the country could establish a healthier relationship between man and his surroundings. But the optimism was undone by a series of traumatic blows: assassinations of national leaders, an exploding crime rate, urban race riots, duplicitous presidents, and an escalating, winless war in Vietnam—especially the war, for it went senselessly on and on, even as supporters turned into opponents and campuses erupted in protest. Lyndon Johnson's and then Richard Nixon's failure to bring the war to some quick conclusion permitted a poisonous rancor to accumulate, increasingly corroding the national spirit. Many disparate grievances—over military policy, racial prejudice, pollution, and other issues—thus had time to coalesce into a much more generalized malaise. There developed a revulsion, often not fully articulated, against the entire American military-economic-industrial system. Those searching for a humane vision inverted the fifties' ways of thinking. The technological became ever more suspect. Many Americans became less concerned with the newly fulfilled dream of rocketing to the moon than with the prospects for going to the country and living close to the land. Shaken by so much tumult, many people wanted to connect themselves to forces of stability and permanence. Few things could be more stable than a dead past, nostalgically recollected, or more permanent than earth and nature. Chain restaurants attuned themselves to the new frame of mind by offering landscaped, calmly horizontal, earth-toned exteriors with traditional materials (natural products like brick and wood especially) and by shifting to darker interiors furnished with plants, natural textures, and old-time decor.

This was not the first time the man-made environment of the United States had been subdued by a generalized sense of trouble. The urban historian Lewis Mumford termed the period from 1865 to 1895 "the brown decades." Of that period—ushered in by assassination, riots, and fratricidal war, and characterized as it went on by racial strife and harsh industrialization—Mumford observed: "The nation not merely worked differently after the Civil War: the country *looked* different—darker, sadder, soberer . . . . The inner world coloured the outer world." Heavy mansard roofs arrived along with brownstone walls, dark walnut furniture, and somberly wallpapered interiors that swallowed up the light.

It is impossible to put boundaries around deeply felt, widely shared emotions. Just as the disturbances of the late nineteenth century altered the entire environment of that period, the distress of the 1960s and 1970s seems to have affected the outlook of architectural review boards, municipal planners, restaurant designers—all sorts of organizations and individuals, regardless of whether they consciously recognized the sources of their attitudes and tastes.

The everyday environment changed, nowhere more so than in chain restaurants, for chain restaurants were superbly prepared to embody popular expectations. The designer of a chain restaurant, unlike the architect of a church, a museum, or some other serious cultural monument, can respond wholeheartedly to the spirit of the times without worrying about how the colors, textures, and forms will function thirty or fifty years in the future; in the restaurant industry, it's assumed that the daily wear and tear on the interior, not to mention the periodic need for a fresh scheme of decoration, will mandate renovation within a few years. Chain restaurants were free to act as a barometer of public mood. Exteriors offered somewhat more resistance to change than did the interiors, but they, too, adapted at least partly to new conditions, as McDonald's demonstrated when it put shingles and bricks on the original golden-arched restaurants. Moreover, because of the industry's rapid expansion and its continuing need for restaurants with enlarged or reduced seating capacities, drive-thru windows, or other features, chains constantly tinkered with their designs and thus were in a position to register the latest shifts of attitude and behavior almost immediately. By the middle of the 1970s, restaurants recorded an entirely different mood from that of twenty years before. Americans felt more in need of solace than of stimulation. The country was dispirited, and it wore its feelings on the roadside.

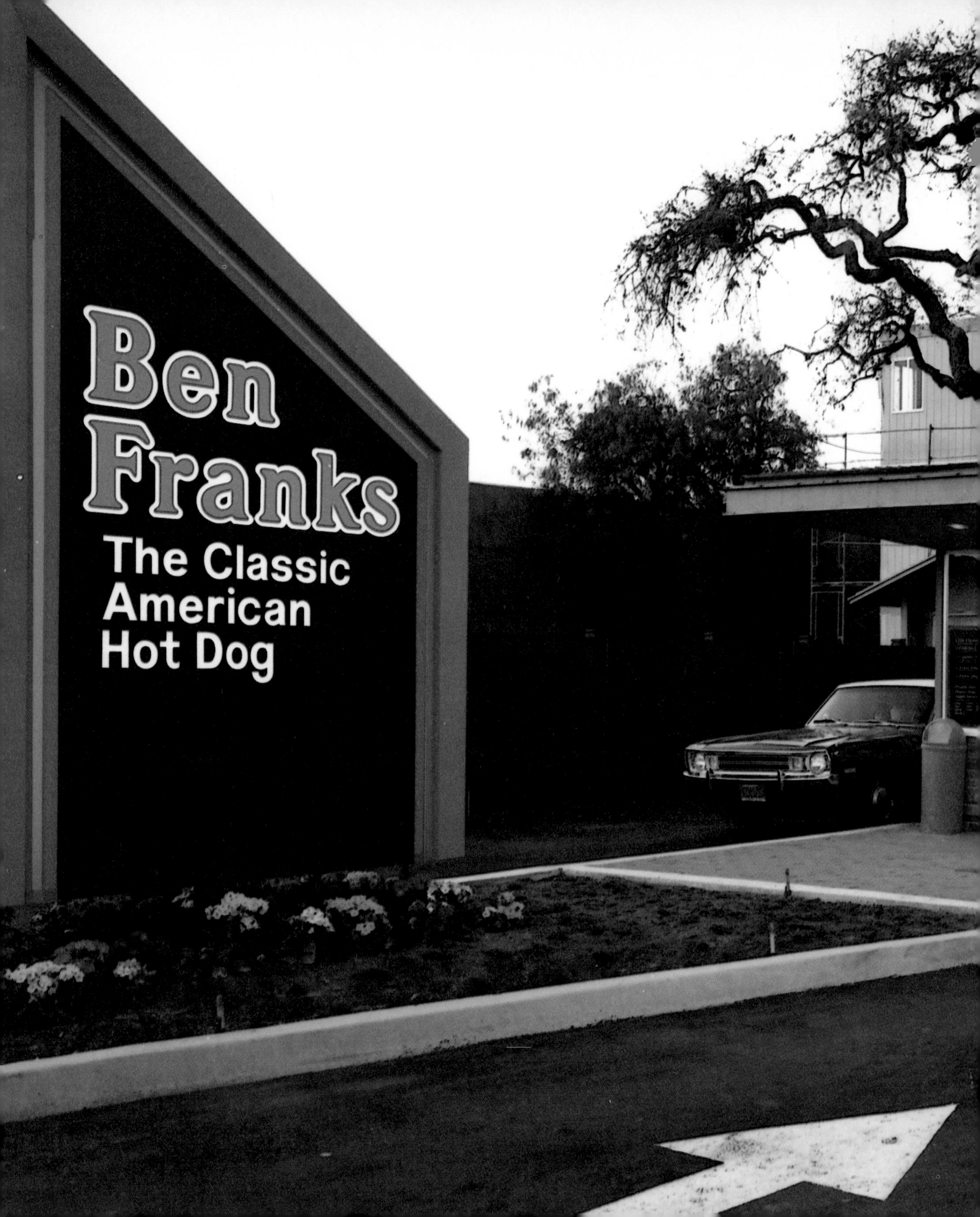
Ben
Franks
The Classic
American
Hot Dog

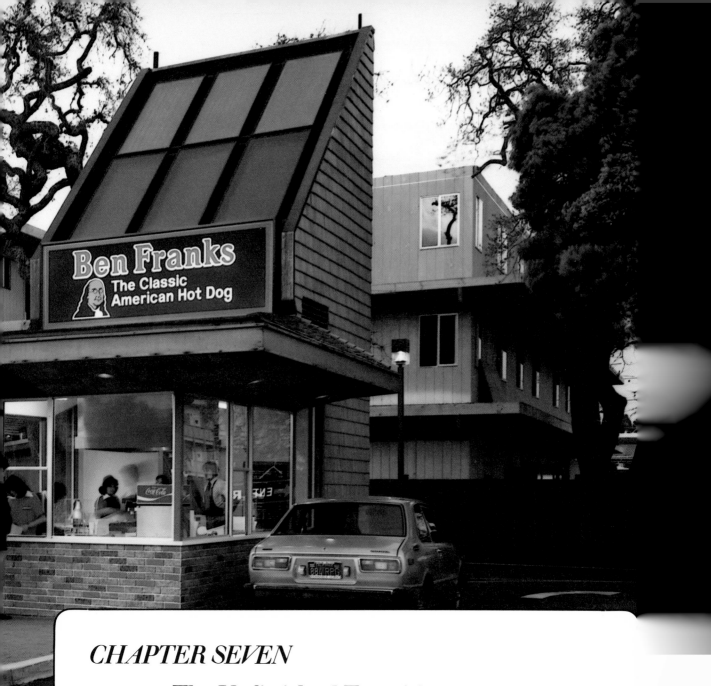

CHAPTER SEVEN

The Unfinished Transition:
Design Since 1975

Overleaf: *First Ben Franks hot dog stand, built in 1979 on El Camino Real, Redwood City, Calif.*

In 1961 TWO BUSINESSMEN IN THE SMALL TOWN OF Rocky Mount, North Carolina, Leonard Rawls and Jim Gardner, bought a restaurant called Hardee's in another North Carolina town, Greenville, about forty miles to the southeast. Wilbur Hardee had opened the restaurant a year earlier, patterning it after McDonald's, with a self-service system and a menu featuring fifteen-cent hamburgers, and Rawls and Gardner recognized its potential for growth, especially in this section of the South where fast food was not yet commonplace. The new owners kept the Hardee's name and used it on new restaurants which they soon began building—some with their own money, most with franchisees'—elsewhere in North Carolina. They ran the chain from two rented rooms above Rocky Mount's Western Auto store, but it wasn't long before the company outgrew such limited quarters. Within fourteen years Hardee's had developed into a major fast-food firm, still based in out-of-the-way Rocky Mount, an hour's drive east of Raleigh, and still headed by Rawls, but now with 900 restaurants spread well beyond the South, into a total of thirty-four states.

As it grew, Hardee's adapted to changing tastes in architecture, using a red-and-white-striped building like McDonald's in the early 1960s, then shifting to a brick building with a large, steeply sloped "mansard" fascia late in the decade. If the mansard had been brown or beige, the company could have continued to use it in the middle and late 1970s, but the mansard was bright orange—a color that won few friends on municipal architectural review boards—and it was surfaced in porcelain enamel, once a competitively priced material but in the 1970s several times as costly as one of the common alternatives, asphalt shingles. By 1975, with its loud and expensive orange mansard hobbling further expansion, the company decided to commission Lippincott & Margulies to produce an updated building concept. Until then, Hardee's had consistently tagged along with design trends already well established in the industry; this time it was ready to move a step ahead.

In 1976 Lippincott & Margulies introduced a new Hardee's prototype that solved the company's most pressing design problems. To overcome opposition to Hardee's conspicuous coloring, bright orange no longer dominated the top of the restaurant; now the orange was relegated to broad borders around windows and doors and to the company's lettering. To head off resistance from communities sensitive about having a standard design imposed on them, the new building was offered in a choice of materials. Exterior walls could be surfaced in polished terrazzo concrete block, rough-sawn plywood, cedar shakes, clapboard, or brick. A complementary range of materials, including standing-seam metal and cedar shakes, was made available for the new building's roof.

But neither the range of materials nor the handling of color was what made the new Hardee's distinctive; the striking thing was the rectangular building's unusually crisp profile. At the top was a mansard, but it had a much different feeling than those used by other restaurants. Instead of overhanging the walls and giving an impression of weightiness, Hardee's mansard came down flush against the walls' outer edges; eaves were eliminated. The mansard extended back from the top of the walls at an angle of sixty degrees above horizontal, and this sharp, angular effect was echoed in other aspects of the building. Above each window, an orange border angled inward at thirty degrees below horizontal until it met the sheet-glass, which was recessed four

Right: *1976-style Hardee's on Airport Road, Allentown, Pa. Photo 1983.* Above: *1969-style Hardee's on U.S. 40 in eastern Maryland. Photo 1983.*

feet from the outer wall plane. On the sides of the windows, orange borders formed a similar angled recess, and the same inset was used as a border around the restaurant's doors. Even the edges of the drive-thru canopy and the planters at the base of the building adopted a consistently angular configuration. The combination of sharp angles created a rigorous and austere composition—a decided departure from the heavy and generally soothing esthetic that the chain-restaurant industry had adopted almost in chorus in the late 1960s and early 1970s. Despite the soothingly natural materials available for walls and roof, the new prototype exuded the brusque feeling of "contemporary" geometric design.

Soon Hardee's was not alone. In 1978 Burger King began turning toward a similarly sharpened image. No longer did the typical new Burger King resolutely hunker down beneath a cedar shake mansard. A vestibule that had sat calmly contained under a downward extension of the mansard now thrust abruptly upward. Covering most of the vestibule exterior was tongue-in-groove siding, the grooves angling energetically at sixty degrees above horizontal. One of the restaurant's sidewalls did without the obligatory mansard and instead rose straight up to form a parapet, covered with grooved, rough-surfaced plywood.

At about the same time that Burger King was adopting this livelier look, Minneapolis-based Mister Donut began converting some of its buildings from a backlighted orange-and-white plastic fascia to a fascia of cedar (either genuine or imitation), with the grooves of the wood pattern running at angles—left, right, left, right, all the way around the top of the restaurant.

Energy costs jumped dramatically in the 1970s, and Mister Donut found that a wood or imitation-wood fascia outfitted with a simple neon-lighted sign consumed 30 to 40 percent less electricity than a continuous, fully backlighted fascia of plastic. Likewise, cost-savings provided some justification for Burger King's new look; the company paid less to build a parapet than to continue its mansard all the way around the building. And in the Bay Area south of San Francisco, Ben Franks, a small chain of hot dog stands founded in 1979, used a wedge-shaped roof because it made for optimal placement of solar collector panels, which supplied some of the energy for cooking the wieners. But such expense-reducing rationales only partly explained the shift toward angular architectural motifs. As Ben Franks's founder, Stephen S. Hiller, acknowledged, a sharply angled roof served as "a visual calling card." In the same vein, Raymond M. Poelvoorde, president of Lippincott & Margulies, argued that Hardee's, with an advertising budget a fraction the size of McDonald's, couldn't afford a building as neutral as McDonald's mansard-roofed design; a contemporary, geometric appearance was intended to make Hardee's stand out. Burger King wanted a more contemporary appearance, a look that it labeled the "New Image Burger King."

The esthetic that made its way into these and other inexpensive restaurants in the latter 1970s and the 1980s had shown up earlier in residential architecture. Wood siding had been used on the diagonal by the prominent modern architect Marcel Breuer in the late 1940s, and a generally angular architectural idiom came to be employed in many fashionable individual houses and multi-unit housing developments in the 1960s and 1970s, nowhere with more acclaim than in the Sea Ranch condominium complex that was built along the coast of Northern California in 1965. Sea Ranch, the work primarily of Donlyn Lyndon, William Turnbull, and Charles Moore, who later became dean of Yale University's architecture school, had exterior walls covered in rough, unpainted vertical boards, which culminated in austere shed roofs almost completely shorn of overhangs. The stark roofs, stabbing at the sky, deflected cold ocean winds, but more than that, they exerted a powerful visual impact that helped propel the angular contemporary idiom toward broader acceptance. This was not an architecture with universal appeal in 1965, but after it had been imitated by thousands of condominium complexes across the country in the following decade, thus establishing its cachet, it was ready to be picked up—with varying thoroughness or superficiality—by chain restaurants aiming for a mass market.

As used by a chain like Burger King, the angular, woody style had several advantages beyond simply being economical. The shapes projected a crisper, more energetic personality, while the use of wood provided an ameliorating mellowness. Wood installed at an angle summoned up a variety of largely favorable impressions. It recalled some of the high-style, high-priced architecture of the upper strata of society, yet it also suggested the sturdy, no-nonsense character of vernacular construction— of barn doors, for example, or of mine shafts jutting out of rural land. It seemed casual rather than formal; the texture of wood had a natural feeling, yet its installation at an angle conveyed a sense of being attentive to style. This marriage of the natural and casual with a sense of stylishness held considerable appeal; the same combination of attributes helped sell consumers such other everyday objects of the 1970s as "designer blue jeans." The key lay in creating an impression of informality without descending into drabness. For restaurants, a woody appearance established a connection to nature—important at a time of widespread environmental consciousness—while the sharp geometry imbued the buildings with liveliness. Here was an effective union of opposites: soothing earth tones and natural materials worked into stimulating shapes, rustic functionalism with a sheen of sophistication. The angled shapes generated a brisk vitality that no cumbersome mansard roof could achieve.

Now that the disturbances of the 1960s and early 1970s were receding into memory, the yearning for an atmosphere of calm in the everyday environment began to diminish. More spirited buildings were becoming acceptable.

The shift toward vitality and energy was not restricted to exteriors. Inside, a similar change was taking place. In the mid-seventies, dinnerhouse chains began to abandon their lone-candle-in-the-darkness atmosphere and let both natural and artificial light penetrate the dimness of their dining rooms. Skylights popped through ceilings, and greenhouse–dining room extensions were added to outer walls. These features gained acceptance so quickly that by the early 1980s, fast-food chains like McDonald's and Wendy's were outfitting some dining areas with skylights or greenhouse extensions. Many of these skylights were false, consisting of tilted, translucent panels with bulbs behind them—in accordance with the chains' insistence on minimizing maintenance responsibilities—but nonetheless, they did manage to give the impression of letting the sun shine in. Greenhouses and skylights made settings that also seemed harmonious for plants, which had already become an established part of interior decoration. The result was that a great many restaurant interiors retained a soft, natural feeling even while they became brighter.

In 1981 Denny's began adding glass-roofed, greenhouse-style vestibules and false skylights to its coffee shops, but those alterations were relatively minor. The more noticeable change at Denny's was the shaving back of the broad roof overhangs. Denny's didn't want a tight angularity like Hardee's, but it did want a profile more brusque and aggressive than the prototype the company had used from 1975 to 1980. Donald E. Miller, who left McDonald's in 1979 to head Denny's architectural program, said of the low-slung 1975–80 building: "It's too soft. It's too low in silhouette. It's too fitting to the terrain." Such softness gave the impression that Denny's might be a dinnerhouse, with higher prices and more leisurely service; the earth-hugging building didn't effectively communicate its purpose and its price level. "You could go to most of them and look at the building," said Miller, "and if it weren't for the signage, you might understand it to be a savings and loan."

To be sure, ambiguity in restaurant imagery was not an entirely new phenomenon, nor was it a problem peculiar to Denny's. After World War II, Friendly Ice Cream, based in Springfield, Massachusetts, began using modified Georgian designs which, as they grew increasingly dignified in the 1950s and 1960s, came to look more like branch banks than places serving hamburgers and banana splits. Some of the employees made jokes about people coming to Friendly's take-out window to make a deposit or pulling up to a branch bank and ordering an ice-cream cone. Still, Friendly's superabundance of dignity seemed to be no real problem as long as the chain

Burger King exterior design introduced in the late 1970s, and an early 1980s interior.

expanded at an unhurried pace across southern New England. It was when Friendly went from New England into the Midwest in a rapid expansion drive in the early 1970s that the disparity between outside and inside became a serious handicap. The new Friendly outlets in Ohio may not have been mistaken for banks, but they were certainly not understood to be restaurants with a small menu and a minimal level of comfort. People attracted by the meticulously detailed exterior were disappointed to find they had to sit at counter stools, choosing among hamburgers, sandwiches, ice cream, and other common fare. New Englanders knew, by long acquaintance, what Friendly served, and New Englanders often were willing to sit on stools while eating. But in the Midwest, people going to a restaurant, especially one as fancy-looking as Friendly, generally expected the greater privacy and comfort of a table or a booth. After suffering lagging sales for these and other reasons, Friendly modified many of its Midwestern buildings to provide booth seating, and it switched to exteriors with dark brown roofs, dark brown wooden gables, deeper overhangs, dark window trim, and buff-colored brick with dark mortar. It also introduced a larger menu. The new interior proved to be more acceptable, but the exterior still seemed to promise too much. People looking at the Friendly building wondered whether it was a dinner-house with accordingly high prices. Friendly continued to record disappointing sales in the Midwest, and consequently decided in 1982 to introduce yet another design—a more economical building that retained a cupola on the roof but had the overhangs shaved far back. The new building looked less generous, less relaxed. The stiffer, less luxurious exterior seemed to fit the more limited menu that had been the company's mainstay for years and that was going to be emphasized once again.

The ambiguity in the imagery of chains like Denny's and Friendly's stemmed partly from inconsistency about what kind of trade the companies wanted to capture. Friendly and Denny's, in their brown-tone-and-generous-overhang period, were trying to evolve from coffee shops into family restaurants, which seemed to hold greater growth potential. The difference had to do primarily with seating, atmosphere, and the degree of emphasis on dinner trade. Coffee shops served food quickly, and many of the customers ate at a counter, while family restaurants were slower, with larger menus, booth and table seating, a somewhat more soothing atmosphere, and a bigger dinner business. In the late 1970s, Denny's in particular blurred its image even more than Friendly, combining attributes of a coffee shop, a family restaurant, and a dinnerhouse—the latter being a slower, quieter, higher-priced establishment that emphasized the dinner trade. In Denny's outlets, the counter area and relatively fast service of a coffee shop were retained, but the exterior was softened and the dining rooms became more plush to attract customers for evening meals.

In the early 1980s, Denny's decided that had been a mistake, and the company

Late 1960s Friendly in Springfield, Mass., resembling a branch bank.

The 1980 Friendly that looked too much like a dinnerhouse; photographed in Hyannis, Mass.

edged slightly closer to its original coffee-shop emphasis with a bolder look on the exterior. Inside, however, the colors and textures remained muted. Denny's selected cool green fabrics for booths, chairs, counter seats, and carpets—a far cry from the hot pink and orange vinyl seats and orange-tinged carpeting of the late 1960s. The new tabletops of the 1980s were in simulated oak, not pink and orange Formica. Booths, chairs, and counter seats were trimmed with genuine oak, and a range of browns and tans appeared throughout the restaurant. Somewhat more rousing elements of the decorative scheme were a zigzag pattern of brown and tan tile on the walls behind the counter and false skylights in the ceiling, but these, too, seemed mild by comparison to the orange plastic starbursts that had once been splashed liberally on backs of counter seats, booth dividers, and even lighting fixtures. The attempt to create a livelier atmosphere in the 1980s consisted primarily of increasing the interior's openness. Instead of having three separate dining areas, as in the late 1970s, Denny's reverted to a more open arrangement, with much of the seating at tables and chairs instead of booths, and with some of the food preparation in public view. The company's theory was that the hustle of waitresses and the view of the cooks at work would create the "coffee shop" tempo that the decor itself denied.

Neither Denny's nor Friendly nor many other chains had been hampered in the 1950s by disparities between interior and exterior and type of service. Passing motorists looked through Denny's big windows into a brightly lit interior and immediately knew what the restaurant was like inside. Such uninhibited exposure was the keynote of the California coffee shop and it appeared to a certain extent even at conservative Friendly, where large windows, subdivided into large panes, put the restaurant's dining area in plain view. The problem of having a concealed interior developed later—in Friendly's case when it adopted small-paned, more authentically Georgian windows, and in the case of other restaurants when they felt compelled to present a more subdued face to the world. There was little possibility in the 1980s of going back to the bright, see-through façades of thirty years earlier.

The public seemed willing to welcome a more stimulating appearance, but to a limited degree. Designers, lacking the freedom to make restaurants boldly transparent, had to find other, less forthright ways of announcing the restaurants' character, such as making the exterior less sumptuous. The search for an effective image took place primarily by trial and error at Friendly and at Denny's, but there was another way of dealing with the connotations of exterior appearance. It lay in asking the public for its thoughts, typically by surveying a representative sampling of intended customers. By the 1980s, consumer research, long used by advertisers and merchandisers, had come into full flower within the restaurant industry.

Some companies, such as McDonald's, were equipped with in-house research departments capable of measuring national response to designs, but other chains relied on marketing, design, and communications firms like Lippincott & Margulies in New York and S & O Consultants in San Francisco. Such outside consultants, with their elaborate research techniques, were needed by chains that had grown too large for their executives to observe a cross-section of customers. Multi-million-dollar companies, now operating in many instances as subsidiaries of Fortune 500 firms, couldn't get by on instinct. By 1982, for example, Taco Bell had 1,400 restaurants in forty-seven states and five foreign countries. The chain, owned by the conglomerate Pepsico, was intent on moving into regions that were unfamiliar with both Taco Bell and Mexican food, and the company's executives in Irvine, California, wanted to reduce the risk of an embarrassing failure. Consequently Taco Bell commissioned S & O to study the restaurant's image and design and to propose changes.

An S & O subsidiary, Nova Research Group, questioned a total of five hundred fast-food consumers in three metropolitan areas where Taco Bell was well established and in two areas that Taco Bell had just entered. The questions focused on people's feelings about Mexican food in general and Taco Bell in particular. Participants looked at slides of Taco Bell buildings and signs and chose descriptions from contrasting sets of adjectives—clean or dirty, family-oriented or adult, expensive or not expensive, and so on. Three hundred Taco Bell customers took part in visibility studies, watching scenes that, through the use of a device called a tachistoscope, were flashed

Booth service at Friendly in the 1980s contrasts with counter stools in 1957 in West Boylston, Mass.

for a measured, brief duration—a fortieth of a second, a fifth of a second, three-fifths of a second, and a full second. "What did you see?" the participants were asked. The tests showed that people recognized McDonald's golden arches and Kentucky Fried Chicken's bucket at faster exposures than they recognized the Taco Bell sign. The Taco Bell sign was, in researchers' parlance, "not impactful." After the views had flashed on and off and participants had been asked to identify the views, they were then shown a series of views for an extended period—views of the freestanding sign, the bell tower, the small bell in the tower, the arched windows, the red-tiled roof. They were asked to indicate whether they liked or disliked each of those elements.

The research showed that Taco Bell ran a risk of rejection in trying to promote Mexican food to a non-Mexican population, especially in regions where Mexican food was uncommon. The exotic often meets resistance; this was one of the reasons why Lippincott & Margulies had advised Pizza Hut in the mid-1970s to remove the little Italian character from its building and sign. Pizza Hut had to be "Americanized." Similarly, S & O's research showed that many people distrusted Mexican restaurants, fearing they would be dirty. Something would have to be done about Taco Bell's strong Mexican associations.

The surveys showed that people liked most of the Taco Bell building features, especially the arched windows and the red tile roof, but the sign was another matter— 36 percent disliked it, as compared to the 3 percent who disliked the arched windows.

Above: *"Mainstream Mansard" Taco Bell, 1984.* Right: *One of its predecessors in Phoenix.* Near right: *Logo replacing the "sleeping sombrero."*

In tests like these, consumers generally try to say pleasant things about what they're shown. The sign's 36 percent negative rating signaled outright repudiation. On every measure, the sign fared badly. Besides arousing dislike and falling short of instant recognition, it was also confusing; many people didn't know that it represented a Mexican sleeping under his sombrero, on top of a bell. And if they had known, would they have been reassured by a profile of a sleeping Mexican? Hardly.

One result of S & O's work was a clarification of Taco Bell's strategy for attracting customers. The company was not about to change its name or drop the Mexican foods that had accounted for its success, but it began to play down Mexican associations. People at the company's headquarters began describing Taco Bell as "a fast-food restaurant that serves Mexican food," as opposed to a Mexican restaurant. They were intent on securing Taco Bell a place in the American mainstream. On some existing restaurants, a bell logo, manufactured in plastic, was placed where restaurants in earlier years had displayed a real bell in a real aperture at the top of the wall. Eliminated along with the bell tower were heavy wooden outriggers that had projected outward from the walls, in a manner characteristic of Mexican architecture. The color of exterior walls—"dirty brown," in S & O's judgment—was lightened. The two most popular features—the tile roof and the arched windows—were incorporated into the design of a new Taco Bell prototype, but S & O avoided making them seem too authentically Mexican. Instead of covering a long roof pitch, the tiles formed a simple mansard, a short slope above all four walls; this was a roof shape already strongly associated with fast-food and other obviously American retail buildings, so it helped downplay Taco Bell's ethnic image. No bell tower rose from the roof of the new building—referred to by the company as its "Mainstream Mansard" design. The building adopted a dignified symmetrical façade with front and side entrances that projected slightly forward, their arched peaks echoing the arches of the doorways. On the front of the new prototype, the windows were arched and trimmed in brick, but S & O was fearful of featuring the arches too strongly; on the sides, the building used large rectangular windows, which looked unquestionably modern rather than Mexican. Above the doorway, "Taco Bell" appeared in discreet brown letters, accompanied by the bell logo in plastic. There was irony in Taco Bell's embracing plastic at the very time when other fast-food chains were trying to downplay their "plastic look" and achieve an appearance that seemed more natural and authentic. But Taco Bell, like untold numbers of second-generation ethnic Americans, saw foreignness as a troublesome label and grasped at established symbols of American retailing—plastic and mansards—the datedness of those symbols notwithstanding. The result was in most respects a blander image, but one that seemed to reduce the stigma that some people attached to things Mexican. The new sign lacked sombreros and sleeping Mexicans. All it consisted of was a bell, which may have reminded a few people of Spanish or Mexican mission architecture, but it was a natural choice, considering the name of the company and the man who had founded it in 1962, Glen W. Bell. It wasn't an especially interesting bell, but it was clear and easily distinguishable, and that was enough—it was "impactful." So said the people tested on their response to the sign.

The growing use of consultants like S & O and of designs based on consumer research banished some of the amateurishness from roadside enterprises. Standardized-image chain restaurants had, of course, almost always tried to minimize offbeat personal expression, but the growing acceptance of consumer testing made quirky, individualistic designs all the less prevalent; thousands of small business operators now were part of franchise networks that received guidance from marketing, communications, and design firms. As a consequence, some spontaneity disappeared from the roadside.

This is not to say that all restaurants avoided the unusual. Rather, the unusual was welcome only where it was an integral part of the restaurant's theme—a deliberately selected part of the concept rather than an impulsive act. Restaurant themes became more important than ever in the late 1970s and the 1980s, and were sometimes carried to new extremes. S & O devised a restaurant called Orville Bean's Flying Machine & Fixit Shop for the Steak & Ale restaurant subsidiary of Pillsbury—its theme revolving around a fictitious inventor's strange contraptions, such as steam-driven roller skates, an electric fork, and a combination flask/drinking cup/curling iron. Another S & O concept for Steak & Ale was Juan & Only's, a Mexican restaurant displaying an eclectic assortment of old phonograph records, pictures of Mexican revolutionaries, tubas, hats, and other presumably diverting miscellaneous objects.

Some restaurants capitalized on the nostalgic possibilities of period automobiles and related artifacts. At The Filling Station, a small chain founded in Dallas in 1976, waiters dispensed beer from an old transparent gasoline pump. Racks of tires hung above diners' heads, metal signs advertised long-discontinued brands of fuel, and the exterior faithfully replicated the appearance of a 1920s filling station.

Few pushed a theme further than did the Specialty Restaurants Corporation, founded by David C. Tallichet, Jr. in 1959 with a single Polynesian restaurant, The Reef, on the waterfront in Long Beach, California. Over the years, the company opened a growing assortment of dinnerhouses with names like Dockside Broiler, Ports O'Call, Pieces of Eight, and Baby Doe's Matchless Mine Restaurant—the last a reproduction of the above-ground portion of the Matchless silver mine in Leadville, Colorado, in the 1880s.

The challenge was to find subject matter that hadn't already been thoroughly exploited. In 1973 Specialty Restaurants discovered that the public would respond to a war theme, at least if the war was distant in time and uncontroversial. The company established the 94th Aero Squadron, drawing on associations with Captain Eddie Rickenbacker and World War I. After that proved successful, Tallichet developed a series of themes from World War II. The new eating places bore names like 57th Fighter Group, 91st Bomb Group, and 101st Airborne. Airport locations pleased Tallichet, who had piloted a B-17 during World War II. In 1983, within sight of Cleveland's Hopkins International Airport, he opened a 100th Bomb Group, erecting a building that resembled a half-timbered English farmhouse, with ambulances, Jeeps, olive-drab personnel carriers, and strands of barbed wire strewn around the exterior. Inside, propellers and wings hung on the walls, and hostesses wore Red Cross uniforms. The outdoor patio, called "The Bunker," featured a simulated bomb crater. The 101st Airborne—so close to Nashville Metro Airport that diners could feel the rumble of takeoffs—resembled a brick and stucco French farmhouse used by the 101st Airborne during World War II, and it was made more realistic by positioning Jeeps, ambulances, and C-47 aircraft around the perimeter. Under Tallichet's direction, restaurants evolved almost into Hollywood sets. This was an expensive way to attract customers, but not quite as expensive as it looked—Tallichet knew how to get locally issued government revenue bonds to reduce some of his financing costs.

Even children began to be provided with their own theme restaurants. Five years after the first McDonaldland Park opened in a suburb of San Diego, a far more elaborate restaurant-entertainment center for youngsters made its debut in California's Silicon Valley under the auspices of Nolan K. Bushnell, the developer of Atari electronic games. The video games produced by Atari and other manufacturers were the hottest entertainment innovations of the 1970s, but there were few widely acceptable public places where youngsters could play them. The new video game arcades quickly earned a reputation as bad as the old-time pool halls': they were accused of harboring children who should have been in school, of consuming young customers' money so fast that they spawned juvenile crime, and of generally constituting a nuisance. Bushnell saw the potential for a place where children under sixteen could play video games in a family atmosphere. But it would need more than video games, wouldn't it? How about some robot characters who would put on shows? And there would have to be food, not only for the children but for the parents who accompanied them. It should be food with a party-time feeling, food acceptable to all age groups—pizza.

Filling Station, Richmond Avenue, Houston; photo 1983.   *G. D. Ritzy's, Route 50, Orlando, Fla.; photo 1985.*

In 1977 the first Chuck E. Cheese's Pizza Time Theatre opened in a converted toy store in the Town & Country Shopping Center in San Jose, California, not far from Atari headquarters. By 1983 there were more than two hundred Pizza Time Theatres—usually occupying 10,000 to 20,000 square feet of space converted from other retail uses in a strip shopping center. The outside was marked by a bland mansard fascia, just noticeable enough to advertise Pizza Time's presence without causing community protests and consequent delays. Pizza Time Theatre wanted above all to avoid delay; the company was in a race to get its outlets operating in as many communities as possible before the arrival of its imitator, Showbiz Pizza.

The interior was divided into different areas, the game room painted a dark green and most of the other areas loud yellows and oranges. In the dining room, children and parents could look up from their tables to watch performances by automated characters like "The King," a guitar-playing lion who sang Elvis Presley numbers, and, of course, the restaurant's host, the genial eight-foot rat Chuck E. Cheese.

There was a danger that a restaurant theme, like any novelty, would attract crowds for a while and then lose its appeal. The more unusual the theme—the more it dominated the dining experience—the greater the risk that it would turn into a hindrance. Pizza Time Theatre, a chain with more than two hundred restaurants in 1983, went through bankruptcy proceedings in 1984, partly because its robotic characters and video games possessed less long-term drawing power than the company had anticipated. Victoria Station, another once-hot theme restaurant, fell into financial trouble by 1978, nine years after its start. Its menu, heavy on meat, had lost favor about the same time that its railroad theme had gone stale. What could a restauran-

The Café in Arlington, Texas, 1984, combining bulky old furnishings and an abundance of neon.

teur do with a collection of used boxcars and cabooses? These were not the sort of structures that allowed much flexibility for the future. Victoria Station managed to survive, but more in spite of than because of its railroad ambience.

From the owner's point of view, there was an advantage in using structures without such troublesome uniqueness. R. David Thomas considered himself shrewd to have put Wendy's restaurants in basic rectangular boxes. "We could change from a Gay '90s theme to a space-age theme almost overnight," he bragged.

Conversion of restaurants to new and fresher themes became a widespread practice. S & O's development of Juan & Only's and Orville Bean's Flying Machine was a response to the wearing out of Steak & Ale's original, heavy Old English theme. This was salvage work, and like most salvage operations, it carried no guarantee that it would succeed on a long-term basis. "When you're just in the business of extending a property's life," explained Michael Purvis, a vice-president of S & O, "the rule of thumb is that a theme will last two to three years. You've got to make your payout in a year and get your profit in the next one to two years." According to S & O's calculations, customers might go to a theme dinnerhouse like Orville Bean's about five times, exploring parts of the decor they hadn't noticed the first time, but unless the restaurant's menu was especially appealing or other attractions proved compelling, the customers then moved on.

The restaurant themes that lasted longest were those that complemented the food that was served. An elegant antebellum Southern theme or a down-home Southern theme could have staying power if it were combined with the appropriate Southern cooking. But few chain restaurants, regardless of whether they had an acknowledged theme, could afford to remain the same indefinitely. Most designers felt that if a restaurant didn't change, customers would tire of it and drift off to restaurants offering newer sensations. A major renovation should be undertaken every few years, many designers insisted. Not that the designers were entirely correct. Numerous local, individually operated restaurants have prospered for long periods without a change of decor, because the quality of their food or the attractiveness of their prices has won them a loyal following. Some chains, like White Castle, have also gone decades without substantially altering the character of their interiors. But such constancy has been the exception. As a practical matter, successful restaurants—especially in the fast-food and coffee-shop segment of the industry—have usually had to undertake a major refurbishing every few years just to overcome the wear and tear from serving thousands of people each week. The need for repair or replacement of seats, tables, carpet, and other materials has given designers plenty of opportunities to make changes in the restaurants' decorative schemes. Some designers recently have contended that there has to be a continuous introduction of at least small modifications, freshening the restaurant both to attract customers and to keep up the spirits of the staff.

The implication of this sort of thinking is that restaurants should shy away from anything permanent except for basic structure, and should get by with low-quality materials except where they would be noticed or would need repair before the first regularly scheduled renovation. Earl McKinney, a partner in Hamill & McKinney in Lexington, Kentucky, one of the most prolific designers of chain restaurants in the 1980s, noted that the industry strongly prefers rectangular buildings because they can be most easily adapted. Buildings with unusual shapes, such as the tall, sharply pitched "chalet-style" roofs adopted by the International House of Pancakes chain in the 1960s, are frowned upon because they can't be changed without difficulty. Hamill & McKinney occasionally has designed restaurants with curved corners, but the curves are achieved through prefabricated panels that can be removed. Awnings have sometimes been used to stylize the exterior, but they're never tied into the building's structure in a way that would prevent their being dismantled.

The transitory nature of chain restaurants is now built in from the start. Chock Full o'Nuts coffee shops in New York had customarily been built to last for the length of their twenty or twenty-five-year leases without substantial alterations. They used tough, high-quality materials—marble, bronze, terrazzo, stainless steel, and Carrara glass. At some Chock Full o'Nuts shops, the bottom frames of the plate-glass windows were buried in the sidewalk, concealing the screws and giving the façade a cleaner look; the construction techniques were premised on longevity. "I would never do that again," a Chock Full o'Nuts executive said in 1983. "I think a store should be given a new look every ten years. People want to see a new look."

In practice, such a revised way of treating design and construction has meant that people would not often see an *old* look. Little would be built to last, and the span of visible history in America's commercial districts would be foreshortened all the more. While restaurants historically have not been intended as monuments, surviving for generations, they do acquire emotional and cultural significance as time goes on. Early White Castles have recently been added to the National Register of Historic Places, and the oldest existing standard McDonald's with arches through the roof— the unit built in Downey, California, in 1953—has been nominated to the Register. Campaigns, often unsuccessful, have been waged for preservation of drive-ins and other once-common commercial structures. For many Americans, apparently, the structures of the everyday landscape hold considerable importance; imbued with memories and with the tastes and manners of an era, these buildings anchor people to a sense of time and place. The growing tendency to design buildings for ease of alteration removes a minor but noticeable element of stability from the commercial environment.

Chains, with a few exceptions such as White Castle, have generally been happy to see their old buildings remodeled or replaced. If impermanent materials have made it easier for established chains to drop outmoded fashions and respond to new trends—in essence, to make themselves permanently transitional—this has seemed an advantage for restauranteurs in the 1980s, a time of shifting esthetics. Why build for the long term when a company might end up being embarrassed by the continuing presence of its early restaurants? McDonald's constructed approximately five hundred buildings with arches through the roofs and red-and-white tile on the walls from 1953 to 1963, but by 1985 fewer than twenty of them survived intact, for the company was committed to molding the entire system to fit its current image. The problem was not only that the early buildings lacked the seating capacity and other amenities of the new outlets; it was that the persistence of yesteryear's image contradicted the basic business emphasis on the present and the future.

Yet despite the widespread emphasis on change, the most dramatically different designs rarely have been introduced by major chains. Big chains have preferred to change incrementally, so that there would be some consistency between units that were newly built and older units not yet due for major alteration. The most striking departures in the 1980s have been pioneered by independent restaurants and small chains, just as, in the 1950s, the flashiest styles were ushered in by upstarts like

McDonald's and Googie's and Denny's, not by established chains like White Castle and White Tower.

A number of new entrepreneurs and organizations, aiming for young adults, have created restaurants with the atmosphere of a neighborhood soda shop or a neighborhood bar-and-grill. G. D. Ritzy's, an "upscale" fast-food chain founded in Columbus, Ohio, in 1980 by Graydon D. Webb (whose initials were at least one source of the "G. D." in the restaurant's name), uses tabletops of silvery Formica with aluminum edges, like those still found in some small-town cafés, and light fixtures shaped into stepped concentric circles, inspired by the styling of the thirties and forties. The dining-room ceiling glows pink with reflected light, and in the window hangs a neon sign. Designed by Hamill & McKinney, G. D. Ritzy's is, like Wendy's, a simple rectangular structure, but with curving metal awnings over the windows and a curving roof over the vestibule for a quasi-streamlined character.

Hamill & McKinney also designed The Cafe, a restaurant in Arlington, Texas, that makes exuberant use of neon—intended for customers not old enough to have regarded neon as irretrievably ugly. Cool blue neon glows through glass blocks surrounding the streamlined, rounded windows. Snaking along upper portions of interior walls is a line of pink neon. A delicatessen area is furnished with hefty old objects—a white-enameled butcher case and soft-drink dispensers with ponderous rounded corners and with logos in raised lettering, bulbous and substantial.

An early- to mid-twentieth-century commercial flavor—neon signs, black-and-white tile floors, marble counters, and white glass hanging lamps—has been re-created in Dalts, a chain started in Indianapolis in 1980 by TGI Friday's. Ed Debevic's, a chain restaurant that made its initial appearances in Phoenix and Chicago in 1984, is fashioned as a nostalgic version of a fifties diner. The thirties, forties, and fifties have recently become prime territory for revivalist restaurant design aimed at people from eighteen to their mid-thirties.

Design with a residential character maintains a considerably broader appeal. In fact, residential feeling has always had an appreciative market among restauranteurs. A houselike character had been used in the thirties and forties by Toddle House and Hull-Dobbs Houses, two chains that eventually merged, and the resulting company, Memphis-based Dobbs Houses, continues to run restaurants with a houselike image, Steak 'n Egg Kitchens. New chains, too, have settled on a homey appearance, sometimes including a touch of nostalgia, as at Mrs. Winner's Chicken & Biscuits, a Nashville-based chain that introduced a restaurant wrapped in a Victorian-style bracketed veranda, with an ample dormer poking up from its gabled roof.

Bob Evans Restaurant, Brice Road, Columbus, Ohio, soon after opening in 1981.

In 1980 in Columbus, Ohio, Wendy's started a chain called Sisters Chicken &
Biscuits in honor of the sisters of Wendy Thomas who hadn't yet had restaurants
named for them. On the outside, Sisters is much like the Steamboat Gothic–style
restaurants that another Columbus chain, Bob Evans Farms, has been building since
1968, but on the inside, Sisters pushes the nostalgic dimension a step further. A main
dining area is in the center, with carpeting on the floor, chandeliers hanging from the
ceiling, and porch railing defining the perimeter. Beyond and surrounding the railing
is an additional dining area with what the company calls "front porch atmosphere"—
wooden floors, a sloping tongue-in-groove ceiling, and decorative woodwork trimming the windows. Here is yet another variant on nostalgic, homey atmosphere.

Still another approach to restaurant design has emerged in the 1980s: an attempt
to entertain customers while also counteracting renewed public skepticism over what
goes into the nation's food. In the 1970s and 1980s many people have become con-

cerned about chemicals used to prevent spoilage or make foods more attractive or flavorful. Recurrent debate has centered on cancer risks associated with additives. One way of responding to this more critical climate, if not to the specific complaints, is to put the ingredients and the food preparation in public view, a technique adopted in 1980 in San Antonio by a "gourmet [i.e., half-pound, cooked-to-order] hamburger" restaurant. Philip Romano christened his new restaurant "Fuddruckers," remaining vague about what the name was supposed to mean. At Fuddruckers, the first things customers see as they enter are crates of ketchup bottles, ice cream cones, and cheese sauce just inside the door. Bags of flour and sugar are stacked in the middle of the floor, and crates of lettuce, tomatoes, and onions stand next to the condiment display. Fuddruckers' oversized buns are baked in public view, and forequarters of beef hang in the butcher shop, visible through plate-glass windows. Customers can watch butchers deboning and grinding beef. Even visitors unimpressed by the quality of the ingredients have pronounced this sort of near-total exposure an entertaining exhibition, except for those who don't like seeing the blood of a butcher shop. The effectiveness of this approach is confirmed by the company's rapid acceptance. Five years after the first Fuddruckers opened, the company and its franchisees had built additional restaurants in fifteen other Texas communities and in twenty other states and Canada, and there were ambitious plans for further expansion.

In the 1980s, a growing number of people have expressed weariness with huge chains and with the sameness that chains have spread across the country. To a certain extent, Fuddruckers has capitalized on that reaction, offering a more personalized style of food preparation than fast-food places and a less middle-of-the-road decor; customers sit on old wooden chairs at wooden tables in a dining area illuminated almost entirely by the neon of beer signs on the walls. What Fuddruckers has done is give the fast-food idea a new twist—enlarge the portions, downplay the standardization of the food, and gear the decor to young adults who like a fashionably informal atmosphere, yet require the customer to go to the counter not once but twice, first to place an order, then to pick it up. Fuddruckers has carved out yet another niche in the chain-restaurant industry. It has been able to do so because the overall market has grown to immense proportions. Affluence has made it possible for tens of millions of people to go out to eat regularly; the continuing increase in women working outside the home has made it necessary for them to do so.

All this is a substantial change from conditions earlier in the century. In 1931 C. A. Patterson, founder of *American Restaurant* magazine, pointed out, in an editorial entitled "The Chained-Down Chains," that only 3,500 of the nation's 125,000 restaurants were chain-operated. He saw no likelihood that the situation would ever change. "The chain idea simply does not lend itself that readily to a successful application in our industry," Patterson declared. It was too difficult to achieve true chain-wide standardization, he said, and even if it was achieved, chain expansion would soon be limited by the fact that there are only so many people who like any one kind of restaurant. "Restaurants," he insisted, "must have individuality."

What Patterson couldn't foresee was that there would be such a flood of chains that people would be able to find a wide variety of food, service, and atmosphere simply by switching from one chain to another. And "the chain idea"—the notion that each of a company's outlets could achieve an essentially uniform level of quality—has turned out not to be farfetched at all. The chains' proficiency in delivering a predictable product in a consistent atmosphere has in fact made it hard for independent restaurants to compete. Each day, over 6 percent of the American people eat at McDonald's. Two-fifths of all the restaurant employees in the United States now work for chains. McDonald's, which was considered a large chain in 1960, when it had 228 restaurants, entered 1985 with more than 6,500 outlets in the United States and more than 8,000 worldwide; it has recently been adding a new outlet every seventeen hours. In 1985 Kentucky Fried Chicken had 4,500 U. S. restaurants, Pizza Hut 4,300, Burger King 3,500, Wendy's 3,300, and Hardee's 2,400. In all, more than 340 chains were supervising 60,000 fast-food restaurants in 1985, and substantial numbers existed outside the fast-food segment of the industry as well. Denny's, the leader among coffee shops and family restaurants, had 1,100 restaurants.

The profusion of so many chains, each with its own characteristics, satisfied people's needs for a safe, predictable place to eat all across the country. What the chains did not provide was a harmonious or distinctive character for the towns and cities where they did business. Despite the spread of design-review ordinances and despite a surge of interest in accentuating local and regional character, chains in the 1980s have in most instances continued to build their standard designs—with some interior-decor modifications and occasional exterior alterations—throughout the United States. Thousands of cities and towns thus look as if they were put together with interchangeable parts. When Fred Harvey pioneered the chain approach in the nineteenth century, the consistency he provided was a counterpoint to a strange and empty land; moreover, the predictability of a Harvey House lay in its atmosphere, food, and service, not in uniformity of architecture and decor. Today, by contrast, predictable design is the hallmark of most of the nation. A country of varied climate and terrain now looks much the same, in large part because chain restaurants have succeeded in deploying their standardized images from coast to coast.

FRONT E

RIGHT E

CHAPTER EIGHT
The Unsolved Problem

ON

ION

Overleaf: *Chi-Chi's Mexican restaurant prototype, designed by Hamill & McKinney, 1984.*

From the late nineteenth century to our own day, chain restaurants have been a diverse agglomeration. Some chains have served city-dwellers while others have gone after long-distance travelers. A few have aimed for an elevated sense of decorum while a great many more have concentrated on pushing food out fast and cheaply. In some instances, chains have allowed climate and regional architectural traditions to influence their choice of building materials and their relationship with the out-of-doors. Recently, municipal design-review requirements have brought about additional differentiation in chain-restaurant design.

Yet amid the diversity, a few common elements have emerged as keys to chain restaurants' character. One of these is an emphasis on economy and efficiency—in food preparation and delivery, in construction and design, in maintenance of the building and its grounds, and to a lesser extent in the ability to accommodate new layouts and new atmosphere when the original concept becomes obsolete. From the turn-of-the-century urban lunchrooms with their rows of one-armed chairs against the walls to today's fast-food outlets with their seats that induce squirming after a few minutes, lower-priced restaurants have repeatedly relied on design and furnishings to keep customer turnover high. At the same time, they have also tried to avoid any building and site features that would complicate the restaurants' operation—real wood that requires polishing, soft fabrics that get dirty and torn, landscaping that demands frequent attention. "KISS" was one of Ray Kroc's favorite mottoes—"Keep It Simple, Stupid"—and it sums up the still-prevailing attitude in chain restaurants: Concentrate on a few easily mastered techniques. Don't try to do too much. Reduce the level of complexity and the range of responsibilities so that the chain can achieve a uniform level of performance at the tasks that it does take on. This attitude, cherished as the guaranteed provider of a salable hamburger every time, sorely limits the potential for rich or subtle design.

The demand for economy and efficiency is closely tied to the need for consistency and predictability. Some chains have boasted about the varied decor and design of restaurants they've opened in recent years, but rarely are the interiors distinctive enough to generate a fundamentally different atmosphere. A truly divergent setting—one with an unusual level of comfort or a markedly different spirit—would inject uncertainty into the chain's image, and ambiguity of this sort is rarely tolerated by chains. Chain-restaurant design is a kind of quality-control operation; the range of variance is usually confined within narrow limits. Anything below standard threatens to undermine a chain's reputation, but too many designs significantly above the general level could also cause trouble, since they can raise the customers' expectations beyond what the rest of the chain's units are providing. Consistency is critical. On the exterior, predictability is considered almost essential for a somewhat different reason: the building's profile is used as an advertising tool, a corporate sign and symbol. Individualized building designs forfeit some of the wonted advertising advantages; they conflict with the goal of widespread instant recognition.

The drive for economy and efficiency runs up against and is held in check by a countervailing force. This force is, simply, the necessity of winning the public's patronage. In the upper price ranges, this limitation is so well understood as to require little elaboration; chains curb their pursuit of economy and efficiency when they decide to charge higher prices. Layouts, seating arrangements, atmosphere, and degree of comfort may all be altered, and chains will tolerate lower efficiency and slower turnover in return for a larger average check. In effect, the customer pays a surcharge for more pleasant or entertaining surroundings. What needs to be emphasized, however, is that even chains with low prices have to heed factors other than economy and efficiency. Popular preferences have always affected the character of restaurant design, fostering some developments in architecture and decor while dooming others to failure. In the early years of the twentieth century, lunchroom chains felt compelled to create sparkling white interiors because their customers required reassurance about cleanliness. Popular resistance killed the "automatic restaurants" of the 1960s, with their machine-vended foods, and popular preferences in a competitive economy have recently forced fast-food chains to adopt natural-looking materials, indoor plants, interior decoration, and at least a minimal amount of landscaping.

Clearly, popular preferences extend beyond matters of basic physical comfort and encompass popular taste as well. Throughout the twentieth century, restaurant imagery has shifted in tandem with popular taste. The "mansard" roofs of the 1960s and 1970s were a straightforward expression of the popular desire for a calmer, more

Cookie Express prototype, 1984. Individualistic architecture once more as the servant of commerce.

solidly grounded feeling in everyday surroundings. Little of the mansard look was borrowed from high-style architecture of that period; most "serious" architects had nothing but contempt for the windowless, fake mansard. This was a commercial designer's expedient, one that had neither structural honesty nor historical authenticity, but that did present a more soothing building profile, in tune with the popular desires of the time, and did it cheaply.

More often, "serious" architecture has provided ideas that restaurants have eventually appropriated. McDonald's parabolic arches came from shapes used by a significant number of modern architects and engineers beginning more than thirty years earlier. Similarly, the low-slung roof configurations adopted by Howard Johnson's after the Second World War had been used by Frank Lloyd Wright at the turn of the century. Still, popular taste, not the trends within the upper reaches of the architectural world, is the main determinant of chain-restaurant style. Avant-garde architects cannot generate new forms and expect that after an interval, chain restaurants will inevitably embrace what the form-givers have created. On the contrary, the chain-restaurant industry has typically adopted and done well with only those forms that struck a responsive chord with the public—and not everything created by serious architects has struck such a chord. The spare, boxy, rectilinear character of the International Style, for example, dominated hundreds of thousands of offices, schools, and other institutions erected in the 1950s, but it never meshed well with popular taste and so it was generally rejected by the restaurant industry in much the same way that it was dismissed by homebuilders, who similarly had to be sensitive to what the public wanted. Where the forms and spirit associated with a leading designer have made a major impact on chain restaurants, it has been primarily because the designer was working in a mode that had an intrinsically widespread appeal. Wright's Prairie Style, for instance, possessed a powerful sense both of shelter and of harmony with the land, and these strong attributes guaranteed that the Wrightian esthetic would eventually influence popular taste, not only in restaurant design but in the styling of vast numbers of postwar "ranch houses." Similarly, simple parabolic arches may have been handed down from leading European designers, but the main reason they took root on American commercial soil was that they embodied a buoyancy, optimistic futurism, and infatuation with technology that were shared by people at all levels of cultural sophistication. The propaganda orchestrated on behalf of such futuristic design undoubtedly helped make this style more familiar and thus more acceptable, but the underlying reason for the remarkable proliferation of such dynamic architecture was that it fit the spirit of an era of boundless advance, an era in which man was at last making himself master of the heavens as well as the earth. Any esthetic must resonate with a broadly shared mood if it is to prevail in the daily competition that characterizes the restaurant industry.

Finally, a significant influence on chain-restaurant design is also exerted by municipal regulation, particularly design-review ordinances. During the past twenty years, the rise of community review boards and other governmental supervision has generally discouraged the most extreme designs and prodded chains to adopt more subdued exteriors—toning down the colors, limiting the clash of forms, restricting the range of materials, and, as a consequence, dissuading chains from indulging in an especially blatant architecture. Many architects have expressed dislike for design review, portraying it as an obstacle to originality, but, on the whole, review processes have done much more to improve discordant or otherwise deficient buildings than to interfere with new buildings of genuine quality.

These social and institutional forces being what they are, why then do chain restaurants remain such a chaotic class of buildings? One reason, certainly, is the architects' customary willingness, for the sake of economic success, to put their clients' demands above the public's desire for a more satisfying environment. Architecture as an occupation attracts an above-average number of idealists, hopeful about changing the world for the better. But designers don't get far before they find themselves, out of the necessity of earning a living, engaged in producing buildings that serve their clients' needs but fail to bring coherence to the larger environment. Indeed, the inability of architects to create harmony in the man-made environment is one reason why design review has flourished in recent years. Some of the more candid architects within the restaurant industry, such as Larry Ray, a longtime designer for Denny's and other chains, frankly credit municipal design standards for much of the advance that has taken place.

In addition, the architectural profession, perhaps in part as a reflection of its servitude to competitive enterprise, continues to cling to individuality and originality at the expense of community concerns. In the 1980s, the architectural press has been full of talk about contextualism, and many architects have apparently persuaded themselves that designers are now honoring the character of the areas in which they propose new buildings. Yet, in fact, the profession's affinity for brashly self-centered designs is far from extinguished. The process by which architects win awards and gain publication in the professional journals is still weighted toward novelty.

One example from the awards given by *Progressive Architecture* in 1985 will suffice: a coveted design citation was bestowed on a prototype for Cookie Express—a tiny combination bakery and retail outlet to be erected on the parking lots of strip shopping centers. The prototype was a showy assemblage of shiny parallelograms, triangles, and grids, out the top of which popped a giant, reddish-purple circle. Jurors for *P/A*'s awards evidently were impressed by the prototype's use of techniques that had been explored in Constructivism, an early form of modernism that appeared in Russia in the late teens and early twenties. But why? Even if the shapes and proportions and their relationships to one another were exquisite, these geometric forms have nothing in common with the sites on which the owner of Cookie Express has made it clear that he intends to place them. What the design is geared to do is differ from everything in sight, thus forcing everyone, especially motorists, to notice the building. Indeed, Cookie Express's architect, Hodgetts & Fung Design Associates of Los Angeles, told the jurors, in a revealing choice of words, that this was a "billboard-sized" building heavily influenced by the owner's "desire for visibility." Jurors apparently ignored the fact that the initial locations for the design

An American strip: Charleston Boulevard in Las Vegas, Nevada, about 1975.

were to be in a region—California's Orange County—where many communities for the past twenty years have made a concerted effort to produce a consistent appearance in roadside commercial development and have achieved considerable success.

It seems indisputable that the Cookie Express prototype—if built to a standard design on widely scattered sites, as its architects proposed, without intervention by municipalities—could set off a visual free-for-all as undisciplined as anything seen in the 1950s. It is disturbing to see how little the architectural profession's vision, as exemplified by its publications and awards presentations, has matured since the 1950s.

Architects nonetheless bear only part of the responsibility for the garishness and contentiousness of much of America's commercial surroundings. The disjointedness has more basic causes: the profusion of building materials and construction technologies, the proliferation of cars and trucks, the ceaseless travel and migration throughout the country and the competitive nature of the economy. And the unavoidable fact remains that a popular insistence on economy and convenience often makes it difficult for ordinary commercial buildings like chain restaurants to reflect any more elevated notion of what America's cities, suburbs, and towns could be.

It's clear that chain restaurants have thoroughly mastered the practicalities of design and organization. The question is whether, having dealt successfully with the nuts-and-bolts issues of economy, efficiency, consistency, and convenience, these ubiquitous restaurants can accomplish something greater. There have been times in the past when competing private economic interests came together in the creation of business districts that were both convenient and emotionally satisfying, both varied and coherent. And there are places today where chain enterprises have been integrated into harmonious community design. The issue is whether restaurant chains, now that they have become, in effect, some of America's most influential urban and suburban designers, can be roused to enhance everyday surroundings not only for a few affluent locales but for much of the nation. In the end, it comes down to whether the public is willing to invest a substantial effort in prodding, inspiring, and sometimes forcing restaurant chains to take their social responsibilities seriously. As of now, the most encouraging thing that can be said is that the evolution of chain-restaurant design has not yet reached its conclusion.

NOTES

The information in this book came mainly from two kinds of sources. One was architectural, restaurant, business, and general-interest periodicals, the most important of which are cited in the notes; the other was hundreds of personal and telephone interviews and correspondence that I conducted from 1982 through 1985 with founders, executives, designers, and others associated with chain restaurants. With a few exceptions, this second category of sources is not presented in the notes, since the letters and interviews are not publicly accessible. Among the most significant interviews and correspondence were those with Arthur C. Bender, Harold J. Betzger, Curtis L. Blake, Robert F. Byrnes, Donald Clinton, Keith G. Cramer, Eldon C. Davis, David R. Edgerton Jr., Charles Fish, John Galardi, Paul R. Gershen, Abraham J. Goldberg, Alvin Golin, Tony Grate, James M. Hamill, Robert Hornacek, Carroll Johnson, Jules Kabat, Jack Larson, John Lautner, Leo S. Maranz, Richard J. McDonald, Earl F. McKinney, James W. McLamore, Stanley C. Meston, Jack Meyer, Donald E. Miller, Victor M. Newlove, Rufus Nims, Raymond M. Poelvoorde, Michael F. Purvis, Leroy Raffel, Larry A. Ray, Hank Sherowski, Thomas Wells, and Robert E. Wildman.

ABBREVIATIONS OF PERIODICALS

Am Rest	American Restaurant	FF	Fast Food*
A+A	Arts + Architecture	Fntn Svce	Fountain Service*
Arch Forum	Architectural Forum	FSFR	Fast Service/Family Restaurants
Arch Rec	Architectural Record	H&H	House & Home
AIAJ	American Institute of Architects	ICTJ	Ice Cream Trade Journal
	Journal	NRN	Nation's Restaurant News
Bsns Wk	Business Week	P/A	Progressive Architecture
Chn St	Chain Store Age	Rest Bsns	Restaurant Business*
D&CO	Drive-in & Carryout	Rest Mgt	Restaurant Management
D Rest	Drive-in Restaurant	Sat Eve Post	Saturday Evening Post
DRHC	Drive-in Restaurant & Highway	Soda Fntn	Soda Fountain*
	Cafe	Soda Fntn Svce	Soda Fountain Service*
F&FF	Fountain & Fast Food*		

*These are all names for the same journal at different periods of its existence. *Restaurant Business* is the current name.

CHAPTER ONE: Origins of the Chain-Restaurant Industry

5   *Frederick Henry Harvey:* Architectural information on Harvey Houses is primarily from David Gebhard, "Architecture and the Fred Harvey Houses," *New Mexico Architect*, Jan.–Feb. 1964, pp. 18–25, and July–Aug 1962, pp. 12–17; Virginia L. Grattan, *Mary Colter: Builder upon the Red Earth* (Flagstaff, Ariz.: Northland Press, 1980); James J. Henderson, "*Meals by Fred Harvey*": A Phenomenon of the American West (Fort Worth: Texas Christian Univ. Press, 1969); and photos in Prints and Photographs Collection, Library of Congress, Washington, D.C., and Fred Harvey Collection, Univ. of Arizona Library, Tucson. Additional historical information is from Clifford Funkhouser and Lyman Anson, "Cupid Rides the Rails," *American Mercury*, Sept. 1940, pp. 42–46; Jim Marshall, "The Return of Miss Harvey," *Collier's*, Nov. 17, 1945, pp. 20ff; and series on Harvey by Lowell Parker in *Arizona Republic*, Sept. 13–15, 1976.

9   *horse-drawn cart:* Richard J. S. Gutman and Elliott Kaufman in collaboration with David Slovic, *American Diner* (New York: Harper & Row, 1979), pp. 1–10.

   "*diners*": Ibid., pp. 12–15, and *Diner & Counter Restaurant*, Aug. 1950, p. 22.

   ice cream soda: J. A. Silander, "The Soda Fountain Story," *ICTJ*, June 1951, pp. 30ff; "The Fountain's Role in Ice Cream Progress," *ICTJ*, June 1955, pp. 164ff; and "Veteran of Half a Century Reviews Progress of Soda Fountain Industry," *Soda Fntn*, May 1907, p. 33.

   75,000 . . . 3,500: "Fountain's Role," p. 225; and *Soda Fntn*, July 1908, pp. 34–35.

   "*luncheonette*": "The Luncheonette a Recognized Institution," *Soda Fntn*, Aug. 1912, p. 32; and *Soda Fntn*, Nov. Nov. 1911, p. 34.

10   *Ueata Lunch:* "Feeding Fifteen Thousand Detroiters Daily," *Am Rest*, Oct. 1925, pp. 98–99.

   John R. Thompson: "John R. Thompson, 'One-Arm Lunch' Magnate, Is Dead," *Am Rest*, July 1927, p. 48.

   Baltimore Dairy Lunch: "Then and Now—In the Lunch Business" (J. A. Whitcomb interviewed by C. A. Patterson), *Am Rest*, Aug. 1921, pp. 26–28.

   Childs Unique Dairy Lunch: "William Childs," *World's Work*, April 1928, pp. 530–35; and "Childs Steps Out—and Up," *Rest Mgt*, Mar. 1937, pp. 189–91.

   Waldorf Lunch: Percy E. Woodward, "We Accomplish by 'Pushing On,'" *Am Rest*, Oct. 1921, pp. 29–32.

   size of Thompson's, Childs, Waldorf: Rest Mgt, May 1930, p. 317.

10–11   *lunchroom interiors:* "Unjust Competition," *Am Rest*, Oct. 1925, p. 122; A. E. Merrill, "The Cafeteria," *Am Rest*, April 1922, pp. 26–29; Childs Steps Out," p. 189; "Automatic Cashier Saves Labor," *Soda Fntn*, Dec. 1907, p. 46; and ad, *Soda Fntn*, July 1908, p. 37.

12   *low stools:* John Walker Harrington, "The First Popular-price High-class Lunch Room," *Rest Mgt*, Nov. 1934, pp. 281–82; and ad, *Soda Fntn*, Jan. 1911, p. D.

   connected horseshoes: Lee G. Johnson, "Does Soda Fountain–Coffee Shop Provide an Answer to the All-Important Service Problem?" *Am Rest*, Aug. 1931, pp. 52–53.

13   *advantages:* Reasons for cafeterias' popularity are enumerated in Merrill, "The Cafeteria," *Am Rest*, April 1922, pp. 26–28.

   first cafeterias: "The Origin of the Cafeteria—the Institution," *Journal of Home Economics*, July 1925, pp. 390–93; William Francis Ireland, "Where the Cafeteria Was Born," *Am Rest*, May 1920, pp. 15–19; and William Francis Ireland, "King of Cafeterias," *Am Rest*, Oct. 1922, pp. 48–49.

   Forum, Bishop's, S&W, Morrison's: H. C. Siekman, "Forum's Newest Cafeteria," *Am Rest*, April 1939, pp. 22ff; Brad Church, "Bishop Buffets Had a Modest Beginning," Waterloo (Iowa) *Courier*, Nov. 27, 1980, p. 24; Frank Hann, "Washington's New S&W Cafeteria Sets Pace for Restaurant Industry," *Rest Mgt*, Feb. 1935, pp. 68ff; and *Rest Bsns*, May 1976, pp. 100–02.

14   *public taste:* Daniel J. Boorstin, *The Americans: The Democratic Experience* (New York: Random House, 1973), p. 327.

   "*There's more profit*": Dev Thatcher, "There's More Profit If You Can Get Them to Stand Up," *National Restaurant News and Management*, Sept. 1925, pp. 1–9.

   Linton Lunch: "'Order Boards' Summon Food and Conveyor Belts Fetch It, at Linton's," *Rest Mgt*, July 1931, pp. 16–20.

15   "*eat-as-you-go*": "An Eat-as-you-go Lunch Room," *Literary Digest*, Dec. 24, 1921, pp. 21–22.

   Merry-Go-Round: Ima Wurl, "Merry-Go-Round Restaurants," *Pacific Coast Record*, Sept. 1931, pp. 12–13; *Rest Mgt*, Nov. 1930, p. 342; and *Rest Mgt*, Aug. 1931, pp. 80–83.

page
16   *first Automat:* Jack Alexander, "The Restaurants That Nickels Built," *Sat Eve Post*, Dec. 11, 1954, p. 100.
     Evening Bulletin: "Automat Lunch Room Opens Next Monday," *The Evening Bulletin*, June 7, 1902, p. 12.

18   *"Autometer":* "A Restaurant with Mechanical Brains," *Am Rest*, May 1924, pp. 54–56.
     how disease was transmitted: J. C. Furnas, *The Americans: A Social History of the United States, 1587–1914* (New York: G. P. Putnam's Sons, 1969), p. 908.

19   *new materials:* E. A. Turner, "The Growing Popularity of Monel Metal," *Am Rest*, Aug. 1922, pp. 48 and 59; and "Manufacture and Uses of Monel," *Am Rest*, Oct. 1926, pp. 118–20.
     white, sanitary look: William Childs, "Effective Decoration in the Restaurant," *Am Rest*, Dec. 1922, p. 32; and "Childs Steps Out," p. 190.
     "Sani-onyx": ad, *Soda Fntn*, Oct. 1917, p. 2.
     "Better than marble": ad, *Soda Fntn*, Jan. 1918, p. 13.
     "sanitary lunch chair": ad, *Am Rest*, Jan. 1920, p. 40.
     floors: "What Linoleum Is and How to Use It," *Am Rest*, April 1924, p. 70; and "Composition Flooring Settles This Question to Perfection," *Am Rest*, Dec. 1925, pp. 52 and 76.

19–20   *quality of their air:* Robert C. Nason, "Overcoming Common Faults in Ventilation," *National Restaurant News and Management*, May 1926, pp. 24–27; and Kenneth C. Lovgren, "Air-Conditioned Restaurants Multiply Summer Profits," *Am Rest*, May 1934, pp. 32–34.

20   *"a fresh tradition":* Lewis Mumford, "Machinery and the Modern Style," *New Republic*, Aug. 3, 1921, p. 264.
     Childs: "Childs Steps Out," pp. 189–90.

21   *flashing electric signs:* ad, *Soda Fntn*, Feb. 1907, p. 55.
     "far and near": ad, *Am Rest*, May 1925, p. 103.
     "sanitary": ad, *Am Rest*, June 1920, p. 68.
     expanses of plate glass: Ray Underwood, "Put the Soda Fountain Where It Sells," *Fntn Svce*, May 1945, pp. 16–17.

21–2   *Cleveland Forum:* H. C. Nulmoor, "The Forums Do It Again," *Am Rest*, Aug. 1931, pp. 48ff.

23   *Chicago Forum:* Siekman, pp. 22ff.

24   *"soft materials":* Childs, "Effective Decoration," p. 32.
     away from modern materials: Nels H. Seaburg, "In Old France," *Rest Mgt*, June 1928, pp. 312–14; and T. F. Marshall, "'Old London'—William Childs' Newest Restaurant," *Am Rest*, Dec. 1931, pp. 30–31.

24–5   *Clifton's:* "*Life* Visits Clifton's Cafeteria," *Life*, Nov. 27, 1944, pp. 102–05; and company brochure, "Views of Clifton's," Dec. 1956.

CHAPTER TWO: Standardizing the Image

29–30   *"White Castle":* Most White Castle information is drawn from E. W. Ingram, Sr., "All This from a 5-cent Hamburger!" (New York: Newcomen Society in North America, 1975); "How an Idea Built on Nickels Does Business in the Millions," *Rest Mgt*, Aug. 1935, pp. 81–86; and Maurice F. Benfer, "They Make the 12 'White Castle' Cities in an Airplane," *Rest Mgt*, Sept. 1929, pp. 172–73.

30   *grew fast:* Untitled 1931 White Castle brochure.
     "When you sit": Untitled 1932 White Castle brochure.

33   *movable building:* W. Ray Luce, "White Castle and Preservation," *SCA* (Society for Commercial Archeology) *News Journal*, Sept. 1984, pp. 4–6.

34   *White Tower:* White Tower information, except where noted otherwise, is from Paul Hirshorn and Steven Izenour, *White Towers* (Cambridge, Mass.: MIT Press, 1979).

34–5   *Little Tavern:* Lynne Heneson and Larry Kanter, "Little Taverns: Renovating a Commercial Landmark," *Trans-Lux* (Art Deco Society of Washington, D.C.), Feb. 1983, pp. 1ff.

35   *White Tavern:* The White Tavern chain evolved into Jerrico, Inc., operator of Jerry's Drive-ins and Long John Silver's Seafood Shoppes.
     Toddle House: ad, *Am Rest*, Sept. 1949, pp. 56–57.
     Krystal: Krystal information is from "Rekrystalized," *FSFR*, March 1982, as reprinted by Krystal Co.
     White Hut: "Streamlined for Fast Service," *Am Rest*, Feb. 1956, p. 120.

page   35   *Rockybilt:* "Sales and Sanitation Go Hand in Hand," *Am Rest*, Oct. 1955, pp. 62–63.
            Royal Castle: FF, Sept. 1966, pp. 76–81.
        36   *"It's toddling":* Unpublished interview with Jack Larson by Constance Rossum and Paul McAbee for Dobbs Houses, Inc., Memphis, Sept. 25, 1979.
        38   *Saxe, Saxe, and O'Connell:* Deposition of Daniel J. O'Connell in *White Castle System of Eating Houses Corp.* v. *White Tower System, Inc.*, John E. Saxe and Thomas E. Saxe, District Court, 2nd Judicial District, Minn., 1930, pp. 3–15.

            specifications and plans: Decision 7133 of U.S. Circuit Court of Appeals, 6th District, Cincinnati, May 4, 1937, in *White Tower System, Inc.* v. *White Castle System of Eating Houses Corp.*, as published in E. W. (Billy) Ingram, "High Court Sustains White Castle," White Castle house organ, May–June 1937, pp. 3–4; and O'Connell deposition, pp. 22–28.
        40   *Harry F. Duncan:* "Glorifying the Daily Hamburger," *American Enameler*, Oct. 1931, pp. 3–4; and Heneson and Kanter, "Little Taverns," pp. 1, 3, and 4.
        41   *Legal proceedings disclosed:* Ingram, "High Court Sustains," pp. 3–4; and O'Connell deposition, pp. 34–42.
            Minnesota court: decision of District Court Judge Charles Boechhoefer, 2nd Judicial District, Ramsey County, Minn., July 7, 1930.
            Court of Appeals: Ingram, "High Court Sustains," pp. 3–4.
            increasingly diverged: Hirshorn and Izenour, pp. 9–14 and 60–119.
        43   *Brown Derby:* Margaret Ettinger, "What's in a Name?" *Pacific Coast Record*, June 1933, pp. 8–9.
      43–4   *Chili Bowl:* unpublished manuscript on Arthur Whizin by Jim Heimann.
        45   *Coon Chicken Inns:* "How a Feature Specialty Built a Business During the Depression," *Rest Mgt*, Aug. 1934, p. 76.
            automobile tourism: Warren J. Belasco, "Toward a Culinary Common Denominator: The Rise of Howard Johnson's, 1925–1940," *Journal of American Culture*, Fall 1979, pp. 508–12; and Warren James Belasco, *Americans on the Road: From Autocamp to Motel, 1910–1945* (Cambridge, Mass.: MIT Press, 1979), pp. 7–103.
            "O'Mahony Dining Cars": ad, *Am Rest*, April 1929, p. 36.
            "B/G Eating Inn": "B/G Invades Highways," *Rest Mgt*, July 1931, p. 31.
        46   *Howard Deering Johnson:* Major sources of information on Howard Johnson's include: Jesse Rainsford Sprague, "He Had an Idea," *Sat Eve Post*, Nov. 2, 1940, pp. 34ff; Gordon Gaskill, "That Wild Johnson Boy," *American*, Mar. 1941, pp. 34ff; Jack Alexander, "Host of the Highways," *Sat Eve Post*, July 19, 1958, pp. 16ff; "The Howard Johnson Restaurants," *Fortune*, Sept. 1940, pp. 83ff; and *Landmark* (Howard Johnson's publication), Vol. 14, Nos. 3–4, 1975.
        49   *HoJo's innate dignity:* For an irreverent analysis of HoJo's image and atmosphere, see "Howard Johnson's: Elevating the Host," in Stephen A. Kurtz, *Wasteland: Building the American Dream* (New York: Praeger, 1973), pp. 19–25.
        50   *accused Johnson of copying:* Question of whether HoJo's infringed on Dutchland Farms' designs "was once discussed in lawyers' letters," according to *Fortune*, pp. 83–84.
      50–1   *Friendly Ice Cream:* "Modernizing Tripled Friendly's Volume," *Fntn Svce*, Oct. 1946, pp. 18–19.
        52   *"end up with a barn":* Carroll Johnson, VP of engineering and construction, interview Jan. 17, 1983.
            kept the company alive: "Off the Highways," *Bsns Wk*, June 19, 1943, pp. 60, 65.
        53   *"no more roadside cathedrals":* "On the Road Again," *Bsns Wk*, Aug. 25, 1945, pp. 52 and 54.
            "eighty-nine different . . . styles": Harold J. Betzger, director of design and architecture, interview, Feb. 15, 1984.
        54   *architectural press . . . restaurant journal:* "Howard Johnson Redesigns," *Arch Forum*, March 1955, pp. 162–65; and "Serving 300 Million Customers a Year," *Am Rest*, June 1958, pp. 58–59.

CHAPTER THREE: The Rise and Demise of the Drive-in

        59   *Pig Stand:* "How Pig Stands Started the Drive-in Restaurant," *Drive-in Management*, Sept. 1961, p. 23.
        60   *"A & W":* "Roy W. Allen, Drive-in Pioneer, Dies at 85," *D Rest*, May 1968, p. 58; and undated A&W International, Inc., fact sheets.

<table>
<tbody>
<tr><td>page</td><td>61</td><td>*"Hot Shoppe"*: Robert O'Brien, *Marriott: The J. Willard Marriott Story* (Salt Lake City: Deseret Book Co., 1977), pp. 111–14 and 127–42.</td></tr>
</tbody>
</table>

61   *"Hot Shoppe"*: Robert O'Brien, *Marriott: The J. Willard Marriott Story* (Salt Lake City: Deseret Book Co., 1977), pp. 111–14 and 127–42.
Marriott and Howard Johnson: Greer Williams, "Good Mormons Don't Go Broke," *Sat Eve Post*, June 10, 1950, p. 160.

62   *Carpenter's:* "Los Angeles Lowdown," *Diner*, Sept. 1946, pp. 8–9.
Pig 'n Whistle: Zoe Wolcott, "A Chain Restaurant Tackles the Problem of Service," *Rest Mgt*, April 1930, p. 232.
"EAT": "Circular Drive-in Includes Commissary," *Arch Rec*, Sept. 1946, p. 101.

64   *"carhops":* Jim Heimann, "Drive-up Deluxe," *California*, May 1983, p. 106.

64–5   *"Houston's Drive-in":* *Life*, Feb. 26, 1940, pp. 84–87.
"do's" and "don'ts": For examples, see John B. O'Meara, "Do's and Don'ts for Better Drive-in Service," *Am Rest*, July 1957, pp. 82–85.

66   *Tiny Naylor's:* Alan Hess, "Coffee Shops," *A+A*, Vol. 2, No. 2, 1983, pp. 44 and 48.
Pietro Belluschi: "Drive-in Restaurant near Jantzen Beach, Oregon," *P/A*, June 1947, pp. 61–63.

67   *Steak n Shake:* "2 'Catchy' Items . . . 33 Busy Drive-Ins," *Am Rest*, July 1958, p. 51; and "1,800 Meals Is Daily Average at Steak n Shake, St. Louis, Mo.," *F&FF*, Sept. 1953, p. 50.
Robert C. Wian Jr.: "Robert C. Wian Jr.," *Am Rest*, June 1952, p. 148; and *Rest Bsns*, May 1976, p. 124.
A & W . . . tripled: *Drive-in*, June 1957, p. 9.

68   *J. F. McCullough:* *Rest Bsns*, May 1976, pp. 124 and 126.
Dairy Queen growth: "The 'Dairy Queen' Heritage," company publication, 1976, p. 9.

68–9   *Tastee-Freez:* "2,500,000 gals. of mix for soft-serve products sold by Tastee-Freez in 1952," *ICTJ*, July 1953, pp. 38 and 79.

69   *Richardson:* ad, *Fntn Svce*, May 1948, p. 3.
Frostop: David Markstein, "The Frostop Story," *F&FF*, Sept. 1956, pp. 56 and 58; and *Drive-in*, June 1957, pp. 9–10.
Carvel: "The Carvel Story," *ICTJ*, March 1954, pp. 26 and 28.

72   *provided shade:* John Selby, "Prefab Canopies," *Drive-in*, April 1958, p. 16.
air-conditioning: *F&FF*, July 1955, pp. 30–31.
"Driv-O-Matic": "Drive-in Service Goes Automatic," *Am Rest*, Sept. 1953, p. 89.
electronic ordering systems: Several are described in *Drive-in*, April 1957, pp. 5–14; and *DRHC*, Nov. 1955, pp. 12–17.
Frisch's: *Am Rest*, June 1955, p. 116.

73   *Dog 'n Suds:* See tentative early butterfly roof in "Dog 'n Suds," *Am Rest*, June 1958, p. 63.
increasingly stylized products: "Visual Attraction of Canopy Can Draw More Customers," *Drive-in*, April 1959, p. 34; and these ads in *D Rest*: Nov.–Dec. 1961, p. 24, Oct. 1963, p. 12, Feb. 1964, pp. 30–32, and Nov.–Dec. 1962, p. 36.

74   *social disorder:* Among many reports in *D Rest* is "The Detroit Study of Drive-in Problems," Aug. 1964, p. 12.
serious problems: William R. Brown, "The 'Teen' Problem," *D&CO*, Aug. 1970, pp. 27–30, and Sept. 1970, pp. 28–29.

75   *municipal ordinances:* Municipal reaction grew so widespread that from June 1965 to Oct. 1967, *D Rest* published a monthly "Ordinance Roundup."
automatic gates: Gordon Hunt, "'Call the Mayor, They're Cruising Again!'" *D Rest*, Nov. 1965, pp. 18–22.

75–6   *harsh appearance:* James Snyder, "Roadside Beauty and YOU," *D Rest*, Nov. 1965, pp. 24–26.

76   *"landscaping can help":* Jim Snyder, *D Rest*, Feb. 1966, p. 50.
Kim's: Jim Kimbell, "How Kim's Design Discourages Litterbugs," *D Rest*, Nov. 1965, pp. 27–29.

77   *look of cedar shakes:* ad, *D Rest*, Nov. 1965, p. 17.
coffee shops: "Big Boom Out West: Coffee Shops," *FF*, Nov. 1961, pp. 44–48.
turnover: Frank B. Thomas, "Parking Comments," *D Rest*, March 1963, p. 21.
rapidly declined: "Goodbye, Carhops," *FF*, Nov. 1963, pp. 18–21.
the Sivils: *D Rest*, June 1967, p. 12.
Sonic's profits fell: "City-based Sonic Food Chain Forms New Strategy for '80s," undated Sonic press release.
eating indoors: Bill Marvel, "Savoring the Classics' Sizzle," Dallas *Times-Herald*, Aug. 26, 1984, pp. 1E and 8E.

CHAPTER FOUR: Handlebars, Boomerangs, and Arches That Flash in the Night

page

81 *unglamourous jobs:* Murray Suid and Ron Harris, *Made in America: Eight Great All-American Creations* (Reading, Mass.: Addison-Wesley Pub., 1978), p. 158.

81–2 *1940 and 1947 wages:* "Restaurants: 1940 Style," *Bsns Wk*, Oct. 19, 1940, p. 29; and "Restaurant Blues," *Bsns Wk*, April 5, 1947, p. 30.

82 *Primex: Am Rest*, May 1952, pp. 122–23.
magazine's cover: "One Million Hamburgers and 160 Tons of French Fries a Year," *Am Rest*, pp. 44–45.

83 *September 1952: Am Rest*, p. 27.

84 *Stanley C. Meston:* Alan Hess, "Golden Architecture," *Journal: A Contemporary Art Magazine*, Spring 1983, pp. 28–29.

85 *"Gay colors":* "Eye-Catcher for Narrow Frontage," *Arch Rec*, Oct. 1954, p. 167.
Saarinen's arch: Allan Temko, *Eero Saarinen* (New York: George Braziller, 1962), pp. 18–19.
expression . . . of the twentieth century: The symbolism of the parabola is discussed in Jeffrey L. Meikle, *Twentieth Century Limited* (Philadelphia: Temple U. Press, 1979), pp. 182–83.
farm of the future: Norman Bel Geddes, *Magic Motorways* (New York: Random House, 1940), p. 268.

88 *neon . . . vulgarity:* "Atmosphere for Dining Out," *Arch Forum*, July 1957, p. 153.
"rainbow-shaped": "Hamburger Specialists," *Am Rest*, June 1958, p. 62.
"round hamburger face": "Big Business with Small Menu," *Am Rest*, July 1955, p. 89.

89 *visited by . . . Kroc:* Ray Kroc, *Grinding It Out* (Chicago: Henry Regnery Co., 1977), pp. 6–8.

90 *Des Plaines, Illinois:* "Big Business," pp. 86 and 89. Both this article and various building permits indicate construction of standardized building in San Bernardino in 1955.
gradually rounded profile: "Golden Architecture," p. 30.
Hardee's: "Kitchen Layout and Equipment Design Give Fast Service at Hardee's," *D Rest*, Aug. 1962, pp. 10–11.
Bresler brothers: "Thirty-five Bresler Drive-ins Planned," *DRHC*, April 1956, p. 25.
Henry's Hamburgers: Am Rest, Jan. 1958, p. 51; and ad, *Rest Mgt*, April 1960, p. 21.

91–2 *Burger Chef:* "How Burger Chef Speeds Service," *FF*, Jan. 1959, pp. 33–34.

92 *"the sun and the stars":* Carl F. Zeigler, "Concrete," *Pencil Points*, Jan. 1943, pp. 43–44.
Dunkin' Donuts: FF, May 1964, p. 130.

93 *Mister Donut:* Ibid., p. 146; and Daniel J. Boorstin, *The Americans: The Democratic Experience* (New York: Random House, 1973), p. 431.
"post-war fountain": Roy H. Crane, "How Will the Post-war Fountain Change," *Soda Fntn Svce*, June 1944, p. 15.

94 *first Burger King:* "41 in Florida," *DRHC*, June 1955, pp. 19ff; and "The Insta-Burger-King Success Story," *F&FF*, April 1956, pp. 104ff.

95 *"more than any sign!":* "Desert Motel," *P/A*, Sept. 1957, p. 114.
New Jersey factory: ad, *Am Rest*, March 1962, p. 70.
Stop 'n Treat: Am Rest, Sept. 15, 1960, p. 8.

96 *Wigwam Wieners: FF*, Feb. 1964, p. 17.
Griff's Burger Bar: Am Rest, Nov. 1961, p. 14.
Dari-Delite: FF, Jan. 1964, p. 80.
Whataburger banner: "All That Glitters Is Not . . . Diamonds," *FF*, April 1957, p. 54.

97 *"done more damage":* Russell Kirk, "The Uninteresting Future," *AIAJ*, Jan. 1961, p. 29.
"arbitrary forms": Catherine Bauer Wurster, "Architecture and the Cityscape," *AIAJ*, March 1961, p. 38.
descended into chaos: "Jury Discussion" and "Announcement," *P/A*, Jan. 1961, pp. 154–56.

98 *Red Barn . . . loft: Chn St*, Sept. 1964, p. 103.

99 *Pete Harman:* Kentucky Fried Chicken "50th Anniversary" publication.
Pizza Hut: "The Fast Food Entrepreneur: Four Stories of Success," *Fast Service*, Apr. 1979, pp. 24–26.

100 *"perfect building":* All That Glitters," p. 56.

102 *Speed was a necessity:* Burger King required the customer to pay when ordering, making him "very, very nervous," recalled James McLamore in an interview, May 23, 1983. "And so I'd say to Dave [Edgerton] and the crew that we've got to have the food so fast that by the time we give him his change, he's got his food."

page

103   *Insta broiler: Am Rest*, July 1955, p. 90.

        not to hire girls: "McDonald's Makes Franchising Sizzle," *Bsns Wk*, June 15, 1968, p. 102.

104   *"automatic restaurants":* "Drive-in Vending Comes of Age," *D Rest*, Sept. 1961, pp. 9 and 14; and "White Tower Opens First Automatic Restaurant," *Am Rest*, Jan. 1962, p. 5.

        failure: Walter W. Reed, "Are Vending Restaurants a Bed of Roses?" *D Rest*, June 1963, p. 22.

107   *prohibited . . . services:* "Appealing to a Mass Market," *Nation's Business*, July 1968, p. 74.

108   *downtown Washington: D Rest*, Feb. 1965, p. 34.

        Gino's: Chn St, July 1966, p. 34; and "From Gridiron to Griddle," *D Rest*, Oct. 1961, p. 9.

        Red Barn: Chn St, July 1966, p. 35.

109   *"marathon sit-downs":* Ibid., p. 34.

CHAPTER FIVE: "Googie": The California Coffee Shop

113   *John Lautner:* Esther McCoy, "West Coast Architects V: John Lautner," *A + A*, Aug. 1965, pp. 22–27; and "John Lautner's Houses," *H&H*, Feb. 1952, p. 86.

114   *"Googie Architecture": H&H*, Feb. 1952, pp. 86–88.

115   *Coffee Dan's . . . Henry's Drive-in:* Alan Hess, "Coffee Shops," *A + A*, Vol. 2, No. 2, 1983, pp. 46–48; and Alan Hess, "Always Open," *Los Angeles Herald California Living*, Oct. 23, 1983, p. 8.

        Armet & Davis: Much of this chapter's information about Armet & Davis designs is drawn from "Spectacular Designs Help Increase Restaurant Business" (March 1958 issue of unidentified magazine in Armet & Davis files) and from the following articles in *Am Rest:* "Always Beckoning Customers," May 1957, pp. 214–18; "Eye-Catching Roofs Catch More Business," June 1957, pp. 110–12; "Coffee Shop Created Around the Cook," July 1957, pp. 120–22; and "Big Appeal in a Small Package," Feb. 1958, pp. 74–75.

        Robert C. Wian: "Bob Wian's 'Big Boy,'" *FF*, May 1964, p. 87; and "Bob Wian—A Delicious Joke," *Rest Bsns*, May 1976, p. 124.

117   *Harold Butler:* Bruce Horovitz, "Butler Struggles to Get Naugles Back on Its Feet," *Los Angeles Times*, Mar. 3, 1985, p. V-2.

118   *1956 . . . Peter Pan:* "Inside or Out—Peter Pan Sells," *FF*, April 1957, p. 99.

119   *Sambo's:* Charles Bernstein, *Sambo's: Only a Fraction of the Action* (Burbank, Calif.: National Literary Guild, 1984), pp. 7, 8, 26, and 94; and *FF*, Dec. 1966, pp. 36 and 44.

124   *Harley Earl:* Stephen Bayley, *Harley Earl and the Dream Machine* (New York: Knopf, 1983), pp. 19–25.

125   *Ship's . . . logo:* Leon Whiteson, "Ships: A Relic of an Era When U.S. Ruled the Waves," *Los Angeles Herald Examiner*, Sept. 30, 1984, p. E-10.

125–6 *Bill Knapp's:* Henry S. Ehle, "The Customers Approve," *Am Rest*, Mar. 1951, pp. 50–51.

126   *Ethel Merman:* Murray Schumach, "Ethel Merman, Queen of Musicals, Dies at 76," *New York Times*, Feb. 16, 1984, p. D-26.

127   *Azar's Big Boy:* "Azar's Ten Years of Growth Is Based on a Diverse Approach," *FF*, Feb. 1964, p. 71.

        Frisch's experimented: FF, Feb. 1967, p. 75.

CHAPTER SIX: The Browning of America

133   *Waikiki Snack Shop:* "Restaurant Near Waikiki Beach," *Arch Rec*, July 1961, p. 158.

136   *"neighborhood Denny's":* Denny's evolution appears in Denise Garbedian-Brennan, "Vern Curtis' Grand Slam Market Strategy," *Rest Bsns*, June 1, 1982, pp. 119–31.

139   *In 1963 McDonald's:* David Morton, "They Did It All for You," *P/A*, June 1978, p. 64.

        Kroc heard: Ray Kroc, *Grinding It Out* (Chicago: Henry Regnery Co., 1977), p. 117.

140   *Howard Johnson's . . . lawsuit:* "Cross Country Rundown," *Am Rest*, Apr. 1, 1960, p. 8.

142   *A & W . . . landscaping:* Jack McDowell, "Shrubbery Guidelines at A&W," *FF*, May 1973, p. 109.

page   143   *"Carefree Shrubbery":* ad, *FF*, May 1973, p. 209.

        144   *"landscaping as a backdrop":* William Cook Murphy, "Creating a Total Site Environment," *FF*, May 1973, p. 150.

                R. David Thomas: Charles Bernstein, *Great Restaurant Innovators* (New York: Lebhar-Friedman, 1981), pp. 5–20.

                "parking space": D. Daryl Wyckoff and W. Earl Sasser, *The Chain Restaurant Industry* (Lexington, Mass.: Lexington Books, 1978), p. 100.

                46 percent: Rest Bsns, May 15, 1979, pp. 62–63.

        145   *Kentucky Fried Chicken's:* Robin Ashton, "Heublein's Bright Young Men Learn How to Run Chicken Stores," *Institutions*, Dec. 1, 1980, reprinted by Kentucky Fried Chicken.

                drawing power: Philip Langdon, "Fast Foods Follow Flock," Buffalo *Evening News*, Feb. 9, 1981, p. 11.

        148   *Big Boys . . . vote:* Mark Potts, "Marriott Pops a Big Question: The Fate of Big Boy," Washington *Post*, Dec. 10, 1984, p. 19.

        149   *organize . . . into clusters:* "A Strip on the Square," *D&CO*, May 1970, pp. 48–49; and Kenneth I. Helphand, "The Landscape of McDonald's," *Journal of American Culture*, Fall 1979, pp. 360–61.

        150   *McDonald's . . . half-measure:* "An Architect's Approach to McDonald's Menu and Decor," *Fast Service*, July 1978, pp. 24–27.

                Ann Arbor: Mary Timmins, "Controversial McDonald's Wins Community Approval," *Rest Bsns*, May 1, 1982, pp. 132 and 136.

        152   *Desmond Morris:* Desmond Morris, *Manwatching: A Field Guide to Human Behavior* (New York: Abrams, 1977), p. 303.

        153   *"not particularly comfortable":* Wyckoff and Sasser, *Chain Restaurant Industry*, p. 100.

                Lippincott & Margulies: Sharon Pavlista, "Hardee's Hoists a New Image," *Rest Bsns*, Mar. 1976, pp. 82–83.

        155   *"decor packages":* Ann Arbor *Observer*, Nov. 1979, p. 44.

        156   *McDonaldland Park: NRN*, Nov. 6, 1972, p. 2.

                Bob Evans: Abby Mendelson, "Bob Evans Farms: Cashing In on Quality," *FSFR*, May 1982, pp. 46–51.

        157   *"get a truckload": Rest Bsns*, May 1, 1981, pp. 204–05.

                Ponderosa: Chn St, Aug. 1966, p. 15.

        159   *Victoria Station: Rest Bsns*, Jan. 1, 1981, pp. 90–92; and Wyckoff and Sasser, *Chain Restaurant Industry*, pp. 4–7.

   160–1   *Steak & Ale:* Bernstein, *Restaurant Innovators*, pp. 107–20.

        161   *Chart House:* "Back to Nature," *Rest Bsns*, Sept. 1, 1979, p. 24; and "Upscale Chain Is CHI's Showpiece," *Rest Bsns*, Apr. 1, 1982.

        162   *"lunch in a dinner place":* Hank Sherowski, *VP* of engineering, interview, Nov. 16, 1983.

                "God's Own Junkyard": Peter Blake, *God's Own Junkyard: The Planned Deterioration of America's Landscape* (New York: Holt, Rinehart & Winston, 1964).

                Fortune: Edmund K. Faltermayer, "How to Wage War on Ugliness," *Fortune*, May 1966, pp. 130ff.

        164   *Refined manners:* see Douglas T. Miller and Marion Nowak, *The Fifties: The Way We Really Were* (Garden City, N.Y.: Doubleday, 1977), pp. 384–88.

   164–5   *"brown decades":* Lewis Mumford, *The Brown Decades: A Study of the Arts in America, 1865–1895* (New York: Dover, 1971), pp. 2–3.

            CHAPTER SEVEN: The Unfinished Transition: Design Since 1975

        169   *Hardee's:* Doug McInnis, "Hardy Hardee's: An Appetizing Hamburger Chain," *New York Times*, Sept. 7, 1980; Sharon Pavlista, "Hardee's Hoists a New Image," *Rest Bsns*, Mar. 1976, pp. 82ff; "Hardee's: A New Family Restaurant" (Lippincott & Margulies brochure); and "Hardee's Is Geared for Growth," *Institutions*, Dec. 15, 1973, pp. 37ff.

        172   *Marcel Breuer:* Tician Papachristou, *Marcel Breuer: New Buildings and Projects* (New York: Praeger, 1970), p. 221.

page 172   *Sea Ranch:* Gerald Allen, *Charles Moore* (New York: Whitney, 1980), pp. 30–41.

173   *change at Denny's:* see "Company Profile: Denny's Inc.," *NRN* "Focus," Dec. 7, 1981, pp. 1–24.

174   *Friendly . . . in Ohio:* "Friendly Repositions Itself for the 1980's," *Rest Bsns*, Jan. 1, 1980, reprinted by Friendly.

181   *100th Bomb Group:* Mary Hirschfeld, "A Real Blast," Cleveland *Plain Dealer*, Nov. 4, 1983, p. 40.

     Nashville Metro: Ed Gregory, "101st Theme Restaurant Feels Airport Rumble," Nashville *Tennessean*, Mar. 25, 1982, p. 61.

182   *Victoria Station: Rest Bsns*, Jan. 1, 1981, pp. 90–92.

183   *"We could change":* D. Daryl Wyckoff and W. Earl Sasser, *The Chain Restaurant Industry* (Lexington, Mass.: Lexington Books, 1978), p. 100.

185   *National Register:* "Calamity J. Contracting: A Castle Is Their Home," *Ms.*, Dec. 1984, p. 26; and David Colker, "Pep Boys Attacks Big Mac's Place in History," Los Angeles *Herald Examiner*, Jan. 24, 1984, p. C-5.

186   *Ed Debevic's:* "Second Ed Debevic's Launched in Chicago," *NRN*, Nov. 26, 1984, p. 4.

188–9   *"Chained-Down Chains": Am Rest*, Dec. 1931, p. 21.

189   *6 percent . . . at McDonald's:* E. R. Shipp, "The McBurger Stand That Started It All," *New York Times*, Feb. 27, 1984, p. C-3.

     Two-fifths . . . for chains: Rest Bsns, Mar. 15, 1982, p. 121.

     340 chains: N. R. Kleinfield, "Fast Food's Changing Landscape," *New York Times*, Apr. 14, 1985, p. F-1.

CHAPTER EIGHT: The Unsolved Problem

193   *KISS:* Actually, Kroc borrowed the motto from Colonel Sanders, according to Murray Suid and Ron Harris, *Made in America: Eight Great All-American Creations* (Reading, Mass.: Addison-Wesley Publishing, 1978), p. 163.

197   *Cookie Express: P/A*, Jan. 1985, pp. 124–25.

INDEX

Picture Credits

All illustrations in this book are from the author's collection except for the following, reproduced by courtesy of:

A & W Restaurants, Inc., pp. 60 (both), 66 (left)
Armet Davis Newlove, pp. 116 (Douglas M. Simmonds, photographer), 118 (both), 119 (Jack Laxer Photography), 125, 127 (left), 139 (George Lyons, photographer)
John Baeder, *Big Boy Bop*, copyright © 1985, oil on canvas, 30″ × 48″, p. 147
Art Bender, p. 83 (left)
Joseph R. Blackstock, p. 61
Bob Evans Farms, p. 187
Burger King Corp., p. 103 (left), 174 (both)
Martin Cable, pp. 56–57 (Edwin Schober, photographer), 65 (left)
Carrols Development Corp., p. 91 (left)
Champion Studio, Orange, New Jersey, p. 100
CHE Inc. (Chart House), p. 163
Chock Full o'Nuts, p. 22 (right)
Donald H. Clinton, Clinton's Restaurants, Inc., p. 25
Denny's, Inc., pp. 126, 130, 131, 137, 155, 158 (top)
DeNovo Corp., p. 74 (main photo)
Dobbs Houses, Inc., pp. 39, 40
Drive-in magazine (May 1958), p. 74 (inset ad)
Dunkin' Donuts, p. 154
David R. Edgerton, Jr., pp. 95 (Leo G. Witt, photographer), 96
Far West Services, W. R. Grace, p. 134
Fast Food magazine (May 1973), p. 143 (left)
Foodmaker, Inc., p. 105
Friendly Ice Cream Corp., pp. 175 (both), 177 (both) (all except p. 177 right are by Xenophon A. Beake, photographer) .
Frisch's Restaurants, Inc., p. 128
Richard J. S. Gutman Collection, copy negative, pp. 2–3
Royce J. Hailey, Texas Pig Stands, pp. ii, iii, 76
Hall, Norris & Marsh, Inc., architects, p. 101 (left)
Eileen M. Haller, p. 15
Hamill & McKinney Architects-Engineers, Inc., pp. 151 (top two), 183 (both), 190–91
Jim Heimann (with permission of Arthur Whizin), p. 44 (top left)
Hiller Enterprises, pp. 166–67
Hobbs-Black Associates, Inc., p. 151 (bottom pair, Daniel Bartush, photographer)

Hodgetts & Fung Design Associates, p. 195

Horn & Hardart Co., p. 18 (right)

Howard Johnson Co., pp. 51, 55 (both)

International House of Pancakes, Inc., p. 127 (right)

Steven Izenour, pp. 66 (right), p. 198 (photo by Steven Izenour)

Jerrico, Inc., p. 157

Jules Kabat, p. 22 (left, Robert Damora, photographer)

George and Gail Kallfelz, p. 71

Richard Cooper Kelsey, pp. 11 (both), 18 (left)

Krystal Co., p. 35

Lake County Museum, Curt Teich Collection, p. 44 (bottom)

John Lautner, architect, p. 114

Marriott Corp., pp. 12 (right), 63

McDonald, Richard J., pp. 78–79

McDonald's Corp., pp. 86–87 (logos)

Don E. Miller, pp. 86 (top left) and 87 (top left and center left)

Nation's Restaurant News, Lebhar-Friedman, Inc., pp. 47, 48, 103 (right)

Raymond M. Poelvoorde, Lippincott & Margulies, Inc., p. 102

Leroy Raffel, p. 101 (right)

Red Barn Restaurants, Inc., p. 99 (right)

Restaurant Business magazine, pp. 129, 138

Copyright *Restaurant Hospitality* magazine, Penton, IPC Publishing Co., Cleveland (all reproductions from *American Restaurant*), pp. 12 (left) (Jan. 1925), 23 (both) (Oct. 1931 and April 1939), 83 (right) (Sept. 1952) William Riseman Associates, Inc., copyright © 1956, all rights reserved, pp. 122, 123

S & O Consultants, p. 178 (logo)

T. Brock Saxe, p. 43 (left)

Emmett Shipman, Jr., pp. 110–11

Peter H. Smith, p. 91 (right)

Taco Bell, pp. 146, 178 (left)

Tastee-Freez International, Inc., p. 75

Frank P. Thomas, p. 93

Time-Life, Inc., p. 65 (right)

Special Collections, University of Arizona Library, p. 8

Mrs. Jessie VanTuil, p. 69

Vicorp Restaurants, Inc., p. 120

Victoria Station, Inc., p. 160

Wendy's International, Inc., p. 145 (left)

Acknowledgments

I WOULD LIKE TO THANK THE Architecture, Planning, and Design Program of the New York State Council on the Arts, which in 1982 awarded me an architectural fellowship to study common commercial buildings. It was this fellowship, administered by Educational Facilities Laboratories, a division of the Academy for Education Development, that enabled me to spend time in libraries, at restaurant headquarters, and on the road, doing the research for this book.

Many individuals helped me gather information and put it into perspective. Joseph R. Blackstock introduced me to Southern California, wondrous fount of restaurant architecture. Alan Hess, Jim Heimann, Arthur J. Krim, and Steven Izenour shared their restaurant research, and Daniel Cohen supplied insights into the evolution of the Automat. John Baeder gave me constant encouragement and the use of his painting *Big Boy Bop.* Four editors, Peter Berlinski of *Restaurant Business,* Stephen Michaelides of *Restaurant Hospitality,* and Charles Bernstein and Charles Forman of *Nation's Restaurant News,* graciously provided access to eighty years of restaurant trade publications. Those who have pored through such old trade journals know what entertaining and valuable sources they are.

Many chains and their executives, managers, and designers furnished information and illustrations. Among those who were especially helpful were Richard J. McDonald; Don E. Miller; Thomas Wells; Eldon Davis of Armet Davis Newlove; Gail D. Turley of White Castle; Carroll Johnson of Friendly Ice Cream; and Abraham J. Goldberg of Dunkin' Donuts.

Dr. Paul A. Knights, professor emeritus of history at Allegheny College, and Dr. Warren James Belasco, associate professor of American studies at the University of Maryland–Baltimore County, read the manuscript with great care and made hundreds of suggestions, helping to improve everything from diction to central ideas. Dr. William Graebner, professor of history at the State University of New York at Fredonia, recommended needed refinements in Chapter Six. Much of the credit for the book's comprehensiveness belongs to Martha Kaplan, my editor at Knopf, who believed from the start that the subject should be explored in detail, not reduced—as is often the fate of popular architecture—to a collection of pictures with an abbreviated text.

The staff of the New Haven Public Library offered constant assistance. My parents, Betty and Kenneth Beightol, acted many times as long-distance researchers. Thanks also go to Mrs. Ruth Brautigam, Michael Brill, Martin Cable, Steve Dornfeld, John Fairhall, Walter Needham, Peter H. Smith, Mrs. Jessie VanTuil, Stephen Verderber, and Gerald Weisman. I am grateful to the many contributors of photographs and other illustrations, listed elsewhere in the book. Most of all, I am grateful to my wife, Maryann D. Langdon, who lived with my obsession with restaurant architectural history, magnified my enjoyment of it, and helped bring it to this successful culmination.

P. L.

A NOTE ON THE TYPE

The text of this book was set in Walbaum, a type face designed by Justus Erich Walbaum in 1810. Walbaum was active as a type founder in Goslar and Weimar from 1799 to 1836. Though letterforms in this face are patterned closely on the "modern" cuts then being made by Giambattista Bodoni and the Didot family, they are far less rigid. Indeed, it is the slight but pleasing irregularities in the cut that give this face its human quality and account for its wide appeal. Even in appearance, Walbaum jumps boundaries, having a more French than German look.

Composed by Graphic Composition, Inc.,
Athens, Georgia

Reflective Color separations by Capper, Inc.,
Knoxville, Tennessee

Transparency color separations by
Graphic Process, Inc.,
Nashville, Tennessee

Printed and bound by Kingsport Press,
Kingsport, Tennessee

Typography and binding design by
Tasha Hall